XL

LAST CALL FOR THE DINING CAR

LAST CALL FOR THE DINING CAR

The Telegraph

BOOK OF

GREAT RAILWAY JOURNEYS

Edited by Michael Kerr

FOR AIDAN, WHO LOVES TRAINS

Michael Kerr has been on the staff of the *Daily Telegraph* since 1987. Having been, successively, news features editor, home affairs correspondent and assistant editor of *Weekend*, he is now deputy travel editor. He is the author of *Our Side of the House*, a memoir of his boyhood in the seaside resort of Portstewart in Northern Ireland during the Troubles.

CONTENTS

---

4 The Americas

5 Crossing Continents

6 Close to Home

12 Firsts and Lasts

INTRODUCTION

——————

We didn't get off to the most encouraging start. Railways got a mention in the first column of the front page of the *Daily Telegraph & Courier*, as it then was, on its first appearance on 29 June 1855. Among the late despatches from the seat of war (the Crimean) and the invitations to try Worth's Patent Razor Strop and Dr Locock's Pulmonic Wafers was this advertisement:

RAILWAY ACCIDENT INSURANCE
£16,221 5s has already been paid as compensation for fatal and other railway accidents, by the RAILWAY PASSENGERS' ASSURANCE COMPANY.

EXAMPLES
£200 was paid to the daughter of J.H., killed on 24 October 1854, secured by a payment of 1d.
£50 was paid to E.A.S., who was severely injured on 22 November 1854, secured by the payment of 2d.
£52 10s was paid to S.P., who was severely injured on 25 January 1854, secured by a payment of 3d.

Twenty-five years on from the start of the first regular passenger service, the Liverpool & Manchester Railway, when the MP William Huskisson had died under the wheels of the engine, the train was still a scary enough beast to be a source of premiums. But it was also, as the insurers acknowledged, a source of pleasure. The advertisement went on to quote rates not only for single and return journeys but for the sort of outing that was already synonymous with the name Thomas Cook: the excursion.

Cook had chartered his first train, to take 500 people to a temperance fete, in 1840. As he himself wrote, he carried his customers 'the enormous distance of eleven miles and back for 1s, children half price. We carried music with us, and music met us at the Loughborough station. The people crowded the streets, filled windows, covered housetops and cheered us all along the line with the heartiest welcome ... All went off in the best style and in perfect safety we returned to Leicester; and thus was struck the keynote of my excursions, and the social idea grew on me.'

It grew on others, too. By the year the *Daily Telegraph & Courier* launched, Cook, his profit margins squeezed as the British railway companies went into direct competition with tour operators, was looking farther afield, and took thousands of visitors to the Paris Exhibition. By the early 1860s he was starting tours to Geneva and Mont Blanc, and it was advertisements from the railway companies themselves, rather than the insurers, that caught the eye on our pages. On 2 June 1862, with what were then called the Whitsuntide Holidays coming up, they were all over the front:

MIDLAND RAILWAY – EPSOM RACES and the GREAT INTERNATIONAL EXHIBITION

PARIS in ELEVEN HOURS AND A HALF by the BRIGHTON RAILWAY – DAILY TIDAL EXPRESS SERVICE from London Bridge and Victoria

THE RHINE, GERMANY, and HOLLAND – the cheapest and most direct route is via ROTTERDAM, and thence by DUTCH RHENISH RAILWAY

PORTSMOUTH or Southampton (for the Isle of Wight), Salisbury, Winchester, by SOUTH WESTERN RAILWAY. WHITSUNTIDE HOLIDAYS – On SATURDAY, 7 June, a SPECIAL EXCURSION TRAIN will leave Waterloo Bridge station at 1.45 p.m.

That last advertisement carried this footnote: 'A small carpet bag or port-manteau only allowed as luggage.' Reading that line in a photographed newspaper on screen, in the windowless *Telegraph* archive room above Victoria station, I was catapulted from the excursion train of 1862 on to the bag-measuring, no-frills airline of 2009. It was as if I had switched the micro-film machine to full speed and run through not just one tape but a whole century-and-a-half's worth of reporting on the railways. Off I went, not with the 'shriek, and a roar, and a rattle' of Dickens's steam train, but with the wooomph! of a levitating maglev, away through the tunnel of time: Metropolitan Railway and *Flying Scotsman*, Pullman and sleeping car, Settle-to-Carlisle and Darjeeling Steam Tramway, Orient Express and Canadian Pacific, Lunatic Line and Trans-Siberian, *Burlington Pioneer Zephyr* and *Mallard*, Palace on Wheels and Eastern & Oriental, tilting, coffee-spilling APT and ear-popping, Channel-crossing, aircraft-conquering Eurostar.

As recently as 1961, a writer in the *Daily Telegraph* began an article thus: 'Lovers of trains – and how few of us keep faith in this fevered age of flight …' The train, it seemed then, was destined to go the way of the stagecoach, and with little more lamentation. That, of course, was a decade before the launch in France of the TGV; before there was a need for the coinage 'crowded skies'; before global warming and the realisation of the growing contribution being made to it by aircraft emissions; before 9/11 and the short-term fear and long-term misery it brought to flying; and it was before the opening – in 2007 – of the fast route from London to the Channel Tunnel (13 years behind the French and only 205 years after it had first been proposed).

Much more convincingly than in the 1980s, when Jimmy Savile was paid for his cigar-chomping sloganeering on behalf of the InterCity 125, it can be argued that this is the age of the train. Even close to home, as that great transport analyst Christian Wolmar pointed out in the *Daily Telegraph* in June 2009, 'people are rediscovering the joys of train travel. The days of slam-door trains and smoky carriages are long gone. Britain boasts a modern fleet of trains and, in many cases, stations to match … Record numbers of passengers are using the network, and punctuality has improved, with fewer than one in ten trains running significantly late. It is all a far cry from the nadir of the Beeching era and its aftermath, when whole swathes of the system were closed for reasons that, even discounting the benefit of hindsight, failed to take account of future transport needs.'

The High Speed 1 link from St Pancras to the Channel Tunnel has plugged Britain into the Continent's super-fast railway network, making flight-free travel quick, comfortable and easy. It's not quite as simple to book a train journey as it is to book a no-frills flight, but enthusiasts such as Mark Smith, the former station manager better known as the Man in Seat 61 (after his favourite seat on Eurostar), are doing their best to remedy that. His website (www.seat61.com) has recently spawned a book, one of a growing number of practical guides to seeing Britain and the world by rail.

This book is not one of those. It might be a bit of a let-down to the train-spotters; to men like Mr Peto who, on reading Edward Thomas's 'Adlestrop', expressed his disappointment that the poet had not taken the opportunity to note the name and number of the engine. It is not a history of train travel, nor even a history of the *Telegraph*'s coverage of train travel (though it does record a few milestones along the way). It is a selection of some of the best writing we have published on railway journeys and railways – on everything from the Trans-Siberian to the curling B.R. sandwich. It concentrates on the second half of the 20th century and the start of the 21st, because that is when narrative travel writing about trains came into its own, and when the *Telegraph*'s Saturday and Sunday magazines, and later its travel sections (plump, prosperous and pre-internet), had the space to do it justice.

Paul Theroux, whose *The Old Patagonian Express* was serialised in the *Sunday Telegraph* on its publication in 1979, was an inspiration for many. Reviewing the book in that paper, Colin Thubron welcomed it in these terms: 'A new type of travel book has arrived. Its ancestors are not H.V. Morton or Lawrence Durrell, but Mark Twain and Alexander Kinglake, and its author, most typically, attempts less to immerse himself in a foreign culture than to submit to chance experiences and insights as he moves along his (usually harassed) way.' David Holloway, reviewing Theroux for the *Daily Telegraph*, argued that 'it would be quite wrong to call *The Old Patagonian Express* a travel book. Even more than his earlier success, *The Great Railway Bazaar*, it is a travelling book.'

The same is true, on a smaller scale, of many of the contributions to this book: they are not travel articles so much as travelling articles. The trip, rather than its end, is the thing, with the opportunities it affords to 'submit to chance experiences and insights along the way'. As Paul Mansfield (of whom more later) puts it, having taken five days to travel from London to Lisbon: 'I could have made this journey by plane in about two hours – and missed everything.'

I wonder, though, whether 'submission' quite sums up the attitude of some of the writers whose work appears on these pages. It hardly applies to Sean Hignett, who wasn't exactly ordered to climb on to the roof of the South Orient Express in Mexico just as it was about to enter a tunnel. Nor does it apply to Jonathan Routh (the prankster of *Candid Camera*) who, embarking on a long trip with his wife, and forced to share a compartment with two American women, makes plain his determination to have the pair of them do his bidding.

Routh, from whose lengthy magazine article I have taken only a short extract, was on the Trans-Siberian, which is indisputably one of the world's great train journeys. It features here a couple of times: in its own right in a piece by Sophie Campbell (vodka-sozzled, but far from submissive towards an amorous chef) and as just one stretch in an epic journey by Peter Hughes – all the way from Wick, in Scotland, to Vladivostok.

What is a 'great railway journey'? This compilation offers a liberal interpretation of the phrase. It can be great in length and duration – three weeks, seven countries, ten time zones – and great again in the telling, as with Peter Hughes's. It can be great as in fabled, as in the Orient Express crossing Europe, promising lust, murder, revolution and intrigue – but not much in the way of breakfast or dinner, as Lee Langley discovered in its dying days. (That was before James Sherwood, in 1982, having bought some of the original coaches, started the private luxury train known as the Venice Simplon-Orient-Express.)

A journey can be great, too, in the qualities it reveals among the passengers: on the one hand, the small-scale rebellion by Janet Daley and her fellow commuters against what she calls 'thuglets' on the London Underground; on the other, the heroism of Necdet Kent, who, while Turkish consul general in Marseilles in 1943, risked his life by boarding a train that was taking more that eighty Jews to the concentration camps and refusing to leave it until they had been freed.

It can be great in its delays, frustrations and stoppages, and then great again in the humour or anger with which those are recounted, whether by Craig Brown, in a skit on 'The Night Train' 're-re-re-crossing the border', or by Boris Johnson, prevented by Midland Mainline from keeping an appointment in a television studio, and giving way to his 'internal John McEnroe'.

Boris Johnson wanted only to get from A to B as quickly and comfortably as possible. The average railway traveller, even while on holiday, has similar ambitions, though he will put up with a few signal failures if there is something interesting to look at along the way. The travel writer, however, is not the average railway traveller. He or she has a vested interest in things going wrong. (As, nearer home, does the transport correspondent – at least these days. It's instructive to compare the schoolboyish enthusiasm with which we greeted in the 1800s the London Metropolitan Railway, the world's first underground, and the City & South London, the world's first deep-level electric railway, with our pratfall-anticipating reports of the ATP, the Chunnel and Eurostar.) The great travel writer Norman Lewis, in an interview with the *Daily Telegraph* looking back on his career, said that he had been drawn to countries only if they were 'a bit horrific'. So it is with train journeys: a little horror, when you have copy to write, can be helpful.

I travelled in May this year from London to San Sebastian in Spain by train, a distance of about 820 miles through three countries. It was quick — about twelve hours, centre to centre — clean, comfortable and dull. More than a decade ago, I travelled by 'fast' train in Cuba from Havana to Santiago, the length of one island, and it took 18 hours to cover the 535 miles. It didn't stir until ninety minutes after departure time, which is roughly when the air-conditioning kicked in. There was no running water in the loo, nothing to eat or drink, and when I tried to sleep I discovered that my seat was the only one in the carriage that didn't recline. What's more, my bottle of water was in my suitcase, and my suitcase was above the head of a policeman who was already snoring and might not take kindly to being roused …

I had only myself to blame. The Cubans had tried to talk me out of it, just as the Sicilians once tried to talk Paul Mansfield out of it: 'No one had understood why I wanted to take a train around Sicily. No one in Sicily, that is. "Slow", "unreliable" and "dirty" were the epithets used by the locals to describe their railway network. I put it down to the twin Italian obsessions with the motor car and speed. Take a car away from a Sicilian and he's like a centaur who has lost his body.'

Paul Mansfield liked a challenge (he felt he couldn't honestly cover the bull running in Pamplona without taking part), but he hated planes, which is the reason why there are six articles with his byline in this anthology. There could have been many more, but I thought it only fair to give a few other writers a look-in. Paul died of cancer in February 2009, aged fifty-three, before I had really begun to trawl the archives. He would have enjoyed disputing, over a bottle of Rioja, what was and wasn't worthy of its place here.

He had been writing for *Telegraph Travel* for years before I moved on to the desk (in 1994), so I knew even before I started that I would find a few pieces of his on train journeys. There were many more than I expected, and they are among the best things he ever did for us. Those I have chosen include one on the Marrakesh Express, in which two of his great loves, trains and music, came together; and one on the Sunset Limited, in which, en route from New Orleans to Los Angeles, he found himself in the company of a Walter Mitty character known only as Texas Bob — the sort of fellow traveller Paul could always be relied on to fall in with. I am indebted to his wife, Judy, for permission to use Paul's work again here.

Shortly before his death, Paul told a friend and colleague: 'Look, mate, let's face it: you and I are dinosaurs. No one's interested any more in what we do [travel writing], and no one's prepared to pay for it.'

I think he was wrong on the first point and that this book will prove it. It's harder to argue with him on the second, certainly in the short term. Newspapers (or, these days, media organisations) are finding advertising harder to come by. Budgets have been cut, there is less money to pay travel writers, and so little incentive to take long train journeys. Why spend more than a week researching one article on the Trans-Siberian when in the same space of time you could make a couple of hops by no-frills airline to the Continent to pen some undemanding city-break pieces – assuming, that is, you can secure a commission even to do the city-break pieces?

This is a tough time to be a freelance writer, and tougher still for free-lance writers whose job entails being away from home for long, uneco-nomic stretches on the road or on the rails – the sort of people whose work provides the heart of this book. Had I been forced to confine my choice to the work of staff writers, this would have been a thinner anthology in more senses than one, so I would like to say thank you again here to all those who said I could consider their work for inclusion, whether it made the final edit or not. Many were friends, whom I have been commissioning for years, but there were plenty who have written for sections other than travel, whom I was encountering for the first time and who had no reason to go out of their way, as they did, to help me. And a big thank you, too, to my staff colleagues, bylined and anonymous, living and dead. It may be my choice, but it's their work. I hope it will give readers as much pleasure as I have had compiling it – and I look forward to seeing noses buried in it on the train.

Stoneleigh, Surrey
August 2009

A NOTE ON THE CONTRIBUTIONS

Most articles appear in this anthology at much the same length as they did in the *Daily Telegraph* or the *Sunday Telegraph* (which began publishing in 1961) or in its supplements. Here and there I have made cuts and tweaks. Where I have used an article at much shorter length than the original, I have marked it as 'Extract'.

For readers unfamiliar with the *Telegraph* and its ways, it might be useful to know a couple of things about our diary columns. In the *Daily Telegraph*, 'London Day by Day' was originally signed 'Peterborough', which later became its title, so for simplicity I have labelled all contributions drawn from it as 'Peterborough'. The diary is now entitled 'Mandrake' – a name originally given to the diary in the *Sunday Telegraph* and still in use in that paper.

CHAPTER I
EUROPE

———————

15 NOVEMBER 1974

SHATTERED WAGON-LIT DREAM

LEE LANGLEY FINDS REALITY TRUMPING FANTASY
ON THE ORIENT EXPRESS

Writers have drawn on the Orient Express like priests quarrying the Bible for their weekly sermons: for almost a century its history, its mystery, its glamour, its splendours and disasters, have provided them with the jumping-off point for another book, another adventure, another literary daydream to feed the ones we all secretly drift into at the very mention of its name: kings, queens, diplomats, millionaires, svelte creatures swathed in furs and hinting at scandal; seductions in the sleeping car, eroticism rampant.

There may be people, clodlike creatures, whose imagination remains unstirred, pulse unquickened, spirits unmoved by the words 'Orient Express'. I suspect they are few and have no wish to meet them. For the rest of us, resigned to acquiring in other areas the painful maturity that comes with disillusioning experience, we still cling to one innocent dream: the great express rushing through the night, long corridors swaying, deserted; the secretive, closed doors of the wagons-lits, sheltering a mysterious elite of polyglot travellers. In our minds we have been there already, we know the whistle of the steam locomotive (though it's all electric and diesel these days) ... the madonna of the sleeping cars looking for adventure (now more likely to wear a haversack than a mink on her back) ... the spies (in reality either second-class seedy chaps out in the cold or ex-public school defectors already safe in Moscow) ... the Queen's messengers (who take their pouches by air now) ... the luxury, the crisp white sheets of the wagons-lits; the hand bell of the steward, tinkling down the train as he announces 'premier service!', summoning us to dinner in the restaurant car. Eating on such a train must be a special experience – the glinting silver, sparkling glasses and spotless cloths; the stylish waiters. The breakfast of hot coffee and croissants on a silver tray to be enjoyed, blearily, in the cosy intimacy of the sleeper ... and above all, the possibilities, the endless possibilities, of three days cut off from the world, thundering across Europe, with who knows what in store.

'Then it seems,' said Poirot slowly, 'as though we must look for our murderer on the Istanbul-Calais coach ... the murderer is with us – on the train now ... ' Agatha Christie, *Murder on the Orient Express*

Legend and history, myth and reality, where does one end and the other begin? So many books, so many films (even a tune, a foxtrot) inspired by the Orient Express: *Sleeping Car to Trieste; Stamboul Train; From Russia with Love; Orient Express; The Lady Vanishes; Victoria, Four-Thirty; Madonna of the Sleeping Cars; Night Train to Munich* ... and of course, Agatha Christie's exquisitely fashioned whodunnit, *Murder on the Orient Express*, which, having baffled readers for forty years, is now being filmed. And perhaps this is a particularly good moment for it to appear, a gloriously unreal slice of high life, a bravura exercise in elegant escapism at a time when everyday life is offering all too little in the way of treats.

The line separating truth from invention is a shaky one; difficult sometimes to distinguish between the two. Is it fact or fiction that a bunch of wild musicians once invaded the Orient Express at some remote station, filling the restaurant car with whirling colours and pulsating rhythms while the train sped through the Balkan countryside? Fact and fiction. It actually happened, on the inaugural trip. But the incident also appeared in a film, *Orient Express*, the screen version of Graham Greene's novel *Stamboul Train*.

And the fateful snowstorm in *Murder on the Orient Express*. That too had its roots in fact: in February 1929, the Simplon-Orient Express was blocked by a snowdrift at Tcherkeskeny for eleven days. Nor is violence confined to the fiction shelves: in 1949, Eugene Karp, a U.S. naval attaché, fell to his death from the same train under circumstances which have never been satisfactorily cleared up.

The present Turkish ambassador to London remembers using the Orient Express as a young student in the 1930s: 'Some people wore gloves when they went into the corridors so that they should not dirty their hands on the dusty windows.' The passengers learned from the waiters little tricks of trainmanship like how to pour their wine without spilling it ('you lift both glass and bottle off the table').

The Orient Express was the brainchild of a Belgian engineer, Georges Nagelmackers, who saw on a brief trip to America the shape of railways to come, and decided to do something about it. He managed to get his first contract signed, for the Paris-Vienna section, in 1872, and in 1876 founded the Compagnie Internationale des Wagons-Lits et des Grands Express Européens, with help from an American railway expert, Colonel Mann. The Paris-Constantinople service opened on 4 October 1883. Once established, the Orient Express had three 'arms', one to Warsaw, one to Bucharest, and one – the Simplon-Orient – to Istanbul. Today that train, now known as the Direct Orient, is the principal means of rail communication between western Europe and Istanbul, with a daily connecting service.

Miss Christie's characters travelled this route, meeting death and nemesis on the Calais coach. It is a journey I have dreamed of, and am now to experience. The tickets are bought, the carriage reserved, and one of those sleeping cars to Istanbul is mine.

Victoria Station, Wednesday 3.30 p.m.: It begins well – almost too well. Beneath the sign saying Orient Express, the intriguing words 'Agent's Special'. I have a momentary vision of a group outing of Bonds ... a package of Poirots ... do they travel in gangs now, the men of mystery?

Calais, and there at the platform – the two Calais coaches of the Orient Express, those for Trieste and Belgrade. I gaze round the cosy dining car with a feeling of warm anticipation. Little do I know that this is to be my last proper meal for three days.

Paris, 11.50 p.m.: My travelling companion and I (I love the slightly dated, risqué connotations of that phrase. Actually it's my husband, but one must try to keep up improper appearances on the Orient Express) investigate the two-berth wagon-lit compartment. The beds are made up, white sheets gleaming against warm, red-checked blankets. The decor is not inspiring. The compartment is so tiny it is like making your home in a public convenience cubicle. Perhaps this lack of space has something to do with the sleeping car's reputation for amorous activity, literally throwing people together? Propinquity can have its advantages. Well, we shall see.

The French wagons-lits conductor in the trim brown uniform hands us customs forms to fill in, and I ask about breakfast. The conductor's smile falters. He is, it seems, not too sure about breakfast. The most he is committing himself to is that he will 'do his best'. *Do his best*?

It is at this moment that reality for the first time clashes with my fantasy image of the journey: I had pictured leisurely meals, skilfully mixed cocktails and the odd late-night liqueur sipped in the company of fascinating fellow travellers. But not only is there no elegance, there is not even a restaurant car.

Like Hercule Poirot before me, I request a mineral water and retire for the night.

Some things at least have not changed: the short, heavy chain on each compartment door is still lagged with soft leather to prevent any disturbing rattle; the coat-hangers still have rubber stoppers to stop them clattering. The deep blue night-light still glows softly above the door, turning the cramped compartment into a shadowy, mysterious cave. And, as always, the steady, rhythmical movement of the train casts its spell: rocking, easing tension, soothing, lulling ... the intimacy of the sleeping car, like no other.

Thursday, 8a.m.: The conductor's smile is cautious. There is, he regrets, no breakfast. 'The train is not what it used to be.' Swiss countryside slides past: laundry-neat landscapes, each field folded and pressed just so. Little houses with pointed roofs. Each, no doubt, with a kitchen where they are all sitting down to huge Swiss breakfasts. The Byronic romanticism of Chillon Castle takes my mind off my stomach for a minute or two. We rush into the Simplon Tunnel: cold, with a smell of wet stone. Blackness. The warm red blankets are comforting.

Domodossola, 9.49 a.m.: The train stops here for eighteen minutes and our conductor decides to retrieve the honour of the company. 'Follow me!' he mutters, locking our sleeper door with his curious cylindrical key. We leap off the train and head for the station buffet across the tracks. Large, clean room; foaming cappuccino, freshly filled cheese rolls. God bless the Italians.

Already the train is taking on the personality of its different sections: at one end are the Yugoslavs, with lots of headscarves and bunchy skirts. Families asleep in untidy heaps, legs and arms flung out, relaxed. A smell of oranges. The Turkish coach overflows with curly-haired, black-eyed, brigandish-looking young men. These are the euphemistically named 'guestworkers' going home on holiday after a year working in Switzerland or Germany. There is a spicy smell, and pungent tobacco fumes.

The Italian coaches bound for Milan and Venice have a well-groomed, stylish air; the passengers are uncrumpled, coiffures unruffled, even on those who have sat up all night. They talk rapidly and confidently, and their coaches are perfumed headily with aftershave lotion, cologne and fragrant Italian cigarettes.

The scenery rolls past like an endless holiday snap: brightly coloured lakes, Como, Maggiore; the islands, the curving waterside, the little lakeside houses and terraces, boats. The sun sparkles on every bright surface.

Milan, noon: The conductor suddenly becomes vague about lunch. There may, after all, be no lunch. Perhaps we should stock up at Milan. Just to be on the safe side. We buy plastic-wrapped rolls, and oranges at about 25p each. Outrageous, but time is short. In the buffet, we spy bottles of Valpolicella clustered darkly on a shelf. We buy Valpolicella and some jolly-looking bars of chocolate.

As we pull out of the station, two young men in overalls, looking like mechanics, appear in the corridor flogging plastic trays of food – 'Plateaux Express'. Hardly haute cuisine but at least food. For lunch we eat the hors d'oeuvres (bean salad with vinaigrette in a plastic bag) and save the bit of cold chicken. Shortage makes hoarders of us all.

Venice: We say goodbye to our French conductor, who is replaced by a Yugoslav. Venice station must be the best sited in the world: down the steps and straight on to the Grand Canal, with the Palazzo Foscari across the water and the Rialto just round the corner to the left. We are late, and no one knows quite when we leave, but they must change the engine, take on Yugoslav personnel and disconnect the Venice coaches. Forty minutes later we leave Venice behind. We could have bought food there, the town was one vast delicatessen counter, but too late we found ourselves without Italian currency.

The first-class coach is fairly international: a Canadian and his wife, bound for Istanbul; a Turkish lady professor; a Yugoslav bureaucrat returning from holiday; an Armenian businessman who looks like Elgar and has six suitcases of samples; a bright-eyed Yugoslav lady; a Bulgarian lady; and a slender blonde who gazes out of the window and doesn't talk to anyone (aha!). There is also Ahmet, a plumping young Turk of immense charm and assurance who wanders the corridors in his Yves Saint Laurent casuals (the only passenger to keep up the old appearances) with a cache of Horniman's teabags and a pocketful of pistachio nuts.

Trieste, 8 p.m.: We are now running nearly two hours late and the rumour is we will have only nine minutes here. The conductor, as usual, knows nothing. We all hang out of the windows gazing longingly at the dimly lit station buffet, thick with smoke and humanity happily stuffing themselves with food. There is only one vendor on the platform and he refuses to look our way. The nine minutes drag on to twenty and the mood is turning ugly. 'Why don't they *tell* us how long we'll be at stations?'

After Trieste, any pretence that we are aboard a great express is abandoned. The train potters along at about 20mph, often coming to a halt completely in the middle of the countryside for long stretches. At last, Zezena brings the Yugoslav police aboard for passport control.

The conductor stokes up his little range and sits back for the night. Our sheets are supposed to be changed each day and beds freshly made, but no one has touched ours for twenty-four hours. We chunter along through the darkness, dawdling, stopping at deserted little stations where steam locomotives are shunting goods trains, their steam white against the night sky. The lighting is dim and sparse, small electric bulbs seeming almost to emphasise the gloom they cannot dispel.

I wander up the corridor and mutter a request for some tea in three languages before the conductor gets my drift. A mere forty minutes later he appears with two plastic jugs looking suspiciously like those containers for urine specimens they hand you in hospital. The liquid inside is pale yellow and evil-looking, with two tea bags floating sadly on the surface.

Friday, 6.30 a.m.: A wonderful night's sleep, rocked gently by the lullaby of track and train. I balance on the edge of the unmade bunk, banging my head against the upper berth, and munch biscuits and gulp tea from a plastic mug with the undemanding acceptance of the long-term prisoner. We are crawling along past shabby Yugoslav stations and rundown-looking houses. In the fields, people working do not look up as we pass. We are all in the corridor by now – it is our promenade, our high street, our local. Those who have supplies eat or drink, sharing with those who have nothing.

Belgrade, 9.20 a.m.: Once again, no one knows how long we will be here. The train is shunted between platforms and again they change engine and personnel, taking off the Belgrade and Athens coaches and joining on an Istanbul section. Taking a photograph of the railway station, we find ourselves being marched silently into the police station. We wait nervously while the uniformed policeman solemnly describes our misdemeanour. The officer at the desk listens wearily, eyes half-closed. Then, bored, he irritably waves us out.

Everyone from the train is rushing about the open station yard to try to buy something to eat. I find some weird cheese pastries, huge, flabby and still warm from the oven. They look like squares of heavy-duty blanket. At the next counter are fat, crusty rolls almost as big as a loaf of bread. Our Italian wine is finished and the new conductor, a Bulgarian, has a flinty, unresponsive face that offers no great promise of consumer delights. On the platform a vendor whose trolley is stacked high with slivovic suddenly finds he has an eager horde of buyers.

By this time, two days out from London, we know most of the people up and down the train who are going all the way to journey's end. In one coach there are two New Zealand girls bound for Istanbul 'because it sounded interesting'; a German boy heading for India and meditation; two ex-student teachers from London who intend to keep travelling until their money runs out. In another compartment, a couple from London; he has been working in the box office of the Odeon Leicester Square, she on the switchboard. They may go on to Cyprus. There are others, with haversacks and a vague mental picture of a world map in their heads.

We leave Belgrade. Ladies in headscarves and thick black stockings sweep through the train corridors bent double, wielding old-fashioned hand brushes, gaily hurling empty bottles out of the windows, just above the notices forbidding bottles to be thrown from windows.

Kreveni-Krsc, 2.15 p.m.: No platforms at this station; the tracks are laid on broken stone and shingle over which the locals stumble and crunch their way to and from the train, pushing cardboard boxes through the windows, hauling themselves up the steep iron steps.

For Muslims, Friday is the most sacred day of the week, and in one crowded second-class compartment, Turkish workers are listening intently to a cassette recording of a religious service.

Dimitrovgrad: Very dim indeed. Narrow platforms, usual dingy station buffet. When the train stops, people try to get off to buy food, but the police push them back brusquely. Only local passengers can alight. We are sealed off from the outside world. Now panic becomes acute as everyone gesticulates from windows, desperately trying to catch the eye of the stolid trolley man.

Just by our window, a second little trolley materialises. A peasant woman in a headscarf sells us the inevitable rolls, some hardboiled eggs, which she fishes out of a large black leather handbag, and bottled beer. Rates of exchange become irrelevant at such a time. People are waving notes of all sizes, just hoping she will accept them. Outside the buffet across the track, a white-coated waiter watches idly. Someone finds out the Croatian for 'cheese' and we all shout it hopefully at him. He reappears, carrying a huge lump of hard, mouldy cheese wrapped in crumpled paper. It looks very nasty. 'Buy it all,' the Canadian urges.

The rotten lump of cheese is unbelievably expensive and we all turn out our pockets to pay for it, in dinars. As the train leaves, we see that the waiter and the vendors are smiling. Later we share the cheese with the Canadians and Ahmet, whose pistachio nuts and tea bags are running low.

The Bulgarian police inspect our passports and say we have no transit visas. We had checked, twice, with the Bulgarian authorities in London before leaving and had been assured no transit visas were needed. The local chaps are unimpressed by this news. 'You need visas! You pay!' one of them screams at us, storm-trooper fashion, eyes blazing with fury. 'You pay!' He flings the passports on the bunks and waits, his uniformed figure blocking the door. Since failure to pay will presumably mean being detained in Bulgaria, and since being detained in Bulgaria constitutes about the worst punishment I can think of, we pay. The visas cost £2 each. In London the same visas, when needed, can be had for 43p.

The police enter the next compartment. Pause. Shouts and protests. 'You pay!' the words reverberate down the corridor. 'You pay!' The Bulgarian countryside, as though trying to make up for its beastly policemen, is ravishing. Green and gold and gently curving. At Mnitniza we move our watches on two hours. East European time. The Bulgarian conductor makes no move to do the beds or attend to our compartment, which by this time is something of a slum on wheels.

Sofia, 7.45 p.m.: A small, neglected-looking station with a trolley of fairly revolting-looking hot dogs selling (to Orient Express passengers, anyway) at around 50p each. A sudden influx of locals: they surge through the train, filling each compartment to bursting point. The new conductor is a Turk. He looks like Genghis Khan, with high cheekbones and slant eyes that glitter. Impassive, remote, silent.

In second class, Cesar the Turkish Cypriot and his friends are feeling the pinch: they have no drinking water, which apparently ran out hours ago, and Cesar even had to pay for a mug of water to shave in. 'You get nothing free on this train,' he says, grinning ruefully. But at least in second class you can get real coffee, sweet, hot and Turkish, in tiny china cups.

The lavatories throughout the train are in appalling condition, clearly untended since Paris. All are littered with discarded paper towels, fragments of toilet paper, cartons. The basins are filthy. In second class they are also awash, scummy water slopping two inches deep on the floor. The stench is lethal.

Supper: Bulgarian rolls, sour cheese and slivovic. I remember the meal the 1883 passengers were given in Turkey – a meal that ended with peaches decorated with almonds and glazed in rose-scented syrup. What will the morning bring?

Woken after 3 a.m. Passport control. Very noisy progress of police down the train. This, thank the Lord, is the last of Bulgaria.

Saturday, 8.30 a.m.: No dining car. No breakfast. Outside, countryside is undistinguished, rather flat, not remotely Oriental-looking. But workers sitting on tractors wave at us and smile; shepherds wave. Children wave. In Bulgaria nobody waved. At last, a minaret! A small one, but still, a minaret.

We bribe our way to another Turkish coffee in second class, and share the last of our now rock-like rolls and cheese with our Turkish friends. We are now running four hours late. The train crawls through the suburbs, stopping every few minutes for local commuters. Gradually, Istanbul approaches; Ahmet, eyes bright with anticipation, does a running commentary: 'Over here! Look, the Blue Mosque! And here, St Sofia! Topkapi is over there.' The mosques grow out of the huddle of houses as if someone were blowing bubbles underground. They sit on the skyline, rounded, massive, graceful. Someone once coined the word 'Bosphorescence!' for Istanbul's special glitter. The light has an extraordinary quality, sharp sunlight fracturing itself against the smog so that the air seems to shimmer.

Sirkecy station, Istanbul, 1.45 p.m.: After three days it seems almost brutal to be going our separate ways so abruptly. Handshakes, hugs, warm good-byes, addresses and phone numbers exchanged. Porters invade the train like termites, stripping it bare of luggage in seconds. Suddenly the train is empty, silent, the carriages strewn with the debris of the long journey. Out of the cool, dark customs hall into sudden blinding sunlight. The station, small and pink and grey, is as lively as a marketplace: police with truncheons almost absentmindedly beat off taxi drivers who descend on passengers like wolves on the fold.

It's over. The journey is at an end. Crumpled, dishevelled – and distended, after a three-day diet of bread and wine – we sever the curious bond with the train. Dusty, streaked with mud, a long, dark green iron monster whose forerunners carried crowned heads. The captains of industry and the kings have departed, victims of egalitarianism and tight schedules, and with them the glory has drained away from the great train de luxe of yesterday. But despite everything there was a weird sort of enjoyment about it all: that marvellous, cradle-rock of the bunk through the night; the way you could *feel* one country taking over from another as you pottered across frontiers. The warmth between passengers that no jet could supply.

And the feeling of serenity, the lack of tension you sense after three nights on the train.

Ronald Hastings

It hardly needs to be said that you do not get the best photographic likeness at a post-mortem, but this seemed to be the aim of James Cameron in *Death of the Orient Express* (BBC 1). Three-and-a-half days in the presence of Mr Cameron going to bed, getting up, shaving, lying in bed, standing in the corridor and leaning out of the window is no one's idea of how to remember this most celebrated train.

The Orient Express, as he said, became synonymous with romance, intrigue, murder and espionage, and for the life of me I can't see how this was commemorated by the sight of Mr Cameron's shaving soap. By the time he travelled the great train had been reduced to two slip coaches and on arrival in Istanbul there were even goods wagons attached.

Smilingly complaining, Mr Cameron covered the subject like a lean, wary chicken picking over an unsavoury rubbish dump and none too sure where it was safe to put its feet.

CHECK EVERYTHING – WITH A NATIVE

THERE IS AN ART TO TAKING RAILWAY JOURNEYS IN ITALY THAT, ONCE MASTERED, PROVIDES AN ENDLESS SOURCE OF PLEASURE, SAYS **TIM PARKS**. BUT FIRST YOU HAVE TO LEARN HOW TO SECURE A SEAT ...

'Mi scusi, signore, questi posti sono prenotati.'

'I beg your pardon?'

Imagine the scene. It's Milano Centrale. You have just settled down in your compartment on the Milan-Rome Intercity, the Michelangelo, no less. You have arrived a little early and taken time to admire the monumental entrance to this most monumental of European railway stations with its weird central inscription NELL ANNO MCMXXXI DELL ERA CRISTIANA (in the year 1931 of the Christian era), a sly allusion to the fact that, back then, the Italians were building another era that they hoped would last just as long: it was year ten of the era fascista.

Keeping half an eye on your watch, you have ridden the escalator up the great marble-and-granite ticket hall, peering at mosaics of mythical warriors and 1930s bas-reliefs of aeroplanes and ocean liners, all half hidden, alas, between vast banners of steamy underwear advertisements. It's a very Italian mix.

Up at platform level, remembering that in Italy you have to stamp your ticket before boarding, you have pushed back and forth through the commuter crowds, until finally you have found one of the little yellow stamping machines that is actually in servizio, even though the date and time it has printed on your ticket are quite illegible.

There's a considerable satisfaction in learning the ropes in a foreign country, isn't there? It feels good. And you still have fifteen minutes before the train starts! Time to listen as you wander up the platform to the wonderful combination of jerky mechanical voice announcements and romantic train names: 'Intercity - sei - zero - otto - ugo foscolo! - diprimaeseconda-classe - delle ore - seidici - e - zero - cinque - conserviziodiristoranteeminibar - per - Venezia Santa Lucia!'

Somehow even the computerised drone communicates a heart-swelling national pride when it reaches the big names: Intercity Vivaldi! The volume goes up a couple of notches. Intercity Tiepolo! Giorgione! Leonardo da Vinci! Here is a country that promises culture galore, even if the TV screens placed every 10m all along the platform are simply showing more and more ads for underwear.

Finally, a carriage that looks fairly empty. You have boarded, enjoyed the old-fashioned business of walking along a corridor and squinting into compartments, seeing how people spread clothes and luggage around to discourage company, or even draw the sickly yellow curtains across the glass door so that you can't know if anyone's in there or not. Never mind. Here's a free one. The little plaque for posting reservation information is reassuringly blank. It's all yours.

So, you've settled, relaxed, pulled out your Italian phrasebook for further study, when along comes this polite little man with his neat moustache and smart grey suit. 'Mi scusi, signore, questi posti sono prenotati.' Ominously, behind him, a group of adolescents can be seen pressing against the glass window of the compartment, transmitting the hubbub you expect of chickens in a battery farm. The guy's a teacher.

'I beg your pardon?'

'Prenotati,' he repeats. He pulls a ticket from his tailored pocket and shows you. The faintly printed figures and abbreviations might as well be hieroglyphics, but at last the word prenotati clicks. That was in the phrasebook: reserved! How can that be? I checked. 'Tutti prenotati, signore.'

The kids are already piling in, with their fluorescent pink backpacks, infectious giggles, personalised ring tones. One phone is buzzing the triumphal march from *Aida* as you beat your retreat.

Yes, two years ago Italian railways stopped bothering to indicate if seats were reserved or not. Where does it say this on the train? Nowhere. They didn't bother to remove the reservation plaques, either. But then they have also left heat-control switches now overridden by central heating, the image of the burning cigarette where it is absolutely forbidden to smoke, warnings not to lean out of windows that can no longer be opened. The past is always present in Italy, like the fascist frieze behind the underwear ads in the station.

So, on this six-hour journey to Rome you change seats five times. You just cannot know if the place you've sat in is already reserved or not. People are polite but firm. 'Questo è mio posto. Ecco il biglietto.' Finally, a bespectacled intellectual reading the pink pages of the *Gazzetta dello Sport* informs you in Oxford English that the seats in compartments seven and eight of every Intercity carriage are always left unreserved. By now those places are taken, of course. If only you'd known. You arrived early enough. In the end, you wait until Bologna and, in the general mill of people getting on and off, manage to grab a seat in compartment seven. Relief.

Except as the train rushes in and out of the tunnels to Florence, a general unease develops. The two businessmen with their busy laptops, the woman with so much to talk about on the phone, the boy with his loud music tinkling under glossy black hair, all are glancing with growing concern at the old lady slumbering by the window. In her eighties, she has raffishly dyed blonde hair under a red hat and brick-bright lipstick. Given the growing heaviness of the atmosphere in the compartment, it also appears that she has recently devoured about half a pound of raw garlic. She is sighing garlic, snoring garlic, sneezing garlic. The air-conditioner fan makes sure her breath is evenly distributed among the six travellers.

Outside, postcards of picturesque Tuscany fling by, pretty campanili and vineyards and stuccoed farmhouses; inside, a toxic gas accumulates. The odour intensifies. Now you understand why garlic is considered a protection against evil spirits. Shortly after Prato, feeling evil, you opt to return to the roulette of empty seats in vulnerable compartments. At least you can try out your phrasebook on the people showing you their reservations.

Or imagine the reverse situation. Imagine you've learnt your lesson now. You know that on Italian Intercity trains it's essential to reserve a seat. And here you are standing, let's say, on the platform at Verona waiting for the train to Milan, early Sunday evening. 'Coincidenza,' announces an urgent voice, 'l'Intercity Francesco Sforza arriva e parte dal binario sei!' Fancy that. It arrives and departs from the same platform. But you've got used to these charming non sequiturs by now. 'In ritardo,' the voice adds. Late. Well, who cares about a little ritardo. I have my place.

But when you climb on board, the carriage is crammed. The corridor is so packed you can hardly get through. You hadn't realised it was carnival in Venice today. The masked Milanesi are returning home. When you've fought your way through harlequins, sheiks and supermen to your compartment, it is to find that your seat is already taken by an exhausted little fairy, half asleep on an ageing witch's knee. The grandmother, perhaps. So do you, with your limited Italian, have the heart, the courage, to start explaining to these good people that actually that's your seat? Look, it says so here on my ticket!

Nope. You don't. So get set for an hour and a half on your feet among the painted faces and the mobile trills. And yet, and yet … I'm going to try to convince you that the train is really the only way to travel in the Bel Paese. It really is.

Take your car any distance in this country and you're sure to regret it: the petrol cartel at the pumps, the rush into sweltering log jams on the autostrada, the prices at crowded tollbooths, even the difficulty of picking up anything decent on the radio, make any long car journey a purgatory. There are times when you feel the circonvallazione round Milan or, worse still, Rome's Grande Raccordo Anulare were designed with the circles of Dante's *Inferno* in mind. You're not supposed to arrive. And when you do there will be nowhere to park.

Nor is the plane an alternative; unless you're on expenses. So long as the Italian government is still the majority shareholder in Alitalia, the policy will be to keep domestic flight prices high. Air-traffic control is ever poised to strike; taxi drivers do their best to ensure this is a prohibitive means of transport; the catering at Malpensa and Fiumicino will not give you the impression it was worth it after all.

But these are not the real reasons why you should be using the train.

The fact is that, as one condemned to travel about 300 miles a week with Trenitalia, I can assure you that it really is a wonderful way to travel, once you know how to use it. And in the process of learning you'll be obliged to acquire a precious insight into the Italian mindset.

Once you've figured out the difference between a EuroCity, an Intercity Plus, an Intercity and a CIT, once you've grasped why there are people standing in a Eurostar when it's a reserved-seat-only train, once you have gone through the rigmarole of the ticket machines, once you've seen how those who have 'forgotten' to stamp their ticket enter into complex negotiations with the inspectors rather than coughing up the fine, then you'll be a bit closer to appreciating how this fascinating country works.

Why, for example, did Trenitalia decide to remove those reservation indicators? Think. Ticket prices here are the lowest among the big western European countries. Only semi-privatised as it is, Trenitalia is not allowed to raise prices without government approval. Overmanned, it cannot lay off staff without this becoming a political issue. Desperate for cash, someone comes up with this wheeze: removing the reservation information obliges anybody who really needs a seat to book. And booking costs €3 (£2) a head.

The more people who book, the more everybody else has to book. And since the information no longer has to be posted on the train, the computers can take bookings right up to the last second. The remarkable thing is how little the Italians complain. Instinctively, the rulings of perverse officialdom are accepted as blows of fate, impervious to retaliation.

So how should I use the trains? Two things must be borne in mind. Italians are great commuters. They love to live in their home-town, regardless of how far away they work. If they can't actually live there, they will certainly return home at the weekend, quite probably with a large bundle of laundry for mother's washing machine. Not for nothing all those underwear ads.

So Sunday and Friday evenings, Monday and Saturday mornings are to be avoided at all costs, as is any sort of festa, or any political election (everybody gets the day off to go home and vote).

Fares, however, bear no relation to peak and off-peak periods. Social policy demands that commuter and local trains be cheap and be seen to be so. But to understand what to expect from a train, use of English is a good rule of thumb. If a train has an international-sounding denomination – Intercity, Eurostar, EuroCity – it will stop less often and cost about 50 per cent more than those with Italian names – the Regionale, Interregionale or the now rare Espresso. But in the end, they're all a bargain.

My advice. Trapped inside their respective regions, crawling doggedly from one watering hole to the next, the Regionale trains are a good idea only if your destination is of a size not to be found on maps of ordinary scale, the kind of station where you buy your ticket with a glass of wine from the girl in the café and a charming bell wakes the locals from sleep to warn them that a train might soon be arriving. Connoisseurs of ancient rolling stock might want to hurry before the old brown dinosaurs on some of these lines finally grind into extinction. Here you sit with your knees jammed against those of the person opposite (or even interlocked, as it were), shivering together in winter, mingling your sweat in summer.

For daytime travel, use the super-cheap Interregionali, but at off-peak hours. They rattle and bang about, as a real train should. There is no pretence of style, they are not for international inspection, but heating and air-conditioning are good, you can open the big windows and blow the garlic away if need be, you can sit where you like and stay there (there are no bookings), and over, say, a three-hour journey, which is about the maximum distance these trains go, they are only twenty minutes slower than an Intercity.

String four or five such trips together and you've got the perfect way to go up and down the country. Italy, after all, has a beautiful city centre about every thirty miles, if not less. Just think of the Venice-Milan line. A string of gems. Padova, Vicenza, Verona, Peschiera, Desenzano, Brescia. Price one way: €12.90. If you don't fancy staying a whole night at Desenzano, you can simply get off the train and walk down to Lake Garda for a swim.

And for long trips, forget the Eurostar. Use the Night Espresso. To make it possible for southerners to work up north and still get home with the regularity mamma demands, these most efficient of all trains (because they have so much time to kill) are kept in operation at prices no one could ever complain about. They'll take you the whole length of the peninsula (and remember it is long) stretched out in a comfortable couchette.

No serious Italophile should be ignorant of the splendid seafront at Reggio Calabria, of the sugar-white stone of medieval Lecce. Amazingly, the much-maligned Trenitalia makes these distant cities easy. Travel light and you can even walk to almost any centre from the train station. Just check that you're not riding the night before a big football match. In fact, check everything – with a native. Italy is a country for initiates.

SICILY ON THE SLOW TRACK

DEFYING THE WARNINGS OF LOCALS, **PAUL MANSFIELD**
BOARDS THE 'DIRETTO' AND 'REGIONALE' TRAINS,
AND MEANDERS THROUGH HUMBLE VILLAGES AND
BEAUTIFUL VALLEYS

Mid-afternoon in Sicily. The heat quivered on the fields; there was no sound but the whirring of cicadas, and the tiny station of Enna was deserted as I stepped off the train. High on a ridge, three miles away, I could see the grey stone clusters of the town itself. How to get there?

The hiss of a Gaggia machine announced that the station bar was open. Inside, a barman with several days' worth of stubble poured me an espresso and announced that a taxi was expected soon. I waited outside, where a three-legged dog hopped across the empty platform to make my acquaintance.

I already had the feeling that someone from the Sicilian equivalent of Central Casting had made arrangements for my reception, and this was confirmed by the arrival of the taxi driver, a thick-set individual with fists like hams and a spiv's leather jacket. Wrap-around shades completed the effect. We set off up the hill, twisting and weaving on the narrow roads, before pulling up in Enna's town square with a squeal of brakes. Now that, I thought, was the way to arrive in small-town Sicily.

No one had understood why I wanted to take a train around Sicily. No one in Sicily, that is. 'Slow', 'unreliable' and 'dirty' were the epithets used by the locals to describe their railway network. I put it down to the twin Italian obsessions with the motor car and speed. Take a car away from a Sicilian and he's like a centaur who has lost his body.

On the taxi ride to the stazione centrale in Palermo, we had hooted, lurched and swerved through the gridlocked traffic, as the driver's temperature rose faster than that of the sweltering streets. The Sicilians have an expression for this situation: 'che camurria', which translates into 'I can't stand it! Let's get moving!'

I couldn't stand it, either. I entered the station bar with relief, to be enveloped in the familiar Italian fug of coffee fumes and cigarette smoke. Outside, in a tiny chapel on the concourse, Mass was being said. Bright shafts of sunlight traversed the tracks, and a railway worker was hanging destination plates on the carriages of the 12.05 'diretto' to Enna. We left on time.

The three-carriage train, covered with graffiti outside but clean and comfortable within, ran alongside the sparkling waters of the coast and then turned inland. We climbed up through rolling hills, the fields carpeted with wild flowers. My travelling companions were a clutch of schoolchildren, two peasant women dressed in black and a singular gentleman opposite with a pencil moustache, trilby, white gloves and the air of a theatrical impresario.

He saw me tucking into my station-bought panini and red wine, and asked if I liked fish. He produced a bag of calamari and passed it over, politely refusing my offer of wine. 'I am afraid I drank more than enough wine last night, signore.' He disappeared at the next station, doffing his hat. I had been on the Sicilian rails less than an hour and already felt I was among friends.

Enna is a mountain town, with a remote, frontier feel. Livy described it as 'inexpugnabilis', and for centuries its primary function was as bastion of defence for and against the many invading armies – Greek, Roman, Saracen, Norman – that have tussled over Sicily's territory. The 13th-century Castello di Lombardia dominates the town, with spectacular views over the rugged, windswept countryside and the lake, Lago di Pergusa, where Hades abducted Persephone into the underworld.

I took a room at Enna's only hotel, the Grande Albergo di Sicilia. It had an ugly modern façade, giving way to a charming art nouveau lobby. I fell asleep to the sound of church bells in the clear mountain air – and was promptly awoken by the amorous adventures of the couple next door. At breakfast they were easy to identify: they both had that unmistakable air of being married – but not to each other. From the edge of town, the snow-capped cone of Mount Etna, which last erupted in 1992, was visible, serene and majestic in the distance.

Later I saw Etna close up, from the Circumetnea Railway. This ancient train rattles around Europe's biggest volcano, from the shambolic suburbs of Catania – passing buildings so closely you could almost reach out and touch them – to the open spaces of Etna's lower slopes. Here, citrus plantations, vines and nut trees add splashes of colour to the black lava.

The train (as always) was crowded with the kind of locals unable to afford other forms of transport. A young mother sat with her baby on her lap, with the expression of a renaissance madonna; opposite me, a thin, tragical Arab-looking teenager studied a computing magazine. Just when I thought I might catch up on some sleep after Enna, what sounded like two competing foghorns started up at the end of the carriage. Two grizzled old boys from a mountain village had joined the train. They sat opposite each other, bellowing and cackling in that peculiar Sicilian dialect that adds a granite-like edge to vowels and slurs everything else. When we reached the coast at Riposto I was as wide awake as I've ever been, and my ears were ringing.

At Taormina I discovered the disadvantages of train travel in Sicily. The station is situated on the coast below the town and, with no taxis to be seen, it was a forty-five-minute slog in the midday heat up to Sicily's most famous tourist resort. Perhaps that is why I did not care for Taormina. After the humble villages of the interior, it seemed too sanitised; a pretty enough place with a justly celebrated Greek amphitheatre, but largely dedicated to tourism, trading on its historical associations (D.H. Lawrence the best known) and all too artificial after life as viewed from a Sicilian train. I left after a few hours, rattling down the coast to Syracuse.

If Taormina has lost caste due to mass tourism, it is safe to say that Syracuse went permanently out of fashion nearly 2,000 years ago. In 500 BC this was the most important city in the western world, but centuries of misrule and military adventurism destroyed its power, leaving it a peaceful, sun-baked backwater. In the late afternoon the Ortygia – the small peninsula where the oldest buildings are – was deserted.

I sat contemplating the Duomo – which began life as a Doric temple, and is now a masterpiece of cream-and-white Baroque statuary – and watched a wedding party arrive at the gates. The bride's voluminous veil caught in the wind and nearly asphyxiated her father; country boys in too-big suits lounged around, cracking jokes; an irascible, bow-tied photographer struggled to organise the party in the late afternoon sun. After a while, like most people who have come to Syracuse in the past 2,000 years, I moved on.

Heading inland, the train passed through villages of astonishing beauty, many of them overlooked by tourists. It was a 'regionale' train, the slowest of the slow, stopping every five minutes, and had grimy compartments hung with black-and-white prints of the Italian Riviera. By mid-morning we were in Noto, with its yellow baroque churches covered in scaffolding. After years of neglect, the Duomo collapsed last year, and finally prompted the city fathers into action to save their town's exquisite architecture.

At noon we had reached Modica, where, in a trattoria near the station, I indulged in a Sicilian lunch of stupendous proportions. Baked aubergines, pasta con sarde e finocchio (pasta with sardines and fennel), involtini di carne (ham and cheese wrapped in breaded veal), salad, fruit and cheese. Ten quid the lot. Wine was local vino sfuso, ruby-red and strong. I toiled up the hill to the station, caught the next passing diretto and promptly fell asleep.

When I awoke the train was running through a deep valley, and there, perched high above, were the old and new towns of Ragusa. The 'new' town, dating from the 17th century, was handsome enough; but the old medieval quarter − hewn out of rock and clinging to the sides of a steep ravine − was wonderful. Best of all were the public gardens, cool and shady, hung with acacia, with glorious views across the ravine. On a bench someone had contributed some lyrical graffiti: 'In questo giardino pieno di misteri, sono morto e rinato' − 'dead and reborn in a garden full of mystery'. My feelings exactly.

From Ragusa the train dropped down to the coast, through a landscape of olives, vineyards and great swathes of corn. We rolled through industrial Gela and on towards Agrigento. Here, three magnificent Doric temples stand on a bluff overlooking the sea. The first sight of them was almost hallucinatory; well removed from the town itself, unfenced and mercifully devoid of tourists, they stood, noble, dramatic and serene − the finest ruins of their kind outside Greece.

Time for the long haul back to Palermo. Another diretto, another mobile lunch of panini and wine, and another chance encounter − this time with Lucia, a graphic designer who had lived in Paris and London. She was an odd mixture: deeply traditional and proud of it, yet in other respects − her designer jeans and skimpy T-shirt − thoroughly modern. She talked about Sicily with that blend of resignation and optimism I had come to recognise as typical.

'Things change very slowly here,' she said. There were enormous problems with corruption and bureaucracy; even the recent 'super-trials', which put several hundred mafiosi behind bars in Palermo, would make very little difference. But despite all this, she had chosen to return to her island and live there. 'I am Sicilian,' said Lucia. 'Not European; not even Italian. I can't be happy anywhere else.'

We reached Palermo in the afternoon rush-hour. The city centre was an immobile mass of honking, overheating cars. Even the train was caught up in it, at an unmanned level-crossing blocked by an impatient truck. I watched the trucker and another driver engage in a heated argument, while I finished my lunch in leisurely fashion. 'Che camurria, indeed,' I thought. They don't know what they're missing.

TRAIL OF THE LONESOME PINE

DISASTROUS RAINS SAVED A SMALL
FRENCH RAILWAY FROM CLOSING

Erica Brown

The train slowed as it approached the bridge, finished just days before by engineers from the French Foreign Legion. A patter of polite applause wafted from a group of teenagers behind us.

There are prettier sights in the south of France than this gun-metal-grey steel bridge, slung across a gash in a landscape that will take nature years to heal. But for the people of this corner of Haute Provence, the bridge signified that, after eighteen months, life was back to normal.

In November 1994, after a week of heavy rain, the River Var overflowed and swept away roads, houses and several miles of railway track. The military set about repairing the damage, but it wasn't until May this year that the bridge between the villages of Entrevaux and Annot was completed and the narrow-gauge railway could resume.

The Chemins de Fer de la Provence, nicknamed the Pine Cone Line, has its own station in the centre of Nice and runs ninety miles north and west, and mostly uphill, to Digne-les-Bains. Built between 1891 and 1911, the line was a vital link between otherwise almost inaccessible villages in the Alpes Maritimes and Haute Provence.

By the 1990s, however, the N202 road, which follows its route, had taken most of the traffic from the privately owned railway and its future was in doubt. The 1994 floods threatened to close it completely. But the disaster was to prove the line's saviour.

Locals who had taken it for granted suddenly realised how much they needed it. The original, grand 19th-century station in Nice was sold to raise funds and the government lent soldiers from the army and Foreign Legion to repair the track and replace the bridge.

Railway buffs may be disappointed that steam engines have not been used for many years (except on short stretches a few times each summer), and that the nondescript carriages look like trams. But there's no denying it's an engineering tour de force: twenty-six tunnels blasted through mountains (one is two miles long); sixteen viaducts and fifteen bridges built across deep valleys; and a track rising from sea level to three thousand feet.

Its sheer romance won me over. The train, Provence's own TGV – 'train à grandes vibrations' – rattled out of Nice at 9 a.m., across main roads clogged with rush-hour traffic and closed for our approach. We started to climb along the left bank of the Var. This first forty-five minutes is commuting territory, the least-interesting part of the trip. Then, at La Vesubie, the line turns west, briefly sandwiched by the two sides of the N202 dual carriageway, and the landscape becomes mountainous.

Twenty minutes later, we pulled in to Villars-sur-Var, where the station contained an inviting restaurant complete with terrace, fresh pasta, a 65-franc menu and resident artisan chocolatier. But it was too early for lunch.

Towards Entrevaux there are completely different landscapes either side of the train. To the east, sheer cliffs and mountains, some terraced with olives; to the west a valley, softly green with orchards, salad crops and vines. The first sight of Entrevaux was its citadel perched on top of an almost vertical hill.

Entrevaux was once an important border defence between France and Savoy and as such was heavily fortified in the 1690s by Vauban, Louis XIV's military architect. The small town, a hotchpotch of medieval houses, sits at the foot of the hill in a U-turn of the Var that forms a natural moat. You enter it across a drawbridge, through one of three gatehouses. It looks impregnable, so it's difficult to understand why Vauban went to town the way he did, ringing the place with ramparts.

From here, it was fifteen minutes to Annot, a pretty, small town with a renaissance heart. Here, if the train is on time, there is a five-minute stop at the newly rebuilt station (a chunk of hillside fell on it during the rains). If the driver gets off, you know there's time for a coffee in the station buffet – he'll be having one, too.

Beyond Annot, the track winds in a series of giant S-bends that climb more than three hundred feet in two miles, then passes through a tunnel to St-André-les-Alpes, a popular spot for hang-gliders, windsurfers and whitewater rafters. Now we were in true Alpine scenery – meadows lush with fresh grass and pink, blue and yellow wild flowers; orchards; woodland and mountains, forested for most of their height but still with snow on top. 'Does the train run all year?' I asked the conductor.

'Oh, yes, madame,' he replied, recognising I was English. 'We don't have the wrong kind of snow here.' But the Pine Cone train does have something in common with British Rail. We arrived in Digne seven minutes late.

THE RAIL WAY TO SEE THE CONTINENT

PAUL MANSFIELD COULD HAVE FLOWN TO PORTUGAL
IN TWO HOURS. INSTEAD, HE MEANDERED THROUGH
FOUR COUNTRIES IN FIVE DAYS

To lunch, as a warrior unto battle. Casa Botin in Madrid is the oldest restaurant in the world (1725), and features in several books including Hemingway's *Fiesta* ('We lunched upstairs at Botin's. It is one of the best restaurants in the world').

All of which leads you to assume the place will be an overpriced tourist trap.

But what you get is a venerable building with creaking stairs, ancient furniture and tiled walls. At 3 p.m. it was just beginning to fill with locals. The house speciality is suckling pig: a plate so huge that you feel you probably couldn't pick it up, let alone eat it. As Hemingway observed, you have to drink plenty of wine to get it all down – in his case, a preposterous five bottles. I managed a creditable two of house Valdepeñas. Flushed with success, I stumbled towards the station like a wine cask on legs.

Travelling across Europe by train you notice cultural changes in a way that you don't when travelling by plane – and especially when it comes to food. The farther south I got, the heavier the ingredients became, and the greater the air of excess attending meals.

I'd left London a few days earlier on Eurostar, with a leisurely five days to reach Lisbon. It's a lovely way to travel. We rolled through the south London suburbs, peering into windows an arm's length from the track, and soon were running through the Kent countryside, warm and golden on a sunny afternoon.

My immediate neighbour was an elderly gentleman who spent the journey angrily ripping out pages from his newspaper and summoning the train steward to ask stupid questions. ('How can you tell which is the window seat?' was one). Eventually the old boy fell asleep. At six we were rolling into the Gare du Nord, the heart of Paris, with washing hanging from windows and that unmistakable Parisian smell of Gauloises and drains. I took a taxi across the river.

For years Parisian hotels came in just two categories: palace or flea-pit. That has changed. The Bel Ami in St Germain des Prés is a bright, savvy hotel with a modern interior; computer workstations in the lobby and a stylish cocktail bar. From my room on the first floor I looked out over the crowded streets of shops, cafés and restaurants. As dusk fell I sipped pastis, people-watching on the terrace of Les Deux Magots. Perfect.

Even when they go for a blow-out, the French are careful to retain a sense of proportion. At Chez Paul, an antique bistro in the Bastille with a smoke-darkened interior, I lunched on pot-roast lamb and vegetables. The portions were just right, the cheeseboard varied without being excessive, the half-bottle of St-Emilion strong but not overpowering. The French savour their food, but they don't linger over it for hours. By three, Chez Paul was empty-ing as its regular customers headed back to work.

Leaving the Bel Ami, I was struck by another advantage of train travel. At airports you become passive; checked in and ordered about. Travelling by train you take a cab to the Gare d'Austerlitz, then sit at the terrace bar with a beer until you feel like boarding the waiting overnight express to Madrid.

The train itself was a Talgo 'trainhotel', the Francisco de Goya. You could see immediately this was a Spanish train. As I settled into my single berth, the steward arrived with a choice of dinner sittings: eight or ten o'clock? Ten? 'Spanish hours,' he said with a smile.

And in the dining car that slight formality between waiters and their customers (which in France seems appropriate) was entirely absent. Here the waiters were kindly, middle-aged men, warm and approachable. Would señor care for a glass of Jerez? Señor certainly would. Señor was travelling alone? Bueno. Information was exchanged: about the weather in Spain, about homes and families. The meal was enormous: Mediterranean aspara-gus, each strip thick as a finger; a huge plate of lamb; vegetables, salad, cheese, an apple tart. I sipped ruby-red Rioja and watched the neat fields and hedgerows of Bordeaux flash by.

In the bar two shaven-headed men talked in excited tones about how dull Paris was compared with Madrid, and dropped the names of several fashionable Madrileños as proof. A pony-tailed fellow with leathery skin said he was a musician in a gypsy band and acted the part, leaning into the bar and tipping back draughts of Johnny Walker with a shudder.

Perched on stools were two fresh-faced American backpackers who had managed to get the attention of a beautiful bilingual Spanish girl. She sat chatting to them as they ogled her longingly. Eventually she excused herself, made for the bar – and immediately fell into conversation with the Scotch-drinking musician.

At 3 a.m. I was jolted awake in my bunk. We had reached the Spanish border just before San Sebastian, where the change of gauge between railway networks takes place automatically. Even so, the effortlessly smooth ride of the French side had gone. We bumped and tilted through the rest of the night.

The sun came up on another world; the bare, denuded hills of Castile y León, with their outcrops of rock and pine and air of windswept grandeur. Over coffee I gazed at the walls of Avila, one of the most complete medieval cities in the world, rising like an apparition in the distance. A few miles later it was the Escorial, Philip II's vast monastery-palace, with its sculpted towers and austere, abandoned air.

'Nine months winter, three months hell,' say the people of Castile y León of their climate. Sure enough, we pulled into a Madrid caught in the middle of a heatwave. The city seemed dazed; deserted during the day, with people returning to the streets and parks only at night when it was cool enough to walk around or sit at an open-air cafe. At the Hotel Villa Real near the Prado, I slunk inside, grateful for the air-conditioning.

Arrival at a Spanish hotel is always an event. It's the decorousness – in this case the Villa Real's imposing, stained-wood lobby – mixed with the warmth of the staff. They inquire after your journey, help you settle in in small ways – procuring a table at the ever-busy Botin's, for example. At the Villa Real, as elsewhere in Spain, everything is personal.

Two days later, Portugal proved different again. On the Talgo Express from Madrid we dropped down into the plains of western Spain. It was a scorching day, with hawks wheeling in the clear sky and the fields quivering in a heat haze. The train stopped at village stations decorated with blue tiles. In the dining car the barman was taciturn, and the other passengers – a young businessman and a smartly dressed woman, who smiled demurely like royalty – kept themselves to themselves. Like the French, the Portuguese are happiest keeping a distance.

Lunch was in the station café at Badajoz, near the Portuguese border. The air-conditioning was roaring as the waiter read out the 'menu' (scribbled on his cigarette packet): pasta with chorizo; garlic chicken and salad. A bottle of rusty-tasting red wine was brought from the fridge. The other diners – mostly local workmen – finished their meals, lit up cigarettes as one, then pushed back their chairs and left. I'd come a long way from the leisurely indulgence of lunch in Paris and Madrid.

At six in the evening the train coasted down the banks of the River Tagus, past the 10.5-mile-long Vasco da Gama Bridge, into Lisbon. Five days, four countries, 1,250 miles of track.

Time for one last meal – fiery chicken peri-peri in a Mozambican place below the castle, with washing hanging in the courtyard and children scampering in and out. Then a slow meander back to my hotel, reflecting that, had I wanted, I could have made this journey by plane in about two hours. And missed everything.

YOU'RE ONLY YOUNG TWICE

FUELLED BY A DESIRE TO REPEAT A JOURNEY OF HIS
YOUTH, **PAUL MANSFIELD** BOARDS THE TRAIN IN
LONDON BOUND FOR ATHENS

Three in the morning: the train has stopped, it is pitch-black outside, and someone is tapping on my compartment door. Then thumping. Then kicking.

Oh, God. Struggling into my jeans, fumbling for passport; fumbling with the padlock on the door … Enter three burly Serbian immigration officials, with revolvers and nightsticks, who proceed to go through my bag and papers. Questions are barked, replies met with unfriendly grunts. Pavel, the Hungarian conductor, stands behind them impassively. When they leave, he produces a bottle of brandy, shaking his head in derision. 'It is as I said. Balkans. Bal-kans!' The next checkpoint, he says, will be in half an hour. We clink glasses, and forget about sleeping. It is going to be a long night.

I decided to travel from London to Athens by train for nostalgic reasons. Twenty years ago I'd made the same trip as a teenage InterRailer, and I wanted to rekindle some old memories. But just as the map of Europe has been redrawn, railway networks, too, have been re-organised. It came as a shock to discover that some versions of the current InterRail ticket are not recognised in France – which tends to detract from the 'go-anywhere' spirit of the old days. Perhaps more significantly, for someone engaged in revisiting the scenes of his youth, my ticket also fell into a new and unsettling category: InterRail 26-Plus.

More changes, too, leaving London; setting off not by boat train from Victoria but on Eurostar from Waterloo, 186mph on the way to Paris. I had come to Paris with my wife, and we spent a happy weekend prowling around the sights. But when we said goodbye on Monday – she heading back to London, and me south to Greece – my mood plunged.

In a café opposite the Gare de l'Est, surrounded by backpackers, I sat over a beer feeling anxious and depressed. Anxious, because a rail journey of 3,000 miles – through eight countries and across fourteen borders – allows plenty of opportunities for things to go wrong. I had a visa for the Federal Republic of Yugoslavia, but was unsure if it was valid for Serbia. Macedonia, another new country, at constant loggerheads with neighbouring Greece, presented another problem.

But I was depressed for a different reason. The sight of those cheerful, fresh-faced travellers – bearing nylon packs, clutching plastic bottles of water like athletes on a round-Europe relay – confirmed a simple fact: if not actually old, or even barely middle-aged, I am certainly no longer young.

The EuroCity left on time at 2 p.m., a sleek, comfortable train with a decor of cream and orange. Wandering through the corridor in search of the buffet I was enveloped by a cloud of marijuana fumes. A young black guy, with shades and Walkman, was leaning on the end of a compartment, smoking. Some avuncular advice seemed called for.

'Prenez garde, M'sieu. L'aroma, c'est formidable.'

'Je suis toujours en garde, mon ami.' He gave a crocodile smile, and offered me the joint.

In my compartment was a French diplomat en route to Strasbourg, full of anecdotes about the recent French elections; and a retired German couple, Dieter and Ursula. With her bobbed blonde hair and blue eyes, Ursula bore an uncanny resemblance to Doris Day. She reminisced about her first European train journeys, as a child during the Second World War. 'It was terrible. We had to move home five times to escape the bombing. It was such a bad time. But over forever now, I think, thank God.'

We rolled through the green heart of France, and crossed the border into Germany near Baden-Baden. At 10 p.m. the train reached Munich, to horrible scenes on the concourse. A gang of moody, belligerent drunks milled around the bar, alternately slapping each other's backs, arguing and sulking with each other. One of them, a woman, slid slowly down to her knees and on to the floor. When the station police arrived, the other drinkers abused them. The woman, incredibly, made it to her feet and resumed drinking. I left in a hurry and found my berth. Sleeping through stops at Salzburg and Vienna, I woke once to a cold blast of mountain air coming through the open window. I'd forgotten how high we were.

Budapest was damp and chilly under a misty dawn. But Keleti station – in Communist days a dour, lifeless place – was a revelation. Here was the free market in full swing, in the form of lively bars and cafés, shops, food stalls, innumerable private 'travel agents' and money changers.

No showers here, but at least the chance to wash and shave for 10p in the gents'. I had a cappuccino, surrounded by a group of characters drinking Scotch for breakfast with the collars of their leather jackets turned up against the cold. An old man wandered through the crowd, half-heartedly shouting, 'Polis! Polis!' No one paid any attention to him.

The Danube was grey and sluggish in the morning light. I stocked up on groceries at a supermarket: thick Hungarian bread, salami and cheese, fruit and wine. No one had been able to provide any information – let alone currency – for Serbia, the next stop, and I was taking no chances. Back at the station, the Hellas Express for Thessaloniki was ready for departure at 11 a.m.

For 'express', read 'ghost train'. The half-dozen rickety old carriages, blue and cream in colour, and with grimy brown banquettes, were almost empty. The only other occupants of my wagon-lit car were a young Greek couple who introduced themselves and then withdrew into their compartment. Sitting alone in a six-seat compartment with barred windows, the train rattling through Budapest's suburbs and out into fields of wheat, felt oddly like occupying a mobile cell.

But then Pavel arrived. He poured coffee and introduced what was to become a familiar theme. Travelling through the Balkans, he said, was a difficult business. 'At every stop they make trouble. They are crazy. You will see.'

At the Serbian border town of Subotica, the first of many men in uniforms clambered on to the train. Trouble. My InterRail ticket was deemed invalid within Yugoslavia. Pavel, looking momentarily worried, took the inspector off for a chat, and returned smiling: apparently I could stay on the train. A £10 bribe, negotiated down from £20 by Pavel, had done the trick.

We rolled across lush countryside, passing clusters of grey-stone villages and women in headscarves bent double in the fields, and by early evening we were in Belgrade.

Outside the station the atmosphere resembled a tawdry back-street market. Men in cheap suits approached offering black-market cigarettes; there were stalls selling food, tatty clothes and magazines, and odd, sinuous folk music blasting from speakers. I tried to buy a hot meal but was rebuffed: large-denomination Deutschmarks only – with a sackful of worthless dinars offered as 'change'. Back to the train, then, for another picnic meal and a few glasses of wine.

Though the wagon-lit remained deserted, the other carriages were now overflowing with locals, some sleeping in their seats, others dozing or lounging in the corridors. Many were peasants on their way home from the capital, and personal hygiene was evidently not high on their list of priorities. I abandoned a walk through the train when the odour of sweat became too strong. At dusk Pavel arrived with a padlock and chain. 'Keep the door locked and your money out of sight. Any problems, I'll deal with them.'

Which he did. What a timeless night that was; rumbling and crashing through the invisible Serbian countryside, with stop after stop for customs, immigration and ticket inspection. Serbian at Presevo; Macedonian at Tabanovci; another exit stop at Gevgelija ... Teams of officials lumbered on and off the train, peering into the compartments with torches. At Tabanovci, the Greek couple were taken off and made to pay a fine for some irregularity with their visas. Pavel watched until they were back on board. Dawn was breaking over the black hills, and from far off we heard the drone of the muezzin.

I woke with a start near the Greek border. The train was following a river through a limestone ravine, with blue sky above and glorious translucent light flooding the compartment. We'd left the gloom of eastern Europe behind and were now, unmistakably, in the south. At the border crossing of Idomeni, there were duty-free shops, bars, even a bureau de change. It was as if Greece was demonstrating to the world her superiority over her upstart Macedonian neighbour. But (this being Greece) most of the facilities were closed.

Thessaloniki brought sad goodbyes to Pavel (who nobly kissed the hand of the departing Greek girl); my first hot meal for forty-eight hours; and the appalling realisation that the rank and grimy smell I'd come to associate with the train was now emanating from me.

Perhaps that's why I had two seats to myself on the Intercity to Athens: a long, hot afternoon running through Greece's central mountains, dropping finally down to the plains, with my neighbours engaged in the familiar Greek pastimes of smoking, arguing and puzzling over quiz magazines.

At 8 p.m. we rumbled into Larissis station. The Greek capital was being dug up for its new metro system, a refuse strike had left the streets piled high with rubbish and the cabbie ripped me off grievously for the short ride to my hotel.

None of this mattered. After fifty-four hours on the train, I felt hugely pleased with myself – though desperately in need of a shower. I also, I noted as I stepped under the hot water, suddenly no longer felt old.

THE ALPS WITHOUT ROPES AND PITONS

ANTHONY PEREGRINE TAKES TO THE HILLS IN FRANCE

There are three keys to a successful rail holiday. The first is to travel light —
ideally with just a wristwatch (to check how long it is until, say, 13:27) and a
slim paperback. If this seems impractical, then take only one bag and make
it the smallest you can. You will be grateful beyond words when you are
haring along a platform having discovered that it is already 13:26.

Second, if you must have a companion — by no means obligatory — choose
the less-talkative sort. Though often quite full of people, trains are strangely
unconducive to conversation.

Third, pick a period during which the entire rail system of your chosen
destination will not be going on strike. This is harder to do in France than
in most other countries. Last October, setting off from my home in the
south of the country, I failed.

With the rail network at a full-stop, Marseilles St Charles station — rarely
a relaxing spot at the happiest of times — had become a refugee camp.
Desperate mothers, stranded for twelve hours or more, were offering up
children for adoption. Senior citizens were being barged past as marginally
fitter folk careered after the few trains still operating (my apologies).
Meanwhile, smart ladies in blue SNCF uniforms fielded formidable abuse
from men in suits unable to accept that they were not going to Paris tonight
or, indeed, any time soon.

So, strikes are best avoided. So, too, are chatterboxes and heavy luggage.
Then you'll have a ball. Outside Marseilles, I did. Mainly.

DAY ONE

Lyon Part-Dieu station, my starting point for this shunt round the Alps, is a
symphony of stainless steel and glass, butty bars and noticeboards. And
people. The trouble with public transport, it occurs to me, is the public.
They are everywhere, and disorientated or dashing.

Announcements compound the tension. Pitched at a volume just below
the readily audible, they always start with the five-figure train number,

which only the demented ever recognise or care two hoots about. They then inform me that the front of my train will be going to Geneva, the middle to Evian and the rear to somewhere I don't catch. Sounds like Milwaukee, though this seems improbable. Aaargh. My car never does this to me.

But the build-up of anxiety is vital to the rail experience. Without it, there would not be that flood of relief when one finally finds a seat in the right bit of the right train. Bag stowed, your responsibilities are entirely over. All you have to do is relax, travel — quite often backwards — through the landscape and hope that no one comes to sit next to you. It is most liberating.

The experience is enhanced by the other-worldly politeness of SNCF staff. The ticket inspector, on seeing my British-issue InterRail pass, conducts our exchange in English, gives me useful tips on changes and wishes me 'a very good voyage'. When I do change, at La Roche-sur-Foron, the chap behind the station desk answers further questions as a deputy headmaster might dispense careers advice. These people aren't just rail employees; they are self-consciously custodians of a public service, itself an expression of the gravitas of the French state. Stations we have passed have often been roughly the same size as the villages they serve. They bear the stamp of authority.

Surely, then, this splendid organisation and its admirable servants won't be shutting up shop in a couple of days? Oh yes, they will. A serious public service has serious ups, but serious downs, too.

By now, we are in the Alps proper, mountains towering above comely valleys dotted variously with chalets and cows. My first overnight stop is Annecy, its lake setting off surrounding mountains splendidly. Lakes and mountains do go well together, and Annecy quite fits the frame. An atmospheric squeeze of waterways, venerable buildings and arcades in the old centre opens to elegant acres of greensward and trees by the lake. Here one should meet Jane Austen heroines discussing suitors.

Instead, there are joggers. Dozens of them. To escape, I climb to the basilica dominating the town. This is the last resting place of St François de Sales — patron saint of journalists (and also, interestingly enough, of the deaf and dumb). His remains are in a copper reliquary, before which I ask for a meeting with Lord Lucan and, as usual on such occasions, a little divine indulgence for my expenses claims.

DAY TWO

To St Gervais. Here, I switch to the Mont Blanc Express, a snappy little train in the Savoy colours of red and white, for a fabulous, sunlit, single-track journey into the power of the mountains and an upward haul to Chamonix. It climbs through woodland, along gorges and past settlements scattered across more hospitable stretches. Story-book chalets abound. In their gardens are woodpiles, tomato plants, chickens and children's play equipment. A Wendy house doesn't half give a different perspective to the Mont Blanc massif.

At the village of Servoz, a passenger gets on wearing the beatific smile of one who is thanking the Lord for all this spectacular beauty and is keen to share his joy. He sits next to me and does just that. It is with some pleasure that I leave him for dead on the Chamonix platform.

Chamonix – you'll have heard of the place: Alpine capital overseen by Mont Blanc and other bulky items. It exists essentially to send people up mountains and then feed them tartiflette when they return. This is commendable, but the town does take the job a little too seriously, given that mountain activities are, like darts and hopscotch, essentially leisure pursuits. There is an uncomfortable air of earnestness, what with all those guides, shops full of equipment (sticks, picks, boots, maps, backpacks, goggles) and streets full of people toting it – bearing the grim mien of those about to undergo surgery rather than have fun.

I'm not a mountain-climbing person; I have the head for heights of a chrysanthemum. So my reserve is probably explained by the fact that I'm intimidated by Chamonix and all it stands for, including the Aiguille du Midi cable car. Laughably, this wants to whisk me 12,000ft up to a viewing platform in a Christmas tree bauble. No, thank you; sitting on a café terrace, drinking a beer and staring mildly transfixed up at Mont Blanc quite fulfils my mountaineering needs.

DAY THREE

Chamonix to Chambéry involves a bit of backtracking. We are, after all, in the Alps. You can't just go directly where you want. It also involves the invasion of my carriage by a posse of adolescents intent on shattering my calm.

Other passengers always cause a problem. This is the central irony of rail travel. We all want trains to keep running, be successful, save the planet, etc. But we also want as few people as possible in our particular carriage. In public, we become excessively private.

Teenagers are ill-equipped to grasp this dynamic – or, it seems, to sit normally in seats. But the scenery remains astounding, there is the essentially masculine pleasure of noting the trains leaving exactly on time (11:47, 15:02: bonkers but deeply rewarding) and, as the youngsters later quit the train they all — and without apparent sarcasm — wish me 'Au revoir, Monsieur'. I feel bad and sad about my ungenerous thoughts. It takes a train trip to make me realise I'm a buffer.

Never mind. Upward and onward to Chambéry and another great advantage of rail travel that I have not yet mentioned: no need to park or worry that the car will attract the attention of the criminal classes. Just walk to the hotel, dump the bag and the town is yours. And Chambéry is an especially appealing town to have — all tree-lined boulevards, comely squares and that aura of deep-rooted self-sufficiency worn by the classier French provincial capitals.

I wander all over the place — up to the street-blocker of a chateau once occupied by the dukes of Savoy, back through the rich wriggle of little streets at its base and to the elliptical, Italianate place St Léger to join the rest of the town for aperitifs. At the next terrace table is an attractive lady drinking wine and reading *Le Monde*, while her two infant daughters romp in the traffic-free square in front. Wherever the heart of civilisation might be, it cannot be far away.

DAY FOUR

National strike day. I had expected pandemonium at the station, but it's as calm as a Sunday, peopled by non-striking SNCF staff on hand to counsel travellers. They have clearly taken vows of patience and courtesy. In place of very many trains, they have rustled up a few buses (despite the fact that most of the country's bus network is also on strike).

I jump on one to Grenoble and a second to Sisteron. This is another brilliant upland journey, with mountains, passes and valleys now more companionably arranged. Through the sentinel rocks guarding Sisteron and we are in Provence. Thirty minutes later, we are in Digne — one of my favourite Provençal towns, precisely because it has not a single air or grace.

The setting is grandiose (mountains all around, river round the edge) but the tight-packed old centre remains a place of loaded washing lines, tripe shops and children on bikes rather than potters and Parisian television producers. Shop-fronts from the 1960s announce 'Modern Fashions' and the bar is full of blokes with uncertain cardigans, ill-disciplined bellies and their eyes on the racing on TV. Civilisation takes many forms.

DAY FIVE

Here's a treat. Le Train des Pignes is a privately run single carriage that scuttles through the southern Alps from Digne to Nice. The first of the day is at

7.29 a.m. and rattles down slopes like a bobsleigh. At this hour, the mountains are black masses silhouetted against the lightening blue-black background.

Gradually, the sky clears, turning the clouds an unlikely shade of pink. Mountains and gorges shake off the night, coming up fresh. It is grandiose. One expects God to appear briefly, booming: 'How about that, then?'

Scurrying along ridges and through forests, the train stops at places that aren't places at all, just clearings in the woodland. At one, a family with four children get on. They are obviously on holiday from some unknown country where communication is by screeching. Just as I'm opting for mass murder, they get off at an equally remote outpost.

Back to contemplation. There is something satisfying about rolling through the mountainscape and linking its doughty villages without damaging them. Rail can do that as road cannot. Many of the stations – one platform, one little building – have chefs-de-gare, dignified chaps who come out for a chat with our train driver. Imagine that: a stationmaster for a station with eight small trains a day. It is a career move I could warm to.

This is a happy train. This has been a happy trip. I'm smiling as we zip through the Var gorges and into Nice. I'm still smiling on the SNCF train along the coast to Marseilles. Where I stop smiling. The national one-day strike has been extended here. The port city is living up to its reputation for excess (or perhaps you've never eaten bouillabaisse?).

In the mayhem, I find a vaguely relevant train. I just manage to hurl myself on as it makes to leave. And – here's the thing – the feeling of triumph against insuperable odds is terrific. I've never had that with a car.

TO THE ORIENT, BY THE NOT-QUITE EXPRESS

NICHOLAS CRANE REPORTS ON DR ZHIVAGO, THE FIGHTING POLICEMAN, AND THE REST OF THE COLOURFUL CAST ON THE SLOW TRAIN TO ISTANBUL

Taking the stopping train to Istanbul is the kind of 'good idea' best acted upon before there is time to consider the implications. Quips such as 'You'll probably spend Christmas in a Romanian railway siding' can come true. So we left at short notice with a rucksack full of books and two tickets to Vienna.

While the 11.40 from Victoria to Dover Western Docks loped through countryside the colour of a pub carpet, I turned to our *Thomas Cook European Rail Timetable*. Besides providing the timings of 50,000 trains, this 512-page paperback offers even the nuttiest of train-brains a lifetime of lip-licking perusal.

For less than the cost of two Awaydays to Dorking, it will, for example, tell you that the 21:56 from Helsinki to Joensuu has a buffet-car but stops at Savolinna on Mondays and Saturdays only.

I had already calculated, using the book, that our route from London to Vienna, with a detour to Prague and then on to Budapest, Bucharest, Sofia and Istanbul and then back to London via the safe bit of Yugoslavia, added up to 7,546km and 125 hours of train travel. As a railway novitiate, I clung to our red paperback convinced that its loss would be as fatal as losing one's trousers on top of Everest.

At the far end of a Channel storm we tottered along the platform at Ostende to board a Quink-blue carriage decorated in gold script with the words 'wagons-lits'. Each of our bunks was fitted with a press-button lamp and a tiny elasticated mesh pocket for the bits and bobs you're left with at lights-out, such as spectacles and false teeth. There was also a little hook just above face-level for hanging a wristwatch.

Minutes after we had moved in, an attendant arrived to inquire whether we would prefer tea or coffee in the morning. He took our passports to avoid disturbing us during the night-time border crossings.

We woke in a snow-covered plain. Solid-looking farmhouses slid by, locked to the steppe by a grid of frozen dykes and roads. We converged on a pewter-grey river, broad and sluggish, with heavy black barges and banks lined with frozen poplars as still as stalagmites. Thomas Cook told us that this was the Danube. The track curled around Melk, crowned by the massive monastery that had encouraged Patrick Leigh Fermor as he crossed the plain on his pre-war walk from the Channel to Constantinople.

Vienna's cobbled streets and coffeehouses tinkled with tram bells and laughter. But three hours down the Danube, the capital of Hungary was showing few signs of having come in from the cold. Freezing fog wreathed gravestone-grey buildings and the precinct of Matthias Church on Buda's hill was deep in snow. We found the 19:45 night train to Bucharest waiting in the dark by an empty platform. A man wearing a fur hat, splendid serge overcoat, leather gloves and a face like Omar Sharif's unlocked the door of the only couchette carriage.

Inside, visibility was less than six feet; the dark corridor was so thick with steam that we had to grope our way forward, passing on the way a 10ft-long section of ceiling that had fallen in. We used our torch to find our numbered compartment. Doctor Zhivago lurched out of the swirling mist and unlocked the door to reveal two clammy plastic seats and a floor puddled with condensation. 'At least we're only here for eighteen hours,' said Annabel, whipping the cork from a bottle of 1981 Hungarian Tokaji.

I woke in Transylvania with a terrible hangover. We were near the top of a bleak pass in the Carpathian mountains, crawling through a blizzard. The compartment was as hot as a sauna. I was beginning to understand why Graham Greene chose to write *Stamboul Train* by staying in his Cotswold cottage playing Honegger's *Pacific 231* on the gramophone.

Bucharest station seethed with people. Arriving passengers staggered under the weight of cardboard boxes done up with string. An amputee dragged himself along a platform, his bare stumps scraping in the snow. In the waiting room, a policeman and a gypsy were locked in a tug-of-war, the policeman's boots scrabbling on the wet floor as the gypsy, his grimy, scabbed face snarling abuse, braced his legs against the door-jamb.

We found the station's small accommodation bureau, where a smiling young man who spoke fluent English made a phone call and handed us an address. Mrs Dobrin was waiting on the pavement for our taxi and, after shaking our hands, she hurried us into the block of flats beside the Odeon Theatre. Five floors up she showed us into a room slightly larger than its double bed. It wasn't until the following morning, as we ate a breakfast of salami and boiled eggs in the living room, that we saw the blanket on the sofa and realised that Mrs Dobrin had given us her own bed. It was Christmas Day.

Bucharest looked like a building site on a Sunday. Every street seemed to have its quota of half-finished buildings, the legacy of a dictator who demolished 9,000 houses as part of his masterplan to create the ultimate socialist city. That night we walked to Ceauşescu's House of the People, sullen upon its artificial hill at the end of a boulevard twice as big as the Champs-Elysées. Above the columns and pediment a pathetic dot of light shone from one of hundreds of blank windows in a building of staggering mass which sucked in sixteen billion lei and occupied twenty thousand workers and four hundred architects for six years.

We bought tickets for the 513km ride from Bucharest to Sofia for 4,437 lei, about £11. Bargains in Bucharest for those lucky enough to have hard currency are to be appreciated privately. For Romanians, turbo-charged inflation is making life miserable. Mrs Dobrin received a monthly pension of 4,000 lei, enough to buy a pair of the cheapest shoes.

We left Bucharest on the 'Sofia Express' which, according to Thomas Cook, would do the trip to Bulgaria's capital in 13 hours, an average speed of 40kmph – slower than a bicycle freewheeling down a steep hill. Going to the lavatory was made more hazardous by the carriage door, which flapped open during the entire journey, allowing a slippery snowdrift to block the corridor. When we arrived at Sofia at 9 p.m. the temperature had fallen to −17°C. The following morning the trams were full as they headed for the southern suburbs and the mountain called the White Lungs of Sofia. Vitosha, rising 6,600ft above the city, was sparkling like cut glass under a blue sky.

Half of Bulgaria seemed to have taken to the summits: families with toboggans, lovers giggling as they slithered on ice, school parties of skiers and threesomes of white-haired men with metal spikes strapped to the soles of their leather boots.

The last leg of our journey was a mere fifteen-hour trundle on the 'Balkan Express', down the valley of the Maritsa through Plovdiv to the neck of land squeezed between the Aegean and the Black Sea. We were in a Polish couchette carriage this time, warm, dry and charmingly administered by an attendant from Warsaw called Mark. After daybreak we crossed to Turkey, and the first minaret broke the rolling, muddy horizon north of the Sea of Marmara.

Carriages from Russia, Poland, Czechoslovakia, Hungary, Yugoslavia,

Bulgaria and Turkey were now joined as our slovenly centipede of multinational rolling-stock rattled and rocked towards Istanbul. Shanties wobbled by, then packed commuter platforms, before we glimpsed the sea.

Nine days after leaving London Victoria, we slithered beneath the walls of the Topkapi Palace and into Istanbul station. I patted the red paperback; we'd need it for the journey home.

CHAPTER 2
AFRICA

---

4 SEPTEMBER 2003

CROSBY, STILLS, NASH – AND ME

'MARRAKESH EXPRESS', A DEFINING SONG OF THE HIPPY
ERA, INSPIRES **PAUL MANSFIELD** ON A JOURNEY
'THROUGH CLEAR MOROCCAN SKIES'

In the Riad Catalina in Marrakesh I lay on my bed and marvelled at the seductive power of music. Through the window I could see the minaret of the 12th-century Koutoubia Mosque and hear the muezzin summoning the faithful to prayer with a high, keening call that floated across the rooftops.

But there was a different tune playing on my Discman: a three-minute pop song with a bouncy, irresistible rhythm. Just as the muezzin's voice has drawn worshippers to the Koutoubia for nearly a thousand years, so it seemed appropriate that I should have been drawn here, a thousand miles from home, by another kind of song:

'Looking at the world through the sunset in your eyes
Travelling the train through clear Moroccan skies.'

'Marrakesh Express' by Crosby, Stills and Nash was one of the defining songs of the hippy era, a paean to adventure and travel. This was a song that not only made you want to hit the road, it told you where to go. I was twelve when I first heard its exhortation to 'take the train from Casablanca going south'. It had taken a while, but I had made it.

We all follow in someone's footsteps. Graham Nash, co-writer of 'Marrakesh Express', was himself emulating the members of the Beat

Generation – William Burroughs, Jack Kerouac, Allen Ginsberg – who in the 1950s had made a playground of Tangier, the northern city in which the railway line to Marrakesh begins.

In those days Tangier had its own laws and administration, more than sixty thousand expats and a hundred brothels. Burroughs boasted that he received 'an average of ten attractive propositions a day', mostly from young boys. But it didn't last. Moroccan independence in 1956, followed by a series of scandals, brought an end to Tangier's days of excess.

My room at the Hotel Continental, a Tangier institution that opened in 1865, looked out over the port, permanently swathed in chilly mist during my day there. In the narrow streets of the medina, cobblers, jewellers and tinsmiths squatted in hole-in-the-wall shops, and old men in hooded burnouses passed by like medieval monks.

Down below, the occasional dark shape darted between the ranks of container lorries, to be pursued and chased away by lazy-eyed policemen: illegal emigrants bound for Spain. Tangier has always been a crossroads for drugs and people. It's a border town: a grey and edgy place. I headed for the new Gare de Ville on the edge of town, eager to get started.

The French built the Moroccan railway network in the early years of the 20th century, after establishing a protectorate here in 1912. One track ran east to Algeria, the other due south. As the line headed towards the Atlas Mountains the harsh terrain became impassable: Marrakesh turned out to be the end of the line.

The 9 a.m. Casablanca train left on time, its red-and-cream carriages swaying and clanging across the points outside Tangier. I had a first-class compartment to myself, and watched as we ran through flat countryside with scrubby brown hills to one side and the Atlantic on the other. We stopped at Asilah, where a massive 14th-century Portuguese fort jutted out over the ocean, then jolted forward again. I'd been anticipating these lines from the song:

'Dogs and pigs and chickens call

Animal carpets wall-to-wall'

But Moroccan railways have come a long way since 1969. No animals in the clean and comfortable compartment – just a fierce-looking Moroccan businesswoman in a trouser suit who sat tearing articles out of her newspaper and barking into her mobile phone. She got off in Rabat, the Moroccan capital – a baking grid of administrative buildings, solid, provincial and dull – and I rolled south towards Casablanca, entering the city through the shanty towns that lined each side of the track.

'Casa' was buzzing in the late afternoon, most of its three-and-a-half million people seemingly out on the streets. Along the Boulevard Mohammed V, neon lights were winking on, and an electrical crackle played above the wide, traffic-clogged avenues. Casablanca has a feverish energy. It's a place not of 'sights' – there are none, save for the gigantic Hassan II mosque, which foreigners can visit only by arrangement – but of activity.

The traffic, the noise, the hawkers with their dodgy jewellery laid out on blankets in the street, the lynx-eyed girls in jeans (Casablanca is where western travellers reacquaint themselves with the sight of the female form), the shoals of pedestrians moving as one across the street and weaving through the oncoming traffic … You get caught up in it, moving from café to café, wandering through the art deco district along streets that look much as they did eighty years ago when Casablanca was born, modelled on Marseilles.

At the Restaurant au Petit Poucet, velvet curtains hung above gilded mirrors and other memorabilia imported from Paris. Waiters in white jackets ferried escargots and foie gras to a mainly expat crowd. It felt like an outpost of the French empire; and indeed au Petit Poucet was the favourite watering hole of the aviator and novelist Antoine de Saint-Exupéry on his mail flights to the Sahara in the 1920s.

His letters and doodles, scribbled on the back of the menu, are framed on the walls. The air of nostalgic, exhausted colonialism suited Casablanca perfectly. And there was more nostalgia the next day at Gare des Voyageurs station, where I found myself sharing a compartment with an elderly French couple, Simone and Jo. They were brother and sister, born and raised in Morocco but now retired to Paris and on a pilgrimage to their father's grave in Marrakesh. 'J'habite en France, mais mon âme reste en Maroc,' said Simone, a little sadly. She chatted animatedly in Arabic with the pushcart-boy who sold us tea and snacks.

I, of course, had my Discman out.

'Don't you know we're riding on the Marrakesh Express

Wouldn't you know we're riding on the Marrakesh Expressly taking me to Marrakesh'

But initially the journey was disappointing. All morning we ran through a flat dull landscape, with scrappy villages under a dark grey sky. Then at noon, as if on cue, the sun came out and everything was transformed. The country-side was now emerald-green; the sky was blue, and all around we could see tiny villages of neat ochre houses, their gardens hung with orange trees.

The Anti-Atlas Mountains rose and before them lay Marrakesh sparkling in the sunshine, a medieval city on a plain ringed by snow-streaked hills. I felt like punching the air with pleasure. I'd imagined this moment many times, and I wasn't disappointed. 'Quelle ville merveilleuse,' said Simone.

Marrakesh, like Tangier, is another crossroads city, but one with a languid, southern air. Palm trees wave above the city walls; the air is balmy; orange blossom and hibiscus offset the blue and crimson djellabas of the locals. I trawled the shady alleyways of the medina by day, then relaxed in the calm of the Riad Catalina by night.

This was French-run, with an inner courtyard hung with greenery. Waiters brought dishes of chicken tanjia – a Marrakesh speciality baked in a clay pot – and red Guerrouane wine; vineyards, like the railways, being another fine legacy of French rule.

Each evening I would head to the Djemaa el Fna, the open square that for a thousand years has been a meeting place for tribes from the countryside, and home to a nightly display of music, dancing, drumming, storytelling and acrobatics. To claim, as some guidebooks do, that the Djemaa el Fna has become 'touristed' is a nonsense: 95 per cent of the onlookers were Moroccan.

As the last rays of light drained from the sky the muezzin at the Koutoubia began his long, mournful wail. Behind the minaret the sun was setting in a sky of gold. 'All-ahh ak-bar,' droned the muezzin. 'Had to get away to see what we could find,' sang Graham Nash, in my head. The light died, the crowds grew quiet, and all was well at the end of the line in Marrakesh.

A BRITISH RAILWAY THAT MAKES MONEY

Martin Moore

Lovers of trains – and how few of us keep faith in this fevered age of flight – will rejoice to know that the most romantic railway in the world is probably the most profitable.

In the era of nationalisation and subsidy, in a year when British Railways had a deficit of £84 million, the British-built, British-owned Benguela Railway made £1 million net profit: more than £1,100 for each mile of its single-track line.

What the future holds for the railway that was pushed into the heart of Africa to bring Katanga ores to the Atlantic coast may now depend on the seriousness of the rapprochement between Gen. Mobutu and Mr Tshombe. Hitherto, in spite of – or because of – chaos in the Congo, this traffic through Portuguese Angola has continued to flow and grow.

Climb, at the Benguela Railway's Atlantic terminus of Lobito, into a mahogany-and-green-leather sleeper (with a shower-bath at the end of the corridor and a well-stocked diner behind) and you begin to see a strip of Africa as any country should be seen – at ground level.

It is possible, indeed, to traverse thus the whole breadth of the continent in the same carriage, across Katanga and Rhodesia, detraining eight days and three thousand miles later by the silky waters of the Indian Ocean, at Lourenço Marques or Beira.

The journey begins and ends in Portuguese territory. Until a few years ago it ended as well as started on a British-owned line, for it was only recently that the Portuguese bought out the Beira Railway. The Benguela concession, however, still has forty years to run.

Soon after Lobito comes the climb of which the Benguela engineers are proudest. In only 37 miles the track rises from sea level to nearly 3,000ft. So steep is the first scarp that five miles of the original line were rack-and-pinion. Trains had to be divided, hauled piecemeal up the hill and reassembled at the top; it used to take several hours to negotiate those five miles. But in 1948 the rack-and-pinion was converted to normal track, and traffic sped up.

Not that speed is the prime recommendation for pleasure travel on the Benguela Railway. It affords endless opportunity to relish the unfolding African scene: flamingos, pelicans, partridges, doves, hornbills and shyer birds that are streaks of colour, yellow and red and ink-blue, among the trees, themselves aflame with flowers.

There is plenty of time also to get acquainted with the men who keep the trains moving. Courtesy and cleanliness are the watchwords. Every little halt is neat as a pin and garnished with flowers. Its African custodian, in spotless white uniform, stands to attention, flag under arm, as we draw up, then lifts his topee in salute.

Since there are no signals on this line, safety is assured by a telephone call made at each loop to ascertain that the next section is clear. While the driver is phoning you may stroll along the platform to examine the engine.

It has a festive air, for leafy boughs are lashed between the front buffers. Here is embowered the train crew's dinner, kept fresh in the air-stream. This countrified note is taken up by the tender, stacked not with coal but with billets of timber. Angola lacks coal, and although some oil-burning locomotives are being used, wood is the most economic fuel.

Socially as well as economically, the Benguela Railway is self-contained. It has workshops capable of building its own rolling stock, and model farms to supply its workpeople. It has its own telephone and telegraph service, housing estates, and hospitals.

To find a little Crewe in the heart of Africa is impressive. To hear a Negro schoolmaster, salaried by a British company, leading his class through a full-throated rendering of 'Stille Nacht' in Portuguese, or to watch a social worker teaching railwaymen's wives to sew, touches another chord of imagination.

Once a month the pay train traverses the whole 838 miles of the line. With it goes a travelling shop to serve staff at isolated posts; and isolated many of them remain, in spite of the development that has followed the railway.

When its building began in 1903, for every workman on the job another had to be employed solely to carry drinking water. Such was the difficulty of the task that the Angola section was not completed until 1928, and the connecting link with the Congo finished only in 1931.

Since then it has richly justified the faith of its founder, Sir Robert Williams, discoverer of Katanga's mineral wealth. The handsome city of Lobito is his monument. When he marked this sand-spit as his terminus it had only seven European and a few score African inhabitants. Now there are some forty thousand, and Lobito is regularly served by more than thirty shipping lines to Europe, seven to North America and another six to the Far East.

LONG NIGHT'S JOURNEY INTO DAY

GRAHAM COSTER TAKES THE LAST GREAT TRAIN TRIP LEFT IN EAST AFRICA – NAIROBI TO MOMBASA

The Frenchman was very disappointed. 'Have you seen the compartments? They are small and dusty, and the toilet is a hole in the floor. Already my blood pressure is up.'

'He was expecting something like Eurostar,' said his Kenyan friend wryly. 'I said to him, "Welcome to Africa!"'

The Eurostar, however, does not pull out of Waterloo to the strains of Dolly Parton. Her silvery voice quavered out of Nairobi station's loudspeakers, heralding Kenya Railways' imminent departure for Mombasa. In the morning, when I had bought my ticket, the empty station had seemed cavernous and dowdy: a station without trains is like a theatre fallen dark. But now, as night fell, it was coming alive with a bustle of passengers, parcels and packs.

The furiously smoking Frenchman might have been downcast, but I was upbeat. Dolly's piping country and western struck exactly the right note – somewhere between the jaunty and the wistful – to send off a night train.

It is the one great railway journey left in East Africa, for there are no longer passenger trains between Kenya and Uganda, despite what the guidebooks say, and the service to Kenya's third city – Kisumu on Lake Victoria – has been reduced to economy class only, an uninviting prospect of twelve hours on hard seats with the splendour of the Great Rift Valley blacked out by night.

Over the past ten years, competition from the airline shuttles and cheap long-distance buses has halved the number of people travelling on Kenya's railways, but there is still this one essential ride left. Nairobi, Kenya's capital, is high in its central uplands; Mombasa, with its ancient fort and Portuguese heritage on the sparkling Indian Ocean, is a place of charming, ramshackle antiquity. The obvious way to travel between the two was the daily train.

Nairobi's station, tucked away at the southern end of Moi Avenue, the main street, seemed an afterthought to the city. A gridlock of matatus choked its potholed forecourt. Christened with names such as Ronaldo or Toni Braxton, these metallic-liveried minibuses, billowing blue smoke and blaring their horns, were where the action was now. But a century ago Nairobi did not exist, and it was the railway, fingering in from the coast to serve landlocked Uganda, that created it.

By 1899 the line had reached a swamp called Nyrobi and there, where the railway builders paused to construct some workshops, the metropolis eventually grew up. The Nairobi-Mombasa line is the spine on which the body of the modern state of Kenya took shape.

At the end of the platform, I chatted to a Kenyan called David, bound for Malindi up the coast where he kept a boat. 'They pride themselves on leaving exactly on time,' he told me and, sure enough, at precisely 7 p.m., we began to roll.

I doubt if our French friend would have been impressed by the Kenya Railway Museum but, as a prelude to my night ride, I had stumbled across this touching backwater of railway history just around the corner from the station. Here, slumbering under the warm sun in forgotten grassy sidings, was a collection of Kenya's old steam locomotives.

York, with its National Railway Museum, has a similar juxtaposition of the old and new – you can gaze at *Mallard* before boarding your 125 – but here there was a poignant sense of ancient engines having exhaled one last sigh of steam and then trundled round the corner to the graveyard where they had languished ever since.

These were giant, saurian hulks with designs as improbable as sea monsters – odd push-me, pull-you shapes designed by Beyer-Garratt with tenders front and back. The biggest weighed some 250 tons and were painted mustard-yellow with proud names such as *Masai of Kenya*. This sultry morning, apart from a tabby cat dozing beneath *Mount Shengena*'s wheels and a quizzical heron hunting snakes in the long grass, I seemed to be the only visitor.

Look more closely, however, and, as so often with old trains, the story leads back to Britain. Cast plates on the sides of these outlandish slabs of metal bore the names of foundries and factories in places such as Newton-le-Willows and Oldbury.

Inside the museum's exhibition room the British were still working hardest to furnish its quirkiest exhibits. One of the hairiest was a game-viewing seat: essentially a wooden bench, fixed to the front buffers of a steam engine, providing head-on views of oncoming animals. The Duke of Windsor, in a period photograph, gave a typically imperturbable demonstration. More recently, a Mr John Wall had lent his collection of tickets, which in turn had prompted a letter from Edward W. Jones of Wrexham, offering an English translation of Britain's longest station name, Llanfairpwllgwyngllgogerychwyrndrobwllllantysiliogogogoch. The Kenya Museum has recently been privatised, and needs visitors badly. Hitherto, under state control, the biggest problem has been bits disappearing off the engines – even whole exhibits going for a walk. 'The corporation is broke,' I was told.

Indeed, a first-class ticket on the Mombasa train – the equivalent of £30 for a one-way ride – hardly purchases sumptuous luxury, although the ticket collector was immaculate in khaki uniform and brilliant white turban. The carriages were a faded brown, the leatherette seats were torn, and from underneath the floors came creaking and knocking as though we were at sea in an aged boat.

When I came back to my compartment to find my bed made up – with a sheet so old my toe went straight through it – there was a small unidentifiable object placed thoughtfully on the pillow like a hotel's chocolate mint, cream in colour and sealed in cellophane. A square of white chocolate? A piece of cheese? I was about to nibble this tiny treat when I realised it was a tablet of soap.

But, as Paul Theroux says, railways are 'irresistible bazaars'. On the way to the coast I shared my compartment with a Kenya Railways signals technician who had been to York and Derby for a technology course. 'So many trains … ' he mused in wonder, as he recalled his time in England.

On the return journey my companions were Gitu from Nairobi and his friend Dilip, visiting from Dubai, who turned out to have relatives running a jewellery shop in Luton. They had taken refuge on the train back after enduring 'eight hours of wild driving' on the bus to Mombasa.

But the best bazaar of all was the dining car. So much of modern travel encourages insularity – the airline seat facing the back of the person in front, the individual meal tray, the headphones – but here there was a delightfully traditional requirement to be sociable. A steward came along the corridor banging a xylophone and off we all went; a three-course dinner and a cooked breakfast at dawn were part of the price of a first- or second-class ticket.

Over onion soup, braised beef and three veg, I talked to a Nairobi University business lecturer, visiting his family on the coast, and an American couple, Guy and Jean, taking a holiday from teaching English in Djibouti.

'I've never eaten a meal on horseback before,' reflected Guy, trying to spoon the small square of steamed pudding and custard into his mouth as the train jerked and bounced its way onwards. But there was a sense of civic occasion in the proceedings, with the uniformed wine waiter and stewards dressed in white linen.

On a night train, of course, there is mostly nothing to see, except those ghostly gas-lit tableaux that appear when you clank to a halt in the early hours, unsure whether you have dreamed you saw that lonely man walking off into the night with a hefty sack of maize. But on the best journeys there is the wonder of waking to a new land – and the Mombasa line saved its finest views for last. We settled down in the restaurant car once more for a glass of orange juice and a plate of egg and bacon. The sun rose as the land fell away. The level, scrubby plains outside Nairobi had gone, and we were curving around an escarpment among lush palm trees, tall cacti and red flowers. Green hills rolled to the south; there was blue water in the distance.

Sometimes you can get to a place too fast. This was a reassuring antidote to the sudden beam-me-down transport of a plane. Restore one of those monumental Garratts, panting steam to shuffle you across the causeway into Mombasa, and perhaps even the Frenchman would be impressed.

CHAPTER 3
ASIA

----

11 JUNE 2006

TICKET ACROSS TURKEY

THE TRAIN RIDE FROM ISTANBUL TO ANKARA BEGINS ON THE ASIAN SIDE OF THE BOSPHORUS AT AN ASTONISHING STATION. **BARNABY ROGERSON** WANTED TO SEE IT BEFORE THE URBAN PLANNERS GOT THEIR HANDS ON IT

Hurry! One of the last great railway journeys into Asia will soon be no more. In three years' time the magnificence of Istanbul's Haydarpasha station will be severed forever from the tracks that lead south and east.

If you put a spoon in a small tulip-shaped glass, rattle it vigorously and call out, 'tchay-kahve, tchay-kahve, tchay-kahve' while advancing down a corridor, you will have some idea of how the traveller is woken at dawn as the night train from Anatolia returns safely to Istanbul. When there is no more tchay or kahve to serve, the conductor will set off on another tour of the sleeper cars, rattling his spoon and glass, but this time crying out, 'Stamboul, Stamboul.'

There can be no more romantic sound to the ear of the traveller. Nor can there be a better station to arrive at. Haydarpasha is one of the last temples of rail travel – a vast Saxe-Coburg-Gotha schloss that should, by rights, stand above the Rhine or above a firth in Sutherland, but is instead perched on the banks of the Bosphorus. It is one of the great buildings of Istanbul's Asian shore. The ticket hall, enthroned within massive Renaissance-style vaults, would have impressed a Borgia.

Haydarpasha has always been about first impressions. It was built by

German engineers as a symbol of the Kaiser's alliance with the Ottoman Empire. A very visible fruit of this partnership was the great Berlin-to-Baghdad rail route.

Every adventurer, explorer, archaeologist and filibuster who sought fame and fortune in the Middle East has passed through the station arches, not to mention the greater numbers of the pious: Orthodox pilgrims heading for Jerusalem and Muslims on their way to Damascus to connect with the Haj line to Medina. It is a place tangibly brushed with the romance of the great days of travel: of piles of trunks, of porters, of romantic separations and of chance encounters; a still-living backdrop to an adventure story by Graham Greene or Agatha Christie.

It was targeted by British agents during the Great War, who achieved the spectacular success of 6 September 1917, when they detonated a device in the ammunition depot behind the station. The resulting inferno destroyed a great chunk of strategic rail track, most of the roof and one or two of the station's towers. A year later it was at the Haydarpasha landing station that the British and French chiefs of staff met at the conclusion of the war, having sailed up through the Dardanelles past the now silent guns and entrenched Turkish infantry that had defeated them during the Gallipoli campaign.

On a hill behind the station stands the wooded garden of the Crimean War cemetery (perhaps the most moody, romantic and secretive of all the British burial grounds abroad), for Florence Nightingale's original hospital is also close by, housed within a corner of the vast Selimye barracks. These were built for the reformed Ottoman army after the unruly Janissaries had been massacred in 1826. The very name Haydarpasha commemorates Selim III's reforming general, who had attempted to suppress the Janissaries a generation before but had perished in the attempt.

Despite being surrounded in every direction by such poignant markers of history, Haydarpasha still remains a working station, and has not suffered from the tourist-creep that is slowly transforming Sirkeci, the railway station on the European shore, into an Orient-Express theme park.

But a cabal of developers and architect-engineers has produced a plan to redevelop the docklands on Istanbul's Asian shore. Never mind that their glass and steel towers will literally cast a shadow over the Topkapi Palace, Ayia Sophia and the Blue Mosque, and obliterate a beautiful urban backdrop. The money the project will generate is on a scale, and of an order, that will prove irresistible. There is also talk of a yacht marina to replace the dignified and still busy waterfront, used by the Black Sea ferries and cruise ships.

So I finally hurried into a journey that I had been idly contemplating for some ten years – to the extent that I have twice rehearsed catching the night train from Haydarpasha. These practice sessions involved a ferry journey across the dark Bosphorus, with long evenings in the station's Lokanta restaurant-bar. One door of the station bar opens on to the platform, where the blue sleeper carriages await their passengers, while from a lower door you can look directly out over the waters of the Bosphorus.

On my last visit one table was filled with moustachioed dock workers drinking raki, while a fur-coated traveller of great age, hennaed hair and indeterminate sex studied a table of mop-haired youths watching football.

The local brew is drawn with Guinness-like respect, the waiters are unflappably soigné and the kebabs are properly spiced. Above the drinkers is a high plaster ceiling, painted lilac, pink and gold, while Moorish geometric tiles are hung on the lower walls. It was such a perfect scene of raw unpackaged travel that I half expected to find Jan Morris or Colin Thubron lurking behind a cast-iron column.

On our actual journey we took our seats on the train after supper, avoiding the last-minute rush that my wife normally insists upon as a vital element of true travel. We were both concerned about one of our daughters, who looked very ill, was dehydrated and had lost her appetite. She travelled with her mother while I cared for the seven year old in the next compartment.

Although small, the seven year old has become a remarkably assertive traveller. While I like the window open, the curtains undrawn and the lights off (all the better to experience the chance noises of a night train, the shuntings, grindings and unexpected stops at deserted railway platforms), she likes to turn a 'sleepy train' into a cosy bedroom. We waged war against each other's preferences, but as she had made an early claim to the bottom bunk, I fear she maintained a slight advantage all night. The window must have clonked itself open and shut at least a dozen times before the 'tchay-kahve' wake-up call signalled a close of play.

During a Turkish breakfast – served in the dining car on the fetching blue and red State Railway porcelain – of olives, tomatoes, cucumber, toasted bread, white cheese and a boiled egg, we rattled across the steppes.

Ankara is not on the itinerary of the romantic traveller. As a destination it was more of an excuse for a night train journey than anything else, yet I had been longing to see three things here. I soon added a fourth, for the station is magnificent, a stern essay in national monolithic, all clean marble and polished efficiency.

I shed tears for the fallen at the Atatürk Mausoleum and felt misty-eyed at the relics of the wizened old temple of Augustus, where the Res Gestae inscription can still be traced in a neglected, locked-up compound beside the Haci Bayram mosque. As schoolboys we loved the Res Gestae for Augustus's swanky opening line – 'At eighteen I raised an army and saved the republic' – but now it seemed as poignant as the neglected tomb of Cyrus.

I took turns at child-care with my wife so we both could take our time sketching the mother goddesses in the citadel museum. Illness excused our daughters from drawing the Hittite carvings at Carchemish. Instead we let our children play havoc in the Ankara Hilton, living a life as close to their cartoon heroine *Eloise at the Plaza*, as they have ever dreamed. So it was room service, TV in bed and lots of journeys in the palatial lifts to the spa. Fortunately it was Ramadan, so there were no high-powered guests to complain of the children shrieking with joy in the Jacuzzi.

We loved rediscovering our beds on the sleeper again the following night, and the waiters in the dining car treated us like long-lost friends as we opened up a pack of cards and ordered a late-night meze supper.

Next morning I was awoken by the 'tchay-kahve' call as we rattled along the shore of the Sea of Marmara and looked out of the window over merchant ships lit up at anchor. During breakfast we passed an ancient ivy-clad fortress that did not appear in any of the guidebooks and then we listened for the waiters' magical cry of 'Stamboul' as we approached Haydarpasha.

After a coffee in the magnificence of the station's vaults, we walked down a flight of stone steps straight to the station quay and listened to the reso-nant cries as the landing stations of the European shore of Istanbul were called out, 'Eminonu! Karakoy! Beskitas!'

As we chugged across the Bosphorus we passed a school of ferries criss-crossing the straits in their livery of yellow and white. Standing by the rail-ings, the wind gusting down from the Black Sea, woke us up to the core. It was just then that the morning sun lit up the domes of the Ayia Sophia and the Blue Mosque.

I looked at my wife and daughters shivering in the wind. I asked them if we should do it again before the urban planners banish all this hectic colour into history and replace it with underpasses and gleaming towers of glass and steel. There was a silence, before my wife said, 'Did you notice that there is a direct train from Haydarpasha to Tehran?'

A.S.L.E.F., PLEASE NOTE

Peterborough

'Every time a local train is late by fifteen or twenty minutes, a section of its passengers resorts to violence. Under the impression that the engine driver, fireman and other members of the crew are directly responsible, they belabour them.

'Meanwhile, some of those who are obliged to cool their heels on the platform ... take it into their heads that the station staff are responsible, with the result that these poor folk get beaten up too ... '

I extract the above from a letter in the *Statesman Overseas Weekly*, published in Calcutta.

INDIA: RAIL AND UNREAL

A NEW LUXURY TRAIN TAKING IN MANY OF THE BEST-
KNOWN SIGHTS SOUNDS THE PERFECT INTRODUCTION TO
THE SUBCONTINENT. BUT WHAT VIEW DO YOU HAVE FROM
ITS TINTED WINDOWS?

Nigel Richardson

A railway station in the Indian state of Rajasthan, on a steamy monsoon morning. A man approaches the window of a stationary train and, using it as a mirror, brushes sweat from his eyebrows and cheeks.

On the other side of the window I am sprawled on a bed with a golden quilt, close enough to touch the man. I stare at him and he stares back, but cultural exchange is not taking place. The window allows me to see out while preventing anyone from seeing in. 'Cccchhhhukk!' The man hawks lustily, and turns away.

It strikes me as a good metaphor, this window, for the way in which many western tourists experience India. In temperature-controlled cocoons: hotels, tour buses, vetted restaurants, emporiums of extortion otherwise known as gift and export shops. And now this, the ultimate cocoon: the luxury private train. One footplate up from the Orient Express, this is the Deccan Odyssey.

Its eighteen coaches give a shudder of anticipation, the driver honks his horn with the exuberant pointlessness of a Mumbai cabbie, and we continue on our journey of more than 2,000 miles across the subcontinent, from Mumbai in the west to Kolkata in the east via some of India's — nay, the world's — finest cultural sites.

The Deccan Odyssey has been chartered from the state of Maharashtra and renamed the Viceroy of India Darjeeling Mail for the two-week duration of the voyage. Luxury train travel is not new to India, but until now it has been confined to individual states. It is the achievement of Tim Littler's GW Travel to have bodyswerved through the massed ranks of local, national and corporate bureaucracy in order to inaugurate this first-ever trans-India service.

Along for the ride are some serious train nuts, many of them veterans of previous GW Travel trips, such as the Trans-Siberian Express. Jim, a retired railroad administrator from Norfolk, Virginia, goes misty-eyed at the mention of Doncaster (possibly a first) because the *Flying Scotsman* was built there. Jane, a designer of hotel interiors who lives in Oxfordshire, told me she spent her childhood travelling to Alpine ski holidays in her own wagon-lit compartment. 'I have to say, when I saw that train standing on the platform in Bombay, I came out in goose bumps. It's sooo exciting.'

My wistful window-gazing, on that first morning, was interrupted by Javed, my cabin steward, knocking diffidently on my door. 'Breakfast ready, sir.' Javed, who wears a burgundy kurta and a red turban, attends to needs. On my return from sweaty excursions in non-air-conditioned reality, he will pass me a cooling face towel, followed by a glass of iced mint tea. He folds the end of my lavatory paper into a point and reminds me when to eat. There are thirty-four Javeds to thirty-four passengers, the Everest of staff-customer ratios.

In the breakfast car I address a plate of papaya, pineapple and watermelon, followed by mango yogurt. Shall I have brioches, croissants or muffins? Pondering this ineffable question, I gaze out of the window at a landscape ripened to tangled profusion by the rains.

Through the yellow filter on the glass, the morning sun has the crazed intensity of the *Fighting Temeraire*. There are two other notable things about the windows, besides their being one-way: they cannot be opened and they have anti-glare tints, variously blue or yellow, which cast the outside world in an unreal hue.

All in all, I am feeling a bit like a boy in a fun-coloured bubble. I have been to India plenty of times but have never seen it like this. It's delightful, but it isn't quite real. I am suffering the cultural equivalent of jet lag.

This is why: twenty-four hours ago, before the Viceroy of India Darjeeling Mail started its epic eastward flight and I was still a private-train virgin, I was stepping over open drains in one of India's most notorious slums. The drains run down the middle of the alleyways, as they did in 17th-century London. A contemporary of Pepys, hoiking up his coat tails, would find familiarity in the dirt, noise, press of bodies and cellular industry of the shanty town of Dharavi in the far north of Mumbai.

Six months ago, no tourist in his right mind would have visited this place. This 432-acre sprawl of tin-roofed shacks and capillary-like alleyways, in which more than a million people live and work, had a similar reputation to Soweto in South Africa.

'When I came to Mumbai from Karnataka in 1993 I was scared of Dharavi,' my guide, Krishna Pujari, told me. 'People said, "Don't go there, it is dangerous, it is full of rubbish and poverty."'

It wasn't until last year that he plucked up the courage to go. What he saw confounded and uplifted him. Since then he has gone into partnership with an Englishman, Chris Way, to offer tours of what they call 'the biggest slum in Asia'.

The tours are conducted with exemplary sensitivity, and the co-operation of the residents, and 80 per cent of profits are donated to local charities. In fact, Dharavi is closer to home than you might think in our global economy.

The tour started when my latter-day Virgil stopped our vehicle on a busy street and led me on foot down a narrow alley. Head-high juts of metal, raindrops in the tangled power lines, men on missions in lunghis and headscarves. This is the recycling area, covering ten or so acres, in which alchemy takes place: old ink vats, cooking-oil containers and paint tins returned to gleaming perfection, confetti of trashed plastic converted to pristine pellets, aluminium to ingots.

The extent and ingenuity of the recycling was humbling to this profligate western consumer. Sounding unwittingly like a Hindu mystic, Krishna described the process as 'the beginning and the end, the end and the beginning'. However, Dharavi's main industry is manufacturing. The annual turnover of the many enterprises based here is US$665 million. In the past week you probably wore or used something made here.

An exporter of luxury leather jackets to the west told me: 'The top designers in Europe are coming to Dharavi and showing us what they want. All they have to do is put the garment on a hanger.' Sitting in his first-floor office off Dharavi's main street, he declined to tell me how many people he employs (on piece-work basis) or how much they are paid.

The truth is, these tours of Dharavi are controversial. The week before I arrived in Mumbai, a television programme had run a critical story accusing Chris and Krishna of 'poverty tourism'. Following the programme, a government tourism minister threatened to have the tours shut down, although they are run perfectly legally, with the blessing of the local police as well as residents.

Whether you're on a luxury train or in a slum, India, it seems, is full of uncomfortable realities that some people would rather you didn't see – such as the three young men making belt buckles in a strip-lit cell in Dharavi. They sat on the ground ladling molten metal into moulds, holding the moulds steady with their bare feet. It looked as casual as pouring stock on to risotto rice, but there was no margin for error.

For this expert, highly dangerous work they are paid daily the same as the price of a beer on the Deccan Odyssey. Then there were the women and children making poppadoms in a sunny courtyard – strictly no photos here as the company that employs them does not wish the public to know the conditions in which they work, nor the pay they receive. I was told that the poppadom-makers receive 16 rupees (about 20p) per kilo of poppadoms.

These truths may be uncomfortable all round. But touring a place like Dharavi is an informative experience for anyone wishing to understand India and our relationship with it. It was also hugely enjoyable. The sledge-hammer smells – animal hides, burning plastic, paraffin – were periodically sweetened by the miraculous waft of freshly baked bread. The density of humanity, far from being oppressive, was exhilarating.

A youth with Harry Potter specs whizzed through the throng on a sit-up-and-beg bike, clanking his bell. A boy knelt on a packing case, submitting to a haircut. Blue-uniformed schoolgirls chattered past, with ribbons in their hair. Through a doorway I caught a glimpse of a doctor wearing a stethoscope, seated at a formica-topped table.

In four hours no one begged from me; no one asked: 'Where from, sir?' No one tried to sell me miniature backgammon sets or take me to his brother's 'good price' shop. Nor did anyone question or visibly resent my presence. In truth, they were busy and I was irrelevant. There may have been no one-way window between us but I was still all but invisible.

On the edge of Dharavi, Krishna handed me on to Shirin Juwaley, the communications manager of a charitable organisation called Magic Bus. With Shirin were forty excited Dharavi children awaiting the arrival of the eponymous vehicle. Presently, to a soundtrack of Hindi Bollywood music, we headed off to a playing field in a leafy area.

The brainchild of an Englishman, Matthew Spacie, Magic Bus aims to socialise Mumbai's slum and street children – of whom there are an estimated 2.5 million – through organised physical activity. 'It is all about getting them out of their communities to expose them to other cultures,' said Shirin as we watched those in Dharavi playing football and running relay races.

There is, I discovered, an unlikely connection between Magic Bus and luxury train. Spacie worked for Cox & Kings, the specialist India travel company, as its chief operating officer, before leaving to set up Magic Bus. Cox & Kings continues to support the project, encouraging its clients to take an interest. It is also responsible for all excursions from the Viceroy of India Darjeeling Mail – those unpredictable moments when real life is likely to get stuck to the bottom of one's shoe.

After breakfast on that first morning on the train – and with increasingly dream-like memories of Dharavi and Magic Bus – we venture from our gilded cage for the first time to see the sights of Jaipur in Rajasthan. The Cox & Kings guides are expert chaperones, but even they can't stem the tide of hawkers that rolls towards our party as we descend from our tour bus within the ancient walls of the 'Pink City'.

The brilliant thing about the Dharavi tour was that it showed the poverty and populousness of India in a positive light. Shorn of such context, India can seem brutal and alien, especially to first-timers. And this is the first experience of the subcontinent for more than half the passengers. Zurich it isn't – to the mortification of a smart Swiss woman.

'We've been here two weeks already,' she tells me. 'If it wasn't for the train trip we'd have probably gone home by now. Quite frankly, the dirt has been terrible.' A glamorous Californian woman philanthropises like mad, dispensing 500-rupee tips left and right. At the end of each excursion – marshalled by the stentorian tones of Marina from GW Travel – there is a palpable sense of relief when we return to the mother ship ('Ah, most kind, Javed').

The train seems to me as unreal and glamorous as a stage set – wood-panelled cabins, art deco uplighters, velvet curtain swags – and the dramatis personae are pretty entertaining, too. There are ladies of a certain age and hauteur and men who made their fortunes in 'precision optics' or 'agri-business'. One describes his profession as 'dodging bullets' – of the boardroom variety, presumably.

The role of indomitable oldies is played to perfection by the husband-and-wife team of JC ('That's Jefferson Charles, but everybody jus' call me Jay Cee') and Widgie (no idea) from Mississippi, who whizz up and down ruins with the stamina of mountain goats. Widgie sends herself up – 'Here comes the southern belle, y'all' – and does a fine impression of a poker-up-the-backside English accent.

The unique achievement of the Darjeeling Mail is that it opens up practically the entire jewel box of India's finest destinations in just two weeks – Mumbai, Jaipur, the Taj Mahal and Agra Fort, Delhi New and Old, the holy city of Varanasi, the old Raj hill station of Darjeeling (with optional helicopter ride into the Himalayan state of Sikkim), and Kolkata, formerly Calcutta.

All this in the lap of luxury: food (choice of western or Indian) and service, as provided by Taj Hotels, are superb. There's also a doctor on board, her services being called upon surprisingly often. Many of the passengers are getting on and appreciate this comfort and security – 'I'm getting pretty bad arthritis in my hands and now my knees. And I thought I should do things while I can,' one explained.

Is it enjoyable? Enormously. Is it the best way to experience India while spending this kind of money? Probably not. Given the size of the group, excursions are often perfunctory, and – at least in the four days I was on board before jumping ship in Delhi – we were steered well away from street bazaars in favour of expensive shops where the sell may be more subtle but is just as hard.

Interestingly, the one concerted attempt to see a bit of 'real life' ends in confusion and embarrassment. On our first night in Agra we are bussed to a restaurant where, our guide tells us, 'the locals like to eat'. Actually, the place contains only tourists but the Kingfisher is cold and the kebabs tender. However, Tim Littler, a self-confessed perfectionist, decides halfway through the meal that the service and food are not up to scratch, and we are obliged to stage a walk-out.

Despite being told we are going to the upmarket Oberoi Hotel, we end up in the garishly-lit Hilton for a bland buffet. By the end of the evening, mild mutiny is in the air. 'Too much bussing and rushing,' says one.

It takes the world's most beautiful building to melt the barriers between us and India. On a blisteringly hot afternoon, with shirts varnished to our torsos, we gaze on the Taj Mahal with humility and awe, along with thousands of other, mostly Indian, tourists.

What does the group think?

'Speechless.'

'Yes yes yes.'

Seated on a bench in the shade, Widgie slaps JC's knee. 'Well, was it worth it, hon'?'

'I guess,' replies JC, looking suddenly seventy years younger than his real age.

RIGHT LINES

Peterborough

Travellers in China can vouch for the enormous job the country faces in trying to modernise. A peasant in a remote part of Szechwan province asked a visitor if he had ever seen a train.

Was it true that a train was bigger than a house? Was it painted black as people said and did it really belch smoke and travel great distances in a day? All true, said the visitor.

'One last question,' said the peasant. 'How many legs does it have?'

MARKET RULES

The travel writer Stanley Stewart, last seen waving from the window of a train at Liverpool Street, bound for the Silk Road, has rung from Kashgar, China.

Despite the fact that it sounded as if someone was crisping duck down the telephone line, the dashing Stewart – he looks like something out of a David Lean film – was in good voice.

His adventure saw him recently in the town of Wuwei, which he wished to leave almost as soon as he had arrived. But the female railway clerk was adamant: there were no train tickets. 'Fine,' said Stewart. 'Will you marry me? If I am to stay here for the rest of my life I shall need a wife.'

Covered in several days' worth of dust, he also applied for residency at the local police station. Within minutes, miraculously, a first-class ticket was found on the next train out of town.

Meanwhile, Stewart is biting his tongue after an encounter with the black-market money changers of Kashgar. Fans, to a man, of 'Mrs Dat-chir', they offer particularly attractive exchange rates for sterling. But word of Mrs Thatcher's fall had yet to cross the Karakorams; when Stewart broke the news, the pound in his pocket went into free-fall.

CATCHING UP WITH A LAND ON THE MOVE

MICHELLE JANA CHAN RETURNS TO CHINA AFTER A DECADE AWAY, AND JOURNEYS ACROSS A COUNTRY IN THE THROES OF MOMENTOUS CHANGE

Just over a thousand years ago, present-day Xi'an was arguably the largest, most cosmopolitan and cultured city in the world. Inside the crenellated city walls that still stand today, one million inhabitants spoke in a dozen tongues, including Chinese, Sogdian and Tibetan. Merchants, missionaries and foreign diplomats travelled in and out of the city, westwards along the Silk Road that frays into a hundred threads through the forbidding Taklamakan desert into the 'Stans', Iran and on to Baghdad.

One millennium later, the Silk Road is unravelling again. China is wide open to trade and travel, and commodities as well as cultural influences are being exchanged in both directions.

I lived in Xi'an in the mid-1990s and this was my first trip back. The city looked much the same as it did ten years ago and probably not too different from a thousand years ago. In the street markets there were bolts of silk, raw and refined, on sale in every colour and pattern. Alongside the textile merchants were fruit and vegetable sellers; traders of spices, pistachio nuts and crystallised sugar; butchers splattered in pig's blood; cobblers resoling shoes; mechanics fixing sewing machines.

In between were many stalls selling bowls of spicy noodles and steamed pork dumplings. I could taste chilli powder in the air and feel the wetness of billowing steam lifting lids off the massive woks. After a little more time there, I noticed that the mountains of watermelons once for sale were now mere mounds, and competing with refrigerated cans of Sprite and Magnum ice creams. There was a queue of children with moon-shaped faces and flabby thighs outside Kentucky Fried Chicken.

I saw my first Chinese car park, with spanking new SUVs jostling for space. In the bicycle park were dozens of motor scooters, and some bikes had gone electric. Locals were dressed in bright colours and, without wanting to sound trite, I think they smiled more. The familiar mantra is that China is booming. There is a strong drive to earn, a huge desire to spend – and there are more things to buy.

In every single conversation, I overheard the word 'qian' – Chinese for money (one of the few words locals can say in English). Taxi drivers in Xi'an talked about not having enough of it. Businessmen from Hangzhou boasted about how quickly they could make it. The whole country speaks about China's booming gross domestic product.

Nothing struck me more on my return than the money talk and the incessant trading. I was no longer asked the dated questions about my age and how many people I had slept with. They demanded to know the price of my train ticket, the cost of my bottled water and how much I had paid for pears from the station platform sellers.

'Duo shao qian? Duo shao qian?' Fellow passengers would urgently ask me, 'How much did you pay?' I might get a nod of approval for a fair price, or a smirk if I had been ripped off.

I wasn't sure how I felt about this new country. Was I nostalgic, discomfited by this steamrolling progress? Or was I a little smug, having experienced Old China? I had almost a month to watch China changing, travelling on a train around this vast country of only one time zone but a wildly varying landscape.

Clackety-clack through the paddy fields of Guangdong, across the floodplains of the Yangtse, into the Tarim Basin and towards the foothills of the Hindu Kush. These journeys by plane would have lifted me above everything that mattered. By car, I would have missed out on living side by side with the Chinese.

I boarded my first mainland train in Guangzhou, a couple of hours west of Hong Kong. It is in the train stations of China that you really feel you are in a country of 1.3 billion people. I arrived an hour and a half early, but in the waiting hall it was already standing room only. More than a thousand passengers squashed together with suitcases, crates of food and those nylon sacks in red, white and blue stripes used throughout Asia.

Children sat atop pyramids of luggage like cherries on cakes. More people streamed in and we miraculously made space. I instinctively looked around for a fire escape and realised that if there was an inferno I'd have no chance. The ceiling fans were so slow the air barely moved. I wanted to nudge my neighbour and share my amazement at the crowds, but everyone around me was unfazed.

One stifling hour later, a uniformed official appeared wearing an oversized peaked cap. He paced by the metal barriers penning us in, watching us sweat, before staggering the opening of gates. It was a human cattle market. I funnelled down the gangway on to the platform, joining the sprint to the carriages, elbowing my way down the aisle and landing on my bunk. With thirty-six hours ahead of me, I was already exhausted.

This train was an old green diesel with linoleum floors and ancient coal-fired samovars bubbling away at the end of each carriage. I took a 'hard sleeper' – a comfortable second-class bunk complete with clean sheets and a blanket. Every carriage takes sixty passengers loosely boxed up in compartments of six, with two top, two middle and two bottom bunks.

The top bunk is the cheapest – and I soon discovered why. After hauling myself up an 8ft ladder, I lay back on my pillow within inches of the ceiling. The bright cabin lights and piped music speakers stared back at me. Behaviour on board is strictly controlled by lights-out at 10 p.m.. Before that, we listened to sharp and rousing marching-band music (along with the occasional Carpenters track) from 7 a.m.

Every morning, on cue, passengers sloped bleary-eyed down to the couple of washbasins and the squat toilet. Someone volunteered to fill up the communal flask at the boiling samovar to make tea. We all slurped soupy noodles for breakfast, pushing back the curtains to see the new landscape on show.

Xi'an is the place to begin a journey along the Silk Road. The region's rich history of successive dynasties is chronicled at the Shaanxi History Museum, and an hour away is the 8,000-strong Terracotta Army of warriors built by China's first emperor. From Xi'an, it is twenty-six hours to Dunhuang, the last stop before what used to be the most arduous journey of the Silk Road.

A mother and father in my carriage waved goodbye to their son, an engineering student in Xi'an. All three sobbed. The parents had spent the weekend here after travelling two full days on a train from Korla in the north west. They now faced the same journey back home. Through the tears, they complained about the high price of train tickets and how rarely they saw their only child.

The first few hours out of Xi'an made grim viewing as the train passed through industrial towns such as Baoji and Lanzhou, the latter once the world's most polluted city. But when I awoke the next morning, we had left behind sulphuric smog and smokestacks and the day was rinsed blue. I gazed out at the vivid grasslands of the Gansu Corridor, a skinny province taking me from the heart of China to its western extremity.

This land is gloriously fertile, dotted with farm workers moving along neat furrows of wheat. Long-legged sheep mosey around the hillsides. Corn on the cob dazzles as it is dried on the flat roofs of brick homes. Sunflowers shine out. Shiny apples bob on trees. Later that afternoon, we passed the station of Jiayuguan where China's Great Wall crumbles into the sand and officially ends at its westernmost point. From the train, I could see dark stone watchtowers rebuilt and eroded sand-coloured walls falling softly away. Chinese tour groups left the train, everyone wearing matching baseball caps.

With each mile, the landscape became more arid. The fields morphed into scrubland and the mountains drifted further from the tracks. We passed towns that were closed to foreigners, locals told me, whispering about the Long March rocket launch pad and how the government was scared of spies. Not far from here is the Lop Nur salt flat, where nuclear tests are carried out. On the edge of the Gobi Desert, Dunhuang is an oasis of cotton plantations, red willow and white poplars. It is known for the Mogao cave temples, some of the world's best-preserved Buddhist art and a UN World Heritage Site.

Inside the caves, the religious icons are more than a thousand years old; manuscripts found here — written on silk and linen — may be the oldest printed books in existence. Most of these documents are now in the British Museum, having been carted away by the explorer Aurel Stein in the early 20th century, but the caves are still beautifully decorated with statues and frescoes. Sitting in the darkness, I cowered beneath the world's third-largest Buddha (promoted from fifth place after the twin Buddhas at Bamiyan were blown up by the Taliban).

From Dunhuang, I took the overnight train to Turpan, passing through inhospitable terrain. Turpan is the second-lowest place on earth, notching up some of the world's hottest temperatures. It was 47°C and I felt as though I were roasting in an oven on gas mark nine. I sheltered under vine trellises heavy with grapes, before walking through the old town of adobe mud houses where families scrubbed their clothes clean in gutters along the road.

It was here that I met Pamela, a fiercely ambitious twenty-six-year-old Uighur woman in her penultimate year at dentistry school (the Uighur minority numbers six million in Xinjiang province — where I now was — and speaks a language intelligible to Turks). She complained about the cost of studying in China and the competitive job market.

'The government is no longer interested in finding people work,' she said. 'Now, you have to apply on your own and do interviews.' Pamela said she wanted to go to Germany, where dentistry was more advanced and she was more likely to find a job.

From Turpan, it is twenty-one hours to Kashgar – on new track through the Taklamakan desert, skirting the border with Kazakhstan. The trains are new, too: air-conditioned, double-decker models with frilly sheets and flowers embroidered on duvets. Joyfully, there is a volume control to turn the music down, and a personal night-light.

'Fangbian mian, niunai, mianbao' – noodles, milk, bread – is the familiar cry up and down the aisles as hostesses peddle their wares. Midday meals (meat, rice, vegetables) are packed in polystyrene and cost less than the equivalent of £1. Outside the window, we passed brick-making factories, quarries and rubbish dumps, releasing waste up into the air like tropical birds, and electricity poles strung together like clothes pegs. We passed modern towns, now abandoned because the new railway line means there is no passing traffic any more. It was a desolate picture.

I woke to see the Tianshan mountains catching the early-morning sunlight. Some peaks were 21,000ft high and the snow glittered halfway down the slopes. Rivers were gushing milky-jade with meltwater. When I stepped out at the next station to stretch my legs, it was the first time I'd been cold in weeks.

By the time I reached Kashgar, I was further west than Delhi. I could see the high Pamir mountains, the so-called Roof of the World. To the south, the Karakoram Highway leads off in the direction of the mountain K2. Kashgar really is the meeting point of east and west, where Chinese mix with people who could be Romanian (green eyes, Roma features), even Celtic (red hair, freckles) and where the majority pray to Mecca.

Kashgar's Sunday market is the city's greatest draw. Crowds of merchants converge here from all over western China, as well as from Tajikistan, Kazakhstan, Afghanistan and Kashmir. Any other day of the week, Kashgar reverts to another faceless Chinese city of wide streets and fountain shows choreographed to Strauss symphonies.

I approached the market through streets gridlocked with donkey carts, bicycles, tractors, open-topped trucks, taxis and moto-tricycles. Children ran loose between the vehicles, playing hide-and-seek. I watched a street magician attracting an audience with tall tales and card tricks. A boy volunteered from the crowd but was clearly in on the game.

The open-air market has now mostly shifted inside a modern warehouse, but around the perimeter there is still plenty of atmosphere – including a pen for donkeys, whose urgent braying sounds like whooping cough.

The stalls opened at 9 a.m.. There were carts of marrows, yellow carrots, green peppers, sun-dried chillies and ropes of garlic. There were areas for bicycle fixing and tools, another where fur traders sold silver fox, tiger skins and mink stoles. Entire families manned the stalls, with children cutting cloth or weighing raisins, dried apricots and walnuts.

In the Chinese medicine shops, I saw sacks of ginseng and dried mushrooms, skeletons of starfish and seahorses, as well as spindly goats' legs to boil in soup. Most ingredients, I was told, improved virility, fertility or longevity.

At the food stands, there were sheeps' heads piled in pyramids and buckets of sheeps' hearts. I went for shish kebabs and sesame seed bagels with freshly squeezed date juice.

I bought bags of almonds and Uighur shampoo resembling coal mixed with donkey dung. I bought a skullcap I will never wear and a telescope I didn't really need to be carrying in my backpack ('Russian technology, Chinese-made, very cheap, you can see beyond the stars'). I resisted the tambourines and curved daggers like the ones hanging from the hips of old Kashgari men.

After a day of bargaining here, and 150 hours on trains, I felt that everyone in China had become a pedlar – from the fast-talking traders on the floor of the Shanghai stock exchange to the souvenir hawkers pushing Mao trinkets. The country was heaving with a mass of merchants moving along a new road made of something coarser than silk.

Travelling by train was the most intimate way to experience this great land transforming itself: with people ranging from the chicken farmers on the sluggish, Communist-style locomotives to the entrepreneurs on the east coast express service from Beijing to Shanghai, where every passenger gets slippers, a toothbrush and a hot meal. Like China itself, the trains are getting sleeker and faster and they are expanding their reach.

But perhaps the country's finest metaphor is Shanghai's $1.2 billion (£666 million) airport shuttle, which reaches 270mph, making it the world's speediest locomotive. On the eight-minute journey, the train hardly touches the tracks; instead it uses magnetic levitation to float friction-free downtown. Around corners, the train tilts, even shudders. China may be taking the fastest, most frantic and frankly the most thrilling ride in the world.

THE PINK STEWARDS OF NOT-SO-RED CHINA

MR LI, MR JANG AND **PAUL MANSFIELD** GET THE 'SOFT SLEEPER' TREATMENT ON THE CHENGDU-TO-KUNMING EXPRESS

Mr Li was having trouble with his English – and one glance at his phrasebook was enough for me to understand why: *120 Dialogs for Everyday Use* was one of those American business manuals full of phrases even Americans would do better to avoid. 'Gotta go. Call me tonight ... I'll check you later.' The mangled phrases tumbled forth, and Mr Li looked confused. But the one that floored us both was in the section on 'saying goodbye'.

'You'll be out to see us next year then, as you promised?'

'Oh yeah. Unless something catastrophic comes up, that's my present plan.'

Mr Li turned his polite, inquiring gaze to me. What was 'catastrophic'? And wasn't a 'present' a gift? I was saved by the arrival of the cabin attendant, who announced that dinner was served.

We were on the overnight express from Chengdu to Kunming, a twenty-four-hour journey from China's central plains to the 'city of eternal spring' in the south. It had been cold in Chengdu, the first days of autumn. The leaves were falling from the trees, and the teahouses along the Silk River were full of old men playing mahjong in the fading afternoon sun. Waitresses ferried sooty kettles around the bamboo tables, refilling cups of jasmine tea. Ear cleaners and fortune tellers wandered through the crowd.

Chengdu, capital of Sichuan, is famous for its teahouses, which were among the first to be closed down during the Cultural Revolution. Sichuan has a reputation as the intellectual heartland of China, and its teahouses were deemed especially dangerous. With that nightmarish period now a fading memory, the teahouses are once again open, and it is as if nothing has changed.

But in fact Chengdu is changing quickly. With China's economy now the fastest growing in the world, rapid development is under way and the intellectuals of Chengdu have turned their formidable talents to the pursuit of money. The face of the city has altered almost overnight. High-rise apartments and offices line the wide boulevards; the department stores of Chunxi Road are stocked with every conceivable brand of western goods.

Chic Chinese women, wearing make-up and a style of clothing that owes something to the catwalks of Milan and something else to the King's Road circa 1976, sit talking to shiny-suited businessmen clutching mobile phones. Above the garish window displays and the swirls of neon, Chengdu's remaining gargantuan statue of Chairman Mao is just visible, standing with outstretched arms at the head of the Street of the People. He looks desperately out of place.

In the backstreets, images of old China remain. Coolies with heavy baskets attached to wooden poles plod along; a woman sits before a blood-soaked plank, pulling live eels from a bowl and skinning them expertly, their wriggling heads impaled on a hook. In tiny restaurants, Sichuan hotpot is still cooked in the traditional way, with skewers of meat and vegetables dipped into a cauldron of bubbling chillies. No English – or even Chinese – words can adequately convey the ferocity of this hot dish.

For four yuan (around 30p), I bought my skewers and sat down at an open-air restaurant. Two minutes later I was on my feet, clutching my throat. The owner put me out of my misery with a bottle of the beautifully, and appropriately, named Sichuan Snow Waves, a light, golden beer ideal for burning larynxes.

Which was just as well, for that night Chengdu's 'English Corner' took place in a park by the river. These events, popular all over China, can be tedious affairs, with the local students laboriously practising their English on passing foreigners. But in Chengdu it was different. Thirty or so teenagers were crowded in under the trees, speaking in surprisingly good – and clued-up – English.

What was the most efficient computer operating system, they wanted to know? Was Jack London considered a better author than Jack Kerouac? Yes, they'd heard of *Wild Swans* by Jung Chang, the Sichuan-born author's heart-rending account of life in Chengdu in the days of the revolution, but no one had yet seen a copy of it. Production of my dog-eared copy nearly provoked a riot.

Down at the station the next day the Kunming Express left dead on time, pulling out to a rousing swirl of martial music from the platform speakers. Female carriage attendants in pink trouser suits stood to attention by the train doors; in my 'soft sleeper' berth there were flowers, dark brown carpets and a Thermos flask of hot water, from which Chinese on the move refill jamjars of murky tea.

Also present were Mr Li and Mr Jang. Mr Li was forty-five, and an architect from Kunming; a tall, gangly man with thick wavy hair and a good-natured grin. Mr Jang was his exact physical opposite: tiny, with an elfin face, and hair swept back across his high forehead. But he too was grinning shyly. We sat back as the train headed through the outskirts of Chengdu and up into the mountains, passing horse-drawn carts on dirt roads, and fishing boats floating on shimmering lakes. As is common all over China, every square inch of this fertile landscape had been densely cultivated.

To be honest, I had been wary of Chinese trains, which even experienced travellers seem to regard with special loathing. But the Kunming Express was clean, punctual and blessed with a strangely easy-going atmosphere. Piped music played (the passengers in hard class frequently singing along); the pink-uniformed attendants bustled along the corridors and made chirpy announcements over the Tannoy. There was also a marked disregard of rules – healthy in a society so long entombed in bureaucracy. As I sat in the corridor puffing on a small cigar, a 'pink' approached and directed my attention to the concealed ashtray. It was located directly below the no-smoking sign.

Mr Li invited me to dinner. I had anticipated this, and offered to pay for at least the drinks, but Mr Jang headed me off at the pass. He would pay for the drinks, he announced, even though (it emerged later) he was a teetotaller. We stopped at the tiny town of Pujong, where, in the twilight, some boys were splashing in the river and an old man sat dozing over his newspaper on the dusty platform.

The splendid dining car was framed with net curtains and its tables laid with heavy linen. A squad of chefs toiled over rows of steaming woks; another squad of pinks brought trays of cooked-to-order food to the table. The Chinese are obsessive about food. They consume vast amounts of it; they discuss its virtues, they relate tales of great banquets of the past. They talk about it, in fact, in much the same way the English discuss the weather. (A customary Chinese greeting is not 'hello', but 'have you eaten?')

And the food on the Kunming Express was magnificent: plates of rice, spicy soup, pork, chicken, green beans with chillies, fish ... I began to worry about Mr Li bankrupting himself until I sneaked a look at the bill – the equivalent of £2.50 for three.

Most of the passengers on the train had brought their own food – they sat in the corridors in hard class, slurping from plates of pot noodles and sucking at chicken bones – so the dining car was the preserve of the high-rollers: professionals like Messrs Li and Jang, and a few party cadres, some of them stony-faced men who sat by themselves, smoking steadily and staring around the car. They seemed unamused by the choice of music on the Tannoy – Madonna – but the pinks paid them no attention.

The train rattled on through the darkening countryside, with Mr Jang nobly attempting a glass of Bindao beer, then giving up and passing round his cigarettes. Back in our compartment we broke out the Scotch, the playing cards and – inevitably – *120 Dialogs for Everyday Use.* Mr Li's confidence was growing by the minute. His ambition, he said, was to own his own car, and in two or three years he thought he might manage it. I was, he declared, his 'new Chinese friend'. He was 'most glad' to meet me. As the Scotch disappeared the conversation grew slightly cock-eyed, but at least we had managed to discard the phrasebook. Mr Li's finest moment came with the phrase 'China's new open-door policy is very beneficial to all of us'. As we turned in for the night I thanked him for dinner. 'Not at all,' said Mr Li, from his bunk.

The train rolled through the night, stopping from time to time at some unknown station, with the ghostly lights of a freightyard filtering in through the curtains. In the morning the countryside had changed: the plains had given way to rolling hills and rice fields, with purple mountains off in the distance. The passengers had changed, too. Some time in the night a trio of Americans had joined the train, businessmen with hard, indifferent faces.

Heading back from a breakfast of noodles I overheard one of them berating his Chinese interpreter in the corridor. It sounded as if he had learned his English from *120 Dialogs* ... 'The hell with it. I'll tell you, I don't give a hoot. It's your company gonna lose money, not mine. Listen. You Chinese have gotta get your act together.' Mr Li sat in the compartment listening, a rigidly polite smile on his face.

Finally, after exactly twenty-four hours, we were running through the industrial outskirts of Kunming, where the air was sweet and balmy – Eternal Spring, indeed. Shoals of bicycles flitted alongside the train and huge balloons held up banners saying in Chinese, 'welcome to our foreign guests'.

Mr Li, who was all for welcoming his foreign guests, offered me the use of his office's car for the day and invited me to stay at his home the next time I was in Kunming. I was able to accept his invitation warmly. Yeah, I'll be out next year to see him as promised. Unless something catastrophic comes up, that's my present plan.

At last, we'd found a use for that bloody phrasebook.

MR KIM TAKES A 6,000-MILE
RIDE INTO ABSURDITY

JOHN SIMPSON REPORTS ON A DICTATOR'S TRIP BY
ARMOURED TRAIN TO MOSCOW

It is the triumph of absurdity. Every day for nine days a bespectacled little man with buck teeth, permed hair, built-up shoes and a dark grey uniform out of *Star Trek* has been staring out of the window in a sealed train, gazing at the hypnotically featureless Siberian landscape.

Occasionally on its 6,000-mile journey the train stopped, and the little man got out to inspect something: a tank-building plant, a place where they made an unappetising type of processed meat. The little man seemed keen to buy tanks and processed meat in large quantities. No doubt the hungry people back home will be happy.

Most of the other stations along his route were closed off at his officials' request. The little man does not like taking risks, and is worried that real people – even the sad provincials who turned out to see him in some utterly remote tract of Siberia – might pose a threat. That is why the train was specially armoured, at enormous cost; that is why he took at least two food-tasters; that is why the technical checks could be carried out only by his own engineers.

He brought all his own water, and he has a hundred security men to guard him. Also ten sniffer dogs. If you are Kim Jong-il, the peerless leader of North Korea and the great successor to the revolutionary cause, you probably need all the sniffer dogs you can get.

And indeed the little man was not entirely wrong. Yaroslavl, the Moscow railway terminus where his nine-day journey ended, had to be closed to everyone else at his request, and Muscovites were so irritated that someone phoned in a bomb warning. A search of the station found nothing, of course.

The peerless leader of one of the world's last communist states seems to thinks he's back in the USSR. His schedule included a visit to Lenin's tomb in Red Square, to see the preserved remains of that other peerless leader whom no one much bothers to see any more. (Charmingly, a senior North Korean official said in English that Mr Kim would be going 'to see Lenin's mummy'; as though old Mrs Ulyanova might be around and receiving visitors after all this time.)

The press is full of phrases about bilateral defence ties, regional stability, and assistance in modernising North Korea's industrial base. But that belies the truth of this visit. It is an exercise in fantasy, the whim of an absurdly pampered character in his late fifties who can do anything he wants except live a real life.

He cannot even lead the life of most political leaders – themselves pretty cut off from reality. This, we are told, is because he is afraid of flying. No doubt it is true: a man who takes ten sniffer dogs with him on a sealed train may be peerless but not fearless. He went to Beijing by rail, and now he has gone to Moscow by rail. Presumably he will not be visiting Washington ...

Soon enough the little man from North Korea will be back on his train, looking out at the Siberian plain and never reflecting for a moment how ludicrous the whole trip has been. In his world it is reasonable enough to spend nine days at a time on the train because you do not like flying; and to take ten sniffer dogs along with you.

But even the peerless leader will have to face reality one day. It is just a matter of when.

ALL ABOARD THE RICKETY SADDAM EXPRESS FOR A LONG, SLOW JOURNEY TO NOWHERE

HOW BIG A JOB IS THE REBUILDING OF IRAQ? IN AN ATTEMPT TO FIND OUT, **PETER FOSTER** BOARDED THE TRAIN FROM BAGHDAD TO BASRA

The car park of Baghdad railway station at 7.45 a.m. It is with a heavy heart that we bid farewell to the creature comforts of our four-wheel-drive, with its air-conditioning, stereo system and upholstered seats, and say 'hello' to the chaotic world endured by ordinary Iraqis.

8.15 a.m. – The queue for tickets is among the few orderly things in Iraq. We pay 1,000 dinar (less than 60p) for a third-class ticket to Basra, Iraq's second city. The journey is almost 370 miles. That works out at less than 0.1 pence per mile.

The scheduled departure time is 'not before 08.30', or whenever Abdul, the stationmaster, is ready to wave his flag. Iraqi trains can never be late because they have no published arrival times. Could Abdul guess for us? 'Today,' he says, 'inshallah [God willing].'

9.10 a.m. – Two huge jolts, and we are off, lurching out of Baghdad past the two bomb-craters on platform one caused by a stray stick of coalition bombs aimed at the adjacent army barracks. In the carriage the temperature is already approaching 40°C. There is no air-conditioning on the train, so two men expertly lever the window out of its socket – filling the carriage with clouds of ultra-fine dust.

This is only marginally more irritating to the eyes and throat than the cigarette smoke that had shrouded the carriage seconds previously. Iraqis are devoted smokers. 'We have few other pleasures,' says one, proffering his pack of 'Sportsman' brand cigarettes. Not many Iraqis look sporting; most are proud of their 'Ba'athist pot-bellies' – as modelled by Saddam.

10.10 a.m. – Three more windows have been removed. The air rushing through the carriage is hotter than a hairdryer. The rolling-stock is French, from the 1970s and falling to pieces. Only about two-thirds of the seats are still worthy of the name. The lavatory is a hole straight down on to the tracks.

A woman fanning a sleeping infant with a strip of cardboard explains why she uses the train. It's cheap. A minibus would cost 10,000 dinar (about £6.50 per person), a seat in a saloon car 25,000 (£16). The crumbling industrial suburbs of Baghdad are drifting by outside – a bit like the stretch of line between Sandwell and Dudley and Birmingham New Street.

11.30 a.m. – An old man with only one tooth insists on buying us a Pepsi from the vendor who walks the train. Soon a discussion has broken out about the future of Iraq. Everyone yells at everybody else. Most of the people on the train are poor Shia returning home from job-hunting in Baghdad. We gather the full spectrum of opinion.

Hasim, a twenty-year-old student, wants an Islamic state and sharia law. There are too many thieves, he says, it would help to cut some hands off. Karim, thirty-eight, the ticket collector, who has stopped to join in the debate, says an Islamic government in cahoots with neighbouring Iran would be fatal. The Americans would invade again. It would be the mother of all wars. Mohammed Makry, the old man, says he doesn't mind, so long as there is peace. 'Don't ask me,' he says with a gummy grin. 'I could drop down dead tomorrow. Maybe even today.'

Everyone is agreed on one thing, however: they need money. Some government salaries have not been paid for three months.

12.25 p.m. – At Diwaniyah, our second stop, Karim invites us to the driver's cab. He is on the lookout for baksheesh – everyone has to try to make a living these days. His supervisor tries to intervene to stop us and a savage row breaks out. Karim calls the man a 'friend of Saddam' and 'Ali Babar' – a thief. His insults hit home. The pair of them have to be kept apart by the driver, a corpulent man called Ali Zureyr.

The supervisor has a reputation for being officious, but since the demise of Saddam no one has taken any notice of him. He doesn't like it. 'Didn't you hear? Saddam is finished!' yells Karim at his 'Fat Controller'. Iraq is full of these underlying tensions.

12.35 p.m. – From the driver's window, the effects of years of under-investment in Iraq's civil infrastructure are clear. The track dates from 1968 but is so poorly maintained that at places Ali can drive at only 12mph.

The Chinese-made loco – DEM (Diesel Engine Mainline) 2706 – is almost new. It was delivered from the People's Republic last year. In between blasts of his air-horn aimed at stray goats and donkeys on the line, Ali says the engines are 'rubbish, big rubbish' – very unreliable.

He explains that we will have to stop halfway, at a town called Samawah, to let the train coming from Basra get past us. Only one line is operational.

How long will we wait? Maybe fifteen minutes, he says. Maybe one hour.

12.45 p.m.– 2 p.m.

The heat is insufferable. I awake from a fitful sleep. The old man catches me glancing up at the luggage rack to make sure that my baggage is still there. 'No worry, no Ali Babar. I keep watch,' he says.

2.20 p.m.

Arrive at Samawah. We are on time. No sign of the Basra train, however, and no way to telephone ahead for information. We must simply wait.

3.35 p.m. – Still no train. In the absence of telecommunications, the loco is detached and sent ahead to investigate.

4.35 p.m.

Still no ----ing train. The novelty of being poor for a day is wearing thin. Iraqis come to offer their condolences. Several say they are ashamed that it is 2003 and we cannot run a train. It is Saddam's fault, says one man: he spent all the money on palaces.

5 p.m. – Decision time. We have only two bottles of water left and no food for the night. If we are to reach Basra by nightfall we must leave now. There are no security guards at the station and, with our conspicuous wealth, it is not safe to sleep the night on the platform.

Reluctantly, the order is given to 'abandon ship' – an option which, needless to say, is not open to our fellow passengers. They must sit and wait. Some are frightened. There was a robbery on the line only four days ago. Shamefaced, we cross the tracks and go to look for a taxi.

5.20 p.m. – Speeding towards Basra in a taxi that has seen better days. One decent pothole and we could all be finished. Dangling from the spot that British taxi drivers usually reserve for a scented pine-tree is a golden trinket with an Arabic inscription that puts all our faith in Allah. We are going to need it.

6.38 p.m. – We run up against a convoy of low-loaders carrying American tanks and artillery pieces. From the turret of one tank a US soldier acts as spotter, telling cars when it is safe to overtake. To our disbelief the driver ignores his signal to back off and starts to overtake in the face of an oncoming lorry.

To our double disbelief the US soldier fires a round from his M16 that strikes the road only a yard in front of our right front wheel. We back off.

6.40 p.m. – The three Iraqis in the front say they all hate American soldiers. The US troops do have an unfortunate manner, not helped by their helmets, which look like those worn by the Wehrmacht in the Second

World War. Add a pair of sunglasses and you have a cross between an SS stormtrooper and Darth Vader.

As we head to Basra the driver heaps praise on the British troops – who just wear berets and, as we have observed in Baghdad, are not frightened of chatting to the locals. The young paras on the gates of the British embassy in Baghdad play football with the locals every night on the embassy's front lawn; the Americans hide behind tanks and endless coils of razor wire.

6.50 p.m. – The mad driver is really starting to enjoy himself, pulling out directly into the path of an oncoming 4x4 occupied by US servicemen wearing civilian clothes but carrying guns. They are probably special forces. The driver is not to be moved and the Americans veer into the desert, putting imaginary pistols to their temples. In the front seat, the driver cackles maniacally. I find myself cheering.

8.10 p.m. – It is dark as we drive into Basra. When we reach the train station the source of our difficulty becomes clear. The Basra-to-Baghdad train never even left. The workers are on strike demanding wages they haven't been paid for four months. No one knows whether the train from Baghdad will reach Basra tonight.

In the station car park is our beloved 4x4, which has made the drive from Baghdad in less than six hours. We sink into the plush upholstery and feel the cool breeze of air-conditioning on our faces – the luxuries of rich men.

But somewhere in the darkness – up the line towards Samawah – there is a trainload of stranded Iraqis. They are filthy, hot and hungry and, like all other Iraqis, they are impatient for results.

ROMANCE ON THE EASTERN & ORIENTAL

A LUXURIOUS TRAIN, LUSH TROPICAL SCENERY ... AND A
PASSENGER SINGING 'LADY IN RED'. **ADRIAN BRIDGE**
TRAVELS THROUGH SOUTH-EAST ASIA IN STYLE

The most enjoyable email I've ever written? Well, the following, dispatched from the Oriental Hotel in Bangkok, is certainly a contender: 'Sorry, must dash. I've got a train to catch. The Eastern & Oriental Express, as it happens ...'

It was the last I was going to send for three days and, yes, I did feel a quiver of excitement as I wrote it.

In an age when speed (and 24/7 internet access) is everything, I was relishing the chance to slow down and switch off – to stop worrying about getting from A to B as quickly as possible, but instead simply to enjoy the journey.

That, after all, is what the Eastern & Oriental Express is supposed to be all about – a return to a gentler, more romantic form of travel.

Its very name conjures up an exotic world of lush tropical scenery and plush luxuriousness, of old-fashioned courtesy and conviviality, of adventure and excitement and life-enhancing encounters. I was only too happy to put the keyboard to one side. But would the reality live up to the fantasy?

The beginning certainly did: at Hualampong station in Bangkok, the train had a separate check-in area, an exclusive lounge and porters dressed in the racing green of the train itself who busied themselves with passengers' luggage. Somerset Maugham, who loved travelling in these parts, would have felt at home. He would also have enjoyed sizing up his fellow passengers for the 1,262-mile journey to Singapore, as I did.

We were a mixed crew, in terms of both nationality and age (though there was rather a large Spanish contingent). There were people who had retired early and who were keen to explore parts of the world they missed in their youth; couples celebrating special birthdays and anniversaries; a mother with her twenty-five-year-old daughter; a Japanese couple and their twelve-year-old grandson; a gay couple; an American serviceman enjoying a break from duties in Afghanistan; one or two singles of indeterminate age.

The first glimpse of the train itself didn't disappoint, either. Those racing green and cream-coloured carriages embossed with the Eastern & Oriental Express crest were an evocative sight, as were the attached signs reminding us of our route: Bangkok – Butterworth – Kuala Lumpur – Singapore. The very names (and the script in which they are written) were redolent of another era.

As was the interior. The wood-panelled compartments, of which there are three sizes – Pullman, State and Presidential – match those featured in the Marlene Dietrich film *Shanghai Express*.

Unlike those on the train's older sister, the Venice Simplon-Orient Express, however, these have en-suite shower rooms, complete with Bulgari accessories. Although it feels as though this is a journey our great grandfathers might have taken, the Oriental & Eastern Express has only been plying this route since 1993, and its fittings are of a more modern age.

It all felt rather surreal when, at 17.50, the train pulled out of Hualampong. The heat of the afternoon had been replaced by the balm and gentler light of early evening as we gravitated towards the outdoor observation deck, complete with padded chairs, protective railings, bowls of nuts, and convenient proximity to one of the train's two bars.

As the shining domes of 21st-century downtown Bangkok receded into the distance we passed tiny shacks, families tucking into rice and vegetables and groups of waving children so close we could almost touch them. What they made of us – Champagne glasses in hand – was anyone's guess.

By now passengers down for the first dinner sitting were dressed in evening finery ('Men will feel comfortable wearing jacket and tie. Black tie is optional,' the company advises). We must have made a perplexing spectacle.

Our first port of call the following morning involved a small detour to the west and an early wake-up to peer out at the wooden trestle viaduct at Tham Kasae, one of the most beautiful stretches of railway in Thailand. A little farther on was the place we had really come to see: the bridge on the River Kwai. It's an impressive construction, or rather reconstruction, of the bridge built at such cost to many British and other Allied prisoners of the Japanese during the Second World War, and its history was vividly brought to life by Hugh Cope, an Englishman now settled in Thailand.

He talked us through a map showing the extent of Japanese domination in this part of the world in 1942, in the clipped tones of someone who could have starred alongside Sir Alec Guinness in the 1957 film detailing the building of the bridge.

There was another echo from the film farther downstream at Kanchanaburi where, in the graphically named Death Railway Museum, I caught some rather moving footage of one of the British survivors whistling the Colonel Bogey March.

After that it was a relief to get back on board and continue the journey south. Looking out of the window of my compartment I saw rows and rows of coconut trees and the occasional flash of a temple roof. I caught a tantalising glimpse of the Gulf of Siam. At crossings I saw young Thai men in brightly coloured shirts impatiently revving up their motorbikes.

For company I wandered back down to the outdoor observation deck. A British couple (celebrating his fortieth birthday) told me they loved the fact that they didn't have a busy itinerary.

'It's great to be confined with no choices to make and no need to rush around and see things,' they said. 'For the first time in ages we've had some real time together, time to talk. It's very classy; very romantic.' Even couples for whom having that much time together was no longer such a novelty seemed to be enjoying the chance to sit and do ... not very much.

And there were always the meals to look forward to. Breakfast and afternoon tea were served in the cabin; lunches and dinners, split into two sittings, were rather grander three- and four-course affairs served in two elegantly appointed dining cars complete with gleaming crystal and silverware on white tablecloths.

The food was a fusion (albeit a rather rich one) of Asian and European – spicy chicken and Chang Mai noodles, lamb and vindaloo jus – and, on my journey at least, the dress code was observed, most men opting for the jacket-and-tie option, but some going the whole way with DJs and bowties. It was formal but not stuffy. Some passengers complained about having to dress up – but then why had they chosen this journey, I wondered.

Later on, in the piano bar, ties were loosened and inhibitions shed as one of the female passengers delivered a splendid rendition of 'Lady in Red' ... And all the while the sights and sounds of South-East Asia flashed by.

Once we were in Malaysia, coconut plantations gave way to the luscious tropical rainforest, the rice fields and the rubber and palm-oil plantations to which British entrepreneurs once flocked.

Over coffee, Leesa Lovelace, the train's general manager, revealed that, for all the gentility, there have been incidents of skulduggery on board. 'Murders, oh yes. We've had many murders on board this train: there's blood on the carpet all right,' she said, going on to spoil the story by saying that the train is occasionally hired out for shorter journeys on which passengers can dress up as characters from an Agatha Christie novel and play Murder on the Orient Express – the game.

In real life, the train has been the setting for proposals, a wedding, and 'lots and lots of indiscretions'. I had a feeling that there had been one or two on this journey, but Lovelace was far too discreet to reveal them. She was, anyway, distracted. A derailment farther up the line during the night meant that we could not move for several hours and were well behind schedule. As a result we were not going to be able to stop at Penang – the 'pearl of the Orient' and the place that nearly all of us were most looking forward to seeing.

On hearing that we were also going to be very late arriving in Singapore, one passenger spoke angrily of a 'total lack of organisation'. 'This is a slow train,' said Lovelace. 'We're on a single-gauge rail track. This is South-East Asia.'

Personally, I couldn't get enough of the wonderful palm-packed scenery of Malaysia, though I did enjoy the contrast afforded by a one-hour stop at Kuala Lumpur, where we were able to jump off to explore the fantasy of domes, cupolas and archways described by Paul Theroux as 'the grandest station in South-East Asia'.

Later I tried one or two of the other diversions on board: a Thai girl providing foot massages (I winced only once) and a palm reader who told me in the train's library/games room that I have a good wife (correct), will live for a long time (keep going …) and will have a successful career and a big house (but surely that should have happened already?).

As we crossed into the extraordinary tip of the Malaysian peninsula otherwise known as Singapore, we were struck by the great villas, perfectly manicured gardens and general orderliness for which Singaporeans are famed. 'It's bonsai-perfect,' exclaimed one of my more exuberant travelling companions as we congregated for one last time on the observation deck.

So, did the reality live up to the fantasy? It was time to take stock. Veterans of the Venice-Simplon-Orient Express said there had been less formality here – more intermingling – and that the private bathrooms were a big bonus. For those with mobility problems, however, the narrower gauge meant narrower corridors and a somewhat bumpier ride.

We were all disappointed about missing Penang, but agreed that the scenery had been magnificent and the experience of travelling in the style of another era memorable.

For most, the exhilaration at reaching the journey's end, Keppel Road station in Singapore, was tinged with sadness at having to leave the slow-moving cocoon of the train, with its little rituals of cocktails, sleepy afternoons and convivial gatherings, and to return to the world of emails.

For some, however, the journey had not ended at all. For at least two people on board (and for all I know there may have been more), it really had been a case of romance on the Eastern & Oriental Express. And for them, of course, the journey had just begun …

CHAPTER 4
THE AMERICAS

20 MARCH 1999

STRANGENESS ON A TRAIN

HIGH ON THE ANDEAN ALTIPLANO, **JULIET CLOUGH**
HAS HER BREATH TAKEN AWAY BY THE TRACK EVENT
OF A LIFETIME

The train, a streak of orange crawling across the bleached Andean land-scape, looked rather fetching — a caterpillar on a faded leaf. I felt pleased with the comparison. The snag was that I should have been making it from behind the carriage windows. Instead, I was minibussing perilously across the Altiplano in pursuit, scattering innocent bystanders, llamas and chick-ens like something out of an old Harold Lloyd movie.

I had woken that morning on the tiny island of Suasi near the north shore of Lake Titicaca. Martha Giraldo inherited the island from her grand-mother; and the little nature reserve she was building — its stone lodge grass-thatched and entirely solar-powered — reflected a new trend in Peruvian tourism. Backpackers are all very well, but Peru is increasingly baiting its hooks with gorgeous lures for the better-heeled. Suasi, where we ate lake fish and drank good Chilean wine and sat about admiring Martha's rose garden, represented quality escapism, a place where the environmen-tally conscious could veg out in comfort.

Wrested from this idyll at 4.30 a.m. by the need to catch the Puno-Cusco train, my Peruvian friend Marisol and I crossed the northern tip of Lake Titicaca, westwards, in one of the new motor launches available for hire. The surface of the lake, a bronze mirror held up to seemingly endless sky, reflected drifts of black ibis, the points of white fishing sails, and a fringing of pink flamingos standing among the reeds.

Three hours later, as tassels of waterweed began to reach up through the clear depths to touch our own reflection, it became evident that we would run aground and out of time long before reaching harbour. Locked into a trance-like state by lack of sleep, the pressures of altitude and the heady beauty of morning on the highest navigable lake in the world, I could not have cared less.

My companions, however — Marisol, Martha, driver, guide and boat owner alike — were made of sterner stuff. On being told in Juliaca, twenty-five miles down the line from Puno, that our train had left an hour ago, they announced that we would catch up with it at the next station, Pucara.

And so began the great train journey that almost never was. We hurtled along beside the railway tracks through potholes big enough to shelter whole families of piglets. We hung, Keystone Copwise, out of the minibus's windows for a first glimpse of the fugitive train. Outside, stills from a documentary of rural life flashed by: a shepherdess under a tree, more flamingos, a woman weaving in a farm courtyard. Even the political party symbols, chalked on bare rock faces, seemed Arcadian: pan pipes, a woolly hat with earflaps, a crossed-out spade.

As Pucara hove in sight, so at last did our quarry, apparently putting on an unsporting burst of speed. Would we converge? We overtook a lorry on the near side to hurl ourselves and luggage, seconds too late, out of the minibus and on to the platform. If ever a train had a smug note to its whistle, drowning our imploring shrieks as it pulled out, that one did.

But suddenly a carriage door flew open, causing shouts from the guard, a clatter of police boots and a shuddering halt. 'These are latecomers of my party,' announced a Swedish tour guide from the footplate, with Olympian disregard for truth. We fell in, gratefully, at his feet.

In the world catalogue of great train journeys, the Puno-Cusco railway comes pretty near the top. Literally. If the scenery does not take your breath away, the altitude will. The railway, built by the British in 1907 as part of a network designed partly with the alpaca wool trade in mind, is a key part of the Arequipa-Colca, Titicaca, Cusco triangle — the beat for almost every first-time traveller in southern Peru. The railway crosses the Andes, leaving the sparse grasslands around Lake Titicaca, and heaves itself over the 14,000ft La Raya pass before dropping to the lush greenery of the Vilcanota valley. At an average altitude of 11,500ft, this is one of the world's highest as well as most spectacular train rides.

When I got my breath back, it was to find a vision swaying daintily by my elbow. Standard-class travel means the company of roving chickens and Quechua-speaking card players; middle-class means wall-to-wall rucksacks. Travel Inka class and you get reclining plush seats, grubby red tablecloths and wannabe air hostesses.

The vision and her colleagues wore scarlet, brass-buttoned, micro-mini dresses with plastic gauntlets to protect snowy cuffs. They tottered along the Pullman coaches, genteelly balancing trays of coca tea or brandy-based pisco sours, both trusted panaceas for most of the problems of travel in Peru. On four-inch heels, this appeared no mean feat. Despite the pancake flatness of the passing Andean plateau, the bumpiness of the track sent peaches and pisco sours flying heavenwards. By journey's end, we and the elderly Swedes had all become adept fielders.

The Altiplano stretched towards dun-coloured hills, clad in the odd patch of polylepis, said to be the highest-growing tree in the world. Most of the forest vanished long ago, felled as fuel by the conquering Spanish. Mixed herds of cows, sheep and llamas grazed the sparse ichu grass, their bowler-hatted minders spinning as they watched. From far across the horizon, a black dog streaked towards the train, trying to round us all up before falling back exhausted.

At the next station, Ayavari, the first group of the day's many vendors held alpaca gloves, bananas and statuettes of Santa Rosa up to our windows, to catch the only passing trade of the day. A little band played hopefully from the platform, the sounds of pan pipes, hand drums and a tin guitar fading as we forged on.

Arrival time in Cusco would depend entirely on who was driving and what kind of engine we had, said our Swedish saviour, Per Gunnar. 'Best bet is the driver known as La Flecha Verde, the Green Arrow. Worst bet is El Sapo, the Toad. Today, it's Velásquez, who is somewhere in between.'

Before last year, Gunnar went on, the timetable used to be even more haphazard, with 10 p.m. arrivals and long waits in freezing, unlit carriages par for the course. 'Once, we waited for seventy-five minutes in Juliaca while the driver looked for oil at the right price,' he said.

The engines, like the drivers, also came in various sizes. 'They put the smaller ones on from Puno to Juliaca. Quite often they swap when they meet halfway.' Gunnar disappeared to consult Velásquez, returning with reassuring news. 'Today, ours is the 352, which is OK.'

And OK it was. At the watershed, La Raya, we stopped in a fork of snow-capped mountains for photographs of the sign announcing a summit altitude of 14,166 feet. Here, a drop of water, spilled to the left of the train, would eventually find its way through Lake Titicaca to the Pacific. Splashed on the right side of the tracks, it would head for the Amazon and the Atlantic.

Soon we were working our way downhill into the green embrace of the Vilcanota Valley. The countryside began to look positively French, its tile-roofed villages tucked into the loops of the poplar-fringed river. We had reached Sicuani, well over halfway, before we met the oncoming Cusco-Puno train. Gunnar had clearly posed a challenge to Velásquez's manhood.

Seven hours spent making caterpillar tracks across the high Andes had provided valuable chill-out time; space in a packed week of travel infinitely more varied, rich and stylish than anything I had ever envisaged. The orange thread of the train had linked two very different aspects of southern Peru: the serenity and solitude of Lake Titicaca with the Inca splendours, Spanish glitter and Kathmandu-style tourism of Cusco.

Ahead of us lay the Sacred Valley, Machu Picchu and the jungle – a whole set of other hills to climb.

TYPECAST IN THE ANDES

Mandrake

Growing weak from a diet of bananas and sardines washed down with Inca-Cola, light-headed from lack of oxygen, and driven mad by the playing of a demonic Japanese piano accordionist, the party of British journalists marooned in the high Andes began to make up the headlines that would announce their fate, such as: 'British journalists eat each other in Andes train horror.'

It had started out as the highlight of a most pleasant tour organised by British Caledonian to celebrate the opening of that airline's service to Peru. The Butch Cassidy-type train chugged its way through the dramatic countryside on its way to the remains of Machu Picchu, the lost city of the Incas. On board were tour parties of Japanese, Germans, French and Americans.

Disaster struck in a gorge alongside the sacred Urubamba River, loomed over by snow-topped mountains. The train pulled up beside an adobe cantina (obviously kept by the engine-driver's grandmother) and refused to budge.

Within minutes the Japanese made their takeover bid. Their tour leader, wearing a green golf cap, organised the other passengers into a singsong. Another unslung a piano accordion. How does it come about that a Japanese will carry a piano-accordion halfway round the world and over halfway up it to visit Inca ruins?

First of all, the passengers underwent the bizarre ritual of the Israeli national folk-dance. Then came Neapolitan love songs. And then, horror upon horror, a trainee American opera singer was found and she swung into *Madame Butterfly* – what else?

It all became more and more bizarre. A second accordionist was found, a Frenchman, and soon everybody had spilled on to the tracks and the French had seized their womenfolk and were dancing waltzes, foxtrots and, of course, the tango. The hours dragged by. The music became diminuendo. And the various nationalities began to show their xenophobic teeth. The Americans disappeared into the guts of the engine, determined to show that American know-how could cure it. They failed, of course.

The Japanese went off on an organised ramble. The British, fortified by a bottle of Scotch taken along by Mandrake's colleague Christopher Dobson – more a war correspondent than a travel writer – viewed the scene coldly and made supercilious remarks which enraged one German. He delivered a lecture on British decadence and wasn't it about time we started to work hard again? This, in turn, produced mutterings along the lines of: 'I've met people like you before – at Belsen,' and 'Who are you, Martin Bormann?'

The atmosphere was becoming strained when, after five-and-a-half hours, the engine was pronounced cured. At the same time, another train appeared going in the opposite direction. Passengers could, said the authorities, go on for a shortened tour of the ruins or return to try again the following day.

A mighty squabble broke out then. Tours split, friends parted company. Eventually a carriage was taken off one train and attached to the other. The original train pulled out for Machu Picchu.

Everybody had a splendid time at the ruins. It was made even more splendid by the news that their renegade companions had only steamed some few miles when they broke down again. It took another four hours for them to be rescued by bus.

COMPLETELY OFF THE RAILS

THE LINE THROUGH MEXICO'S COPPER CANYON OFFERS
ONE OF THE WORLD'S MOST SCENIC JOURNEYS.
SEAN HIGNETT RISKS HIS NECK TO ENJOY IT

It was damn windy, damn dirty and damn dangerous riding on that train.
There was only myself to blame. I should have been riding in it.

We were about seven hours into the Sierra Madre, aboard the train that
climbs and loops, pirouettes, ducks and dives and tunnels its way between
the Pacific and Chihuahua, twisting along the rim of the Barranca del
Cobre, or Copper Canyon. The Mexicans proclaim this spectacularly crumpled landscape to be bigger (four times), deeper (not much) and – really
going for it – grander than the Grand Canyon.

This was not the Ferrocarriles Nacionales de Mexico train, the public one
that leaves before dawn, does the whole trip in a day and thus passes through
some of the best scenery in darkness. We had boarded instead the luxury
South Orient Express – which stops overnight and takes nearly three days
over the trip – at the relatively civilised hour of eight, breakfasted in comfort
as we trundled across the coastal plain and, as we wheedled our way up the
mountain, lunched sumptuously on the best food to be found in Mexico.
Then we descended from the restaurant car's glass dome to take some
pictures.

The few pull-down windows in the air-conditioned coaches were jammed
on the scenery side by camcorder queens, hoovering up the world in Hi8.
So I stationed myself by an unwanted, port-side window with its close-up
view of chiselled rock and the occasional bemused butterfly. Then, as the
train curved round a bend, swinging its back end into view, I saw Nik, a
fellow snapper I had met on the train, sticking up from the roof of the
guard's van, camera clicking.

I had checked out the caboose, as the gringos call the rear car, before we
had set off that morning, and noted the ladder in the middle of the cabin, so
I made my way down the train, leant across the buffers and banged on the
door.

A young man appeared, a latter-day incarnation of the hobo rail-riders of the 1930s. I learnt later he was a Slovak student who had missed the public train and sneaked aboard ours. He pointed back and it dawned: the ladder inside the carriage led only to a couple of wooden ledges on which four Mexicans, none of whom appeared to be any more official than the Slovak, had jammed themselves. Nik, the Slovak indicated, had gone out of the back and climbed on to the roof.

Emboldened by the Chilean Chardonnay I had drunk with lunch, I clambered on to the buffers and, swinging dangerously over the rails, heaved myself up. Nik, I could now see, was hanging on to a raised part of the roof, giving the illusion from up front that he was safely sticking out of the caboose rather than standing precariously on top of it.

I crept towards him, the corrugations of the iron crawl-way cutting at my knees, then stood up. The 360° panorama, mountain to one side, river gorge to the other, unobstructed by the camcorder crowd, was terrific.

Wrapping an arm round the smokestack, I pulled my camera to my eye. Nik grabbed me. 'Tunnel!' he yelled. I dived to my knees just in time to avoid losing my head completely and, smothered in trapped diesel fumes, we chugged through what seemed endless darkness.

Out in the light I stood up again. Nik's face and hands were blackened, as I guessed mine now were. 'How old are you?' I asked him. He smiled and told me. 'Snap!' I grinned. 'Don't you think it's time we stopped doing these damn fool things?' We collapsed hysterically. It was the biggest thrill I've had standing up in years.

The Chihuahua al Pacifico railway was conceived in 1872 by Albert Owen, an American hoping to establish a Utopian community at Topolobampo on the Pacific coast of Mexico and link it with the grain belt of the United States. Owen's project collapsed and others tried their hand, including Pancho Villa in his first career as a building contractor. Come the revolution, Villa returned to blow up his handiwork and, by the 1950s, only the easy stretches over the plains at either end of the line had been completed.

Then the Mexican government, determined to show the gringos how, took over. In 1961, four hundred miles, eighty-six tunnels and fifty-nine bridges later, the railway, one of the most scenic in the world, was completed.

Nowadays, only freight trains go down to the sea at Topolobampo. The passenger terminus is a little way inland at Los Mochis, a dusty, industrial, characterless town. To catch the train, though, you have to get to Los

Mochis the day before, so to occupy the afternoon our guide took us across the plain to El Fuerte.

El Fuerte was a delight, a quiet Spanish-colonial village set around a flower-filled plaza. We lunched in one of its mansions, the Posada del Hidalgo, now a small hotel, an antique funeral hearse in the tunnelled entrance-way, old artefacts and writing desks littered about, each airy 19th-century room opening on to a cloistered atrium enclosing a water garden.

If you are riding the public train that stops at every station, El Fuerte would, I suppose, be a better place to spend the night than Los Mochis. It nestles exactly where the railroad begins to rise into the sierra and the train reaches it at the relatively civilised hour of 8 a.m.

Our South Orient Express was not scheduled to stop at El Fuerte, so we returned to Los Mochis. Although we had already crossed the coastal plain forth and back by bus, forth by train was the better, allowing us to walk about, breakfast in hand, taking in the alluvial flats, yellow with palo verde, pink with amapa, green with the bracts of coral vine and orange with field upon field of marigolds – fed to chickens, I learnt, to give colour to their yolks.

By late afternoon we had twisted our way up mounting ravines, breaking out from tunnel after tunnel to reach our overnight stop at Posada Barrancas. Barrancas really is no more than three hotels and a freight stop for the Tarahumara Indians, the so-called 'foot-runners' who lope vast distances across northern Mexico to the growing grounds of the peyote cactus used in their religious ceremonies. They live in niches in the canyon walls, their homes part-cave, part-timbered, part-adobe.

We sampled each of the hotels, putting up at El Rancho, a simple log cabin structure warmed by oil heaters, dining at an extraordinary fake medieval castle, the Mansion, and breakfasting on the lip of the canyon at the relatively new Posada Mirador. From the 'mirador' itself, a roomy boulder hanging vertiginously over the edge, we could at last overlook the canyon from above.

Grand Canyon it was not. There the view is more or less straight down and straight across a single chasm, the drama of which is enhanced by the starkness of the bare and bright rock. In the deepening dusk, the network of canyons that fingered out a mile below and two hundred miles into the distance was made somehow more gentle by its complexity, its abundance of vegetation and a skein of footpaths that appeared to lead safely down.

We saw Tarahumara women descending those paths to their cliff-side homes. Next morning they returned with their woven straw souvenirs to their vending stations on the hotel steps, bringing with them their menfolk who, ankles rattling with seashells, performed one of those tourist folk dances that are an opportunity for the 'folk' to ridicule the 'tourists', in this case by pretending to be chickens, running wildly at the males in their audience and goosing them.

Overnight our train had pulled ahead without us to the absolute 8,000ft peak of the railway at Divisadero. We drove and walked the two miles to the train via the Balancing Rock, a spectacular projection from the rim of the canyon. Divisadero sits exactly on the continental divide and is the point at which a complex of six canyons, only loosely referred to as 'Copper Canyon', comes to a confluence in the most dramatic vista of all. Indeed, it might be tempting fate to use the description 'to die for', so heart-stopping is the drop-off from verandas of the Hotel Divisadero.

From there it was all downhill, through a rocky landscape of boulders as big as box-cars, to our second overnight at Creel. This is one of those unhurried Mexican outposts where the dentist – to judge by the hog grazing before his wooden shack – is paid in pigs and where borrachos (drunks) sit smiling the afternoon away in the plaza, awaiting immortalisation in a novel by Gabriel García Márquez. It is a base for exploring the depths of the canyons rather than their heights.

We headed for the Valley of Mushrooms and the mission church of San Ignacio, where Tarahumara women sat among the strange rock formations in silent contemplation, apparently unconcerned whether we were interested in their basketwork or not. Then it was on to the isolated and magical 18th-century mission at Cusarare, 'the place of the eagles'. This, patterned inside in ochre by its Tarahumara congregation, was furnished only with a rough box of a pulpit, stuck like a crow's nest atop a log, and a birdcage-like confessional, so open and public it seemed more symbolic than secret.

There were symbols, too, in what I presume was the vestry – a bundle of wooden swords, a hat of a thousand feathers and an effigy of the Virgin propped inside a coffin – all part of the strange concoction that the Tarahumara had made of Christianity.

Between Creel and the terminus at Chihuahua, the train wound across a plain planted with apple orchards by the Mennonites who settled here in the 1920s. The climate here, at 5,000ft, is temperate rather than tropical. At the end of each orchard row stood a primitive, rusting diesel stove, a profligate means of protecting the blossom from spring frosts.

'What on earth are those?' a camcorder queen exclaimed. 'They're kind of altars,' I replied; 'the Mennonites use them in their religious ceremonies to ensure the fertility of their apple crops.'

'Can you just repeat that so I can get it on tape?'

NO HIGHER ADVENTURE

GAVIN BELL, WITH A NURSE AND A CLOWN, BOARDS THE
CENTRAL ANDEAN RAILWAY

A nurse was bustling through the carriages with an oxygen cylinder when something odd happened. Having climbed thousands of feet into the Andes, the train shuddered to a halt. Then, imperceptibly at first, but with gathering momentum, it began to slide backwards.

At this point a clown with scary red eyes appeared in a doorway and shrieked. Even by Latin American standards, this was no ordinary railway.

It is, in fact, the Ferrocarril Central Andino (FCR), an improbable feat of Victorian engineering that blasted through mountains, clung to precipices and spanned gut-churning gorges in the Peruvian Andes to climb higher than any standard-gauge railway in the world.

History does not record how many men died in its construction in the late 19th century, but they numbered thousands. In 1872, an engineer reported in the *Chicago Railroad Gazette* that one five-mile section was almost a continuous graveyard. He then gave a succinct description of the terrain: 'Very much of the line cannot be passed over by a biped until a road is made. He would need wings to do it.'

When completed, its sixty-six tunnels, sixty-one bridges and twenty-two zigzag sections led from Lima to a pass 15,681ft above sea level, which is the equivalent of more than halfway up Everest. All for the sake of buried treasure – millions of tons of silver, zinc, copper, manganese and other precious minerals – that had to be transported to the Pacific coast to fuel the Industrial Revolution.

Every year tourists flock to another Peruvian railway, between the Incas' ancient capital of Cusco and their sanctuary of Machu Picchu. Few have travelled on the higher and wilder reaches of the Central Andean Railway, which has recently resumed occasional passenger services after years of neglect, landslides and terrorist attacks. This is a journey on which adventure comes with the price of a ticket.

Peruvians like to celebrate, and the rare departure of a passenger train on the FCR line is as good an occasion as any. There was a festive air as more than 300 people, mostly Peruvians on holiday, waited at the terminus in Lima to board half a dozen carriages in bright red and yellow livery for a journey of about 200 miles to the mountain market town of Huancayo.

Then the mad horn-blower of the Andes appeared. He was a small, stocky character in overalls whose main preoccupation appeared to be to alert all of Peru to our passage by hooting the engine horn continuously whenever anyone was remotely within earshot. His other job was driving the massive 3,200-horsepower diesel charged with hauling us to the roof of South America.

Thus it was to a cacophony of shouts, horn blasts and cheers that we juddered into motion and pulled slowly through a sea of dusty shanty towns ringing the capital that reminded one of South African townships.

The flotsam and jetsam of economic migration is the same the world over. But in bright sunshine our cavalcade of noise and colour became a travelling circus for onlookers who smiled and waved, and ragamuffin children who ran beside us, and barking dogs and startled cattle, and an old man who fell off his bike in shock. He dusted himself off, and gave us a toothless grin. This was a train that made people happy.

It was also a bit of a mystery. Nobody seemed sure when a passenger service had last reached Huancayo, or how long it would take this time. The manager of the South American Explorers' Club in Lima said it would depend on how many landslides we encountered.

A woman who purported to be the commercial director of the enterprise was on board, but curiously she did not consider briefing travel writers to be part of her job. Fortunately we had among us Michael Grimes, a retired lecturer in electrical engineering from Cork, who knew everything you could possibly want to know about this railway and a good deal more.

Thanks to Michael, we learned that the track took thirty years to build, that the zigzag concept was taken from the Great Indian Peninsular Railway, and that daily landslides were virtually guaranteed in the rainy season. 'I love landslides because you can get out and take photos,' he said.

We had begun climbing through steep, barren foothills. Now, glancing at abrupt rock faces above and below us, it was difficult to share Michael's enthusiasm for landslides. The only way up sheer mountains is the stop-start forward-reverse manoeuvre of zigzags, which tends to cause a flutter in the tummy the first time one slides backwards. At 10,000ft, it is a long way down.

This was the level at which our nurse expected to begin dealing with the effects of altitude sickness, ranging from headaches, nausea and gastric wind to hypertension. It was also where a few of us were ejected from our seats by the clown, who displayed symptoms of all of the above for the amusement of bewildered children.

This is not a quiet train. In addition to the competing babble of the clown and mad Captain Hornblower up front, we were regaled with catchy Latin rhythms on the loudspeakers as we rocked and rolled our way into the Andean sky.

Dr Michael Macek, concert director of the Salzburg Festival, was enjoying himself. He had ridden the railways of Egypt, Japan and Slovakia, and considered this the best yet. Gazing from his window at a tumult of peaks and ravines, he said: 'It is really an adventure. This is the crescendo.' And so it was. A soaring symphony of nature at its wildest and most severe.

The climax was a panorama of snow-capped peaks enclosing grasslands to far horizons, and a solitary railway halt with a sign that said: 'Altura 15,681 pies'. This meant feet, not food, of course, but none of the passengers seemed hungry anyway. During a brief stop, some emerged from the train to wander around in a daze, moving slowly in high, thin air where the least exertion caused breathlessness. I felt distinctly woozy and stayed in my seat.

Then I saw the horsemen. There were about a dozen of them, in a stone corral on a distant hillside. As I watched, they emerged at intervals of about a minute, a succession of lone riders cantering along a ridge above a dark lake. Whether it was a game or just free spirits amusing themselves, I have no idea, but it was a stirring image as old as the days of the conquistadors.

A less appealing vision awaited us in the mining town of La Oroya, which can lay fair claim to being hell on earth. The very mountains have been reduced to crumbling, whitened skeletons by mining operations that poison the air and everything that absorbs it. In the heart of this man-made nightmare the train passed through a giant smelter, from which we were observed by workers who were all wearing gas masks like extras in a *Mad Max* film. Curiously our windows were wide open, and train staff were serving lunch of grilled chicken.

Spirits were lifted again near the end of our journey – twelve hours without landslides – in the lush Mantaro Valley, which serves as the bread basket of Lima. A village brass band had turned out in full ceremonial regalia to welcome us with an enthusiastic rendition of its jaunty repertoire, and the platform was overflowing with excited people eager to promote the attractions of the region.

These include rural communities that produce a wide range of handicrafts, and a lake where boys rowing boats with names such as *Titanic* have yet to learn the art of avoiding collisions. The few foreign tourists who make the effort to get here are greeted with courtesy.

In one village I met a Peruvian mining engineer on holiday with his family, who explained why he preferred the Mantaro Valley to the attractions of Cusco. 'In Cusco they want your money, here they want your smiles,' he said.

In the land of 15,000 pies, there are rare treasures at the end of the line.

112mph BY U.S. TRAIN

STREAMLINED AND USING CRUDE OIL: WORLD RECORD RUN

Chicago

After a run of one thousand-and-fifteen miles from Denver in thirteen hours and five minutes, the Burlington Railway's streamlined train, the *Zephyr*, arrived here last night. This, it is pointed out, is the longest and fastest non-stop trip in railway history.

The cost of the fuel – crude oil – consumed by its diesel engines was only about 4gns. The train maintained an average speed of more than 77mph, and at times reached over 112mph. It cut nearly thirteen hours from the regular running time of the Burlington line's regular crack train, the *Aristocrat*.

Between Denver and Harvard, Nebraska, the officials announced that the train had beaten by one hour fifty-three minutes the four hundred-and-one-mile London-Glasgow record set up by the *Royal Scot* in 1928.

Extraordinary preliminary arrangements were made to prepare for the run. All passenger and goods traffic was side tracked, and the points were spiked so as to prevent any possible tampering with them. All stations were guarded by special police, and difficult curves and isolated sections were patrolled by selected railway employees. Section gangs had worked for weeks on the tightening of nuts and the ballasting of the track so as to ensure a perfect road bed.

Over eighty-five passengers made the trip. About 500 gallons of crude oil, costing but tuppence a gallon, were consumed. Zeph, a Colorado mule, was taken along as a mascot, together with a special supply of hay for his benefit.

ROMANCE OF RIDING THE FREIGHT TRAINS IS SHATTERED BY THE HOBO FROM HELL

BOXCARS HAD BECOME THE NEW DOMAIN OF YOUNG ADVENTURERS BUT THEN A DRIFTER USED TRAINS AS A MEANS OF KILLING

James Langton in New York

Angel Maturino Resendiz was the hobo from hell. For twenty years he rode freight trains across the Mexican border into Texas, seeking victims in a trail of slaughter that stretched as far north as Illinois and left at least nine people dead.

After a brief trial that ended late last week, justice caught up with the forty-one-year-old drifter, who was found guilty of the rape and murder of a Houston doctor. The jury must now decide whether to sentence Resendiz to death. He has already indicated that he would prefer the execution chamber to life behind bars.

The case has sent shock waves through the loosely knit community of 21st-century hobos or 'freight-hoppers', a growing number of whom are young adventurers, often middle-class and well-educated, who seek illicit thrills in jumping aboard an empty boxcar.

Using books such as *Hopping Freight Trains in America*, written by a Californian lawyer and the bible of the so-called 'recreational-hobo' movement, as many as twenty thousand people regularly ride the rails each year.

For recreational hobos, the plaintive wail of a train whistle on a sultry southern night has given way to the chirrup of a mobile phone. The rattle of boxcars over points is matched by the chatter of keys on a laptop, while a credit card in the pocket means they can always be sure of their next meal.

Many hold down well-paid jobs, among them Dawson Morton, a law student at New York University, who publishes his exploits on his website and advises beginners to pack earmuffs, suntan lotion and a good book.

Hans-Christoph Steiner, a computer programmer from Manhattan, is also a confirmed freight-hopper. 'The idea has always intrigued me. I like the image of a self-sufficient wanderer who doesn't burden others,' he said.

Confirmed freight-hoppers can also join the National Hobo Association, which has a membership of more than three thousand and publishes a magazine, the *Hobo Times*. The association even offers 'hobo gear', including a monogrammed polo shirt and a waterproof jacket to 'keep out the night chills around the jungle campfire'.

Buzz Potter, president of the association, who rode freight trains while looking for work after the last war, says that the Resendiz murder trial has damaged the image of hobos. 'I'm head of 3,400 guys who wouldn't hurt a flea,' he says. 'You have to be more careful out there, no doubt about it. But I know more guys who have PhDs who ride freight trains.'

The first hobos – the name is thought to derive from 'homeward-bound boys' – were Civil War veterans who hitched rides home in the 1860s. The hobos' heyday was in the Great Depression, when tens of thousands of unemployed men rode across the United States looking for work. Their lives were later immortalised by the writer James Michener, a former hobo, and Boxcar Willie, the country and western singer.

Union Pacific, one of the biggest railways, says it arrested ninety-seven thousand people for trespassing in 1998 but released most with a warning.

RUNNING OUT OF TIME

PAUL MANSFIELD BOARDS THE SUNSET LIMITED, A TRAIN
WHOSE VERY NAME SUGGESTS IT CANNOT LAST

I knew we would have trouble with Texas Bob. He was pacing the platform
at the Amtrak station in New Orleans, tall and rangy in his denim suit and
cowboy boots, arguing with the porter about his suitcases. Bob claimed he
had been working in the city repairing damage from Hurricane Katrina.
'Show a man some respect,' he said to the porter. Later I heard him telling
another passenger about the 'important' new job he was heading to in
Arizona. But would someone in counter-terrorism really announce the
fact to a stranger?

Anyway, with Bob, his massive suitcases and my wife and me safely on
board, the Sunset Limited rolled out of New Orleans at noon, heading
west.

We had arrived the day before by plane from Miami, which wasn't quite
what we had intended. The Sunset Limited has been running between
Florida and Los Angeles since 1894, and is North America's last remaining
transcontinental train. We had hoped to begin our journey on one coast
and end it on another. But the track east of New Orleans has still not been
repaired post-Katrina, and for the moment the train is running a limited
service. Given the ambivalence of the United States about its railway system
– passenger numbers on some routes are up, but Amtrak still makes an
overall loss – many people predict that the original Sunset Limited will
never run again.

There was already a faint air of nostalgia on board, in the two-tier
'Superliner' carriages, with their old-fashioned decor and clunky fittings.
Our cabin had two fold-down bunks, plate-glass windows and a lavatory
with shower. As we rocked across the points outside New Orleans the train
lurched and swayed precariously, but the view from 20ft up was
unbeatable.

We had spent a day in the French Quarter, now once again fully open for
business. Touristy it may be, but the Quarter still has a dark, seductive

energy. The topless and bottomless bars on Bourbon Street made Miami's look like Sunday schools; the gumbo came dark and rich, served by a sassy waitress who called me 'baby'. Music – jazz, rock, Cajun zydeco – blasted from open windows. Twenty-four hours in New Orleans goes a long way.

And now we were heading west across the Mississippi river through a landscape of cypress swamps and bayous. Not the prettiest country in the world but, like New Orleans, possessed of its own appeal. As the Sunset Limited crossed into Texas the sun went down in a blaze of yellow and crimson. Travelling by train reminds you of the size of the United States. Twenty-four hours hence we would still be in the Lone Star state.

Eating alone is not an option on the Sunset Limited: tables in the dining car are laid for four. That first night we were particularly lucky: David and Sheri were documentary film-makers from Boston off to visit relatives in California, and we hit it off immediately. But as we chatted over fresh fish and steak (cooked, not microwaved, in the kitchen below), we noticed the dining car was filling up with an extraordinary mixture of people.

Senior citizens and students, mothers with young children, tourists, ex-military personnel (they travel at a discount), groups of friends, solo drifters such as Texas Bob – black and white, rich and poor, all of the United States, it seemed, was dining here, and everyone was talking to everyone else. This was curiously exhilarating.

By ten o'clock we had reached Houston and stopped in a dingy little station below the glittering office blocks of downtown. I once had to catch a train here and nearly missed it, because no one knew where the station was. It's a sad fact: all across the United States there are people who have no idea they live near a railway. Texas Bob was in the bar drinking whiskey, telling anyone who would listen about the mosquitoes back in Louisiana; big enough, he said, to 'stand flat-footed and rape a turkey'.

The train rocked us to sleep, and we woke to the Texas plains: a landscape of scrub and sagebrush; a sky of flinty blue. Every so often the flatlands would part to reveal a deep chasm in the earth. At Pecos Canyon the train rolled at walking pace across a delicate iron bridge 300ft high. Down below, a cowboy on horseback stood at the river's edge. This country is rich with stories of the old west. We passed the tiny town of Langtry, where 'Judge' Roy Bean once dispensed idiosyncratic justice from the saloon and held illegal boxing contests on a sandbank in the river.

Texas Bob had joined us for breakfast: he tipped his hat to my wife. This part of Texas, he said, was fine country for wildlife. 'Antelope, mule deer, you'll see 'em everywhere. I shot me five in a day. I love venison.' Shortly after that we ground to a halt: a cracked rail ahead needed repair. It turned into a four-hour delay.

But time passes differently on a train. Caught between two distant points, you hand over control. You gaze at the view, read, listen to music, and you talk to your neighbours: about politics, families, work, hopes, dreams – the sort of conversations that rarely happen elsewhere. Perhaps it's the shared sense of adventure; perhaps it's simply the time available. But something happens. In the lounge bar Texas Bob had fallen in with a group of students. He was buying them beer and telling stories, gesticulating wildly. The students looked nervous.

Sunset – another multi-coloured extravaganza – found us in west Texas, passing through Alpine, where the silhouettes of surrounding mountains really did look like the Alps in miniature, and on to El Paso. This is a border town, with neon lights on the American side facing across the Rio Grande to the Mexican city of Juarez. This was a jumble of adobe houses, with dim silver streetlights and the tang of wood smoke. We turned in early as the train rolled through New Mexico and into Arizona, and woke to the most spectacular sight yet: a desert sunrise of high yellow skies, the red earth dotted with cacti, a silver moon hanging high above.

At breakfast, Texas Bob was nowhere to be seen. The conductor shook his head sadly. The students, it seemed, had grown tired of his stories and snubbed him. Bob – who claimed he had spent 'two hunnerd damn dollars' on beer, had protested, grown angry, and been confined to his cabin. He had left the train somewhere in the night. We all missed him – he had been part of the community.

But now the landscape was changing from Arizona high desert to California plains. Two hours past Yuma – the name resonant, the town scrappy – came a surreal sight: a body of blue water, glittering like a mirage. This was Salton Sea, a saline lake largely unknown outside California, and a presentiment of the vast ocean ahead. At Palm Springs, groves of palms and vines were ringed by the San Jacinto mountains, graceful, black and green, their upper slopes dusted with snow.

The train crew was growing excited: 'Los Angeles, one hour!' Time for a last lunch in the dining car, with sad goodbyes to the other passengers. And then we were running neck-and-neck with the rush hour traffic on the Pasadena freeway. After fifty-two hours, two thousand miles, five states and three time zones we pulled into Union station, Los Angeles, at three in the afternoon. An hour later we were on the beach.

It had been a marvellous trip: a glimpse of the United States that even many Americans don't get to see. Will the Sunset Limited survive? I'd like to think so. But the next day we had lunch with a young Californian woman who listened to our enthusiastic train stories with a decided lack of interest. 'You know,' she said airily, nudging the subject to a close (I was already beginning to dislike her), 'I don't think I've been on an American train in my life.'

CHAPTER 5
CROSSING CONTINENTS

28 FEBRUARY 1979

THE 9.30 FOR ADVENTURE LEAVES VICTORIA

Frank Robertson

The announcer at Victoria station intoned in his everyday voice: 'The train at platform one is leaving for Paris, Berlin, Warsaw, Moscow, Irkutsk, Ulan Bator, Peking, Nanking, Canton and Hong Kong.'

Such a statement had not been made before. The old rail route to China, seldom used since the beginning of the Second World War, traversed Manchuria, and did not touch Mongolia.

Climbing aboard the 9.30 train yesterday morning, Mr John Lennox-Cook, fifty-four, who runs a school of English in Cambridge, remarked about fears that the trip could turn out to be a nightmare: 'Waking up is the great thing about nightmares.' Some twenty-five years ago he cycled around the world.

He was one of eight men and ten women, all but one of them British, who left on the world's longest co-ordinated train journey – a distance of 9,333 miles spanning nine countries with overnight stops to ease the pain. It will take the hardy tourists forty-one days to reach Hong Kong, at an individual cost of £1,845, including the flight back to Heathrow from the British colony.

Mrs Ildi Moran, at thirty-three the youngest of the group, is Canadian with an English husband, Michael, a rock musician from Radlett, Herts. He could not find time for the trip. 'Our strictest instruction is that we must not photograph anything in Mongolia, even a tree,' she said. Having driven across the Gobi Desert, which covers much of the Russian-dominated People's Republic of Mongolia, I have told her that she would not be seeing many trees.

The oldest couple travelling are Dr John Shackleton Bailey, seventy-two, a retired general practitioner, and his wife Dorothy, seventy-three, of Moreton-in-Marsh, Glos. 'This is our last big trip. We've saved a bit, and as they say, you can't take it with you,' the doctor's wife said.

Before the war, the overland Trans-Siberian trip was popular with British civil servants and businessmen living in Hong Kong or China. It was cheap, and time was not a factor, since most got six months home leave every three years, with travel time added.

SLIGHTLY FOGGED

Liz Taylor

Move over, Phileas Fogg. Up until now you have been the prince of travellers, but I'm about to lay claim to the title.

I've just come back from the longest railway journey in the world, ten thousand miles from London to Hong Kong, and I reckon the rigours that Mr Fogg put up with pale into insignificance compared with mine.

Shortly before I was due to leave on my six-week trip it dawned on me that I might have inadvertently booked myself a one-way ticket to a war. The Chinese and the Vietnamese had unsportingly decided to start trouble and everyone wondered if the Russians were about to join in. If they did, well-informed people said, they would definitely attack China through Mongolia. And where was I going? Mongolia, of course.

But I had paid for my ticket, and being a parsimonious Scot, I packed my bag, made my will, bought a first-aid kit and went. There was never a shot fired in anger in the conflicts I encountered, but I bear the scars nonetheless.

When our eighteen-strong party left Victoria to the strains of a pipe-band, the press described us as 'intrepid' travellers. In my case, at least, 'idiotic' would have been a more suitable adjective.

Who else but an idiot would pay out good money – more than £1,800 in fact – to suffer the woes of weird foreign flu bugs, boredom, nausea, sleeplessness, homesickness, disillusion with one's fellow travellers, self-induced hangovers and extreme culture constipation?

Who else but an idiot would actually pay to see that nonpareil of nastiness, the lavatory of the train between Warsaw and Moscow? Or would scrimp and save to be hectored by the world's most unlovable person, our Russian guide Anatole? He looked slug-like and sufficiently sinister to be cast in any James Bond movie, and talked like a Dalek.

'You will eat dinner NOW ... '

'But it's only 11 a.m.'

'You will eat dinner NOW.'

And ... 'You will all walk together and NOT STRAGGLE.'

Other people's illnesses were certainly genuine – how else could they cough with such heart-rending conviction and look so ghastly on many occasions? – but I know that twice when I decided to spend the morning in bed it was more from a wish to get off the bandwagon than from genuine illness.

What kind of fool pays money to heave her suitcase in and out of trains while stolid Mongolian tribesmen who could be more gainfully employed stand around gazing hopelessly into space. I heard myself saying: 'This used to be a nation of porters – what's happened to them?'

I knew I sounded retrograde, undemocratic and imperialist, and only Kubla Khan and Marco Polo would have agreed with me. My fellow travellers thought it all very 'infra dig'. And fancy going into Ulan Bator's biggest – and best? – hotel and turning on the bath taps expecting water to gush forth? Who else would send for room service when nothing happened? There was never any water in the Ulan Bator hotel except between 3 a.m. and 4 a.m., and guess which fool left the taps open?

We got fed up with temples after three days. The path through China was littered with lovely, tranquil temples, pagoda roofs, tinkling bells, walled gardens and artistically planted trees. Yet eventually I came to groan 'ABT' when the day's itinerary was announced. ABT means 'another bloody temple'.

Perversely, we arrived home having enjoyed the whole experience. I'd even go back to China – ABTs and all. But I'm not so silly as to contemplate revisiting Russia or taking another trip on the Trans-Siberian Express. You have to be certifiable to do that sort of thing twice.

BACK ON BOARD

POST 9/11, **SOPHIE CAMPBELL** JOINS THE AMERICANS
REDISCOVERING THE VALUE OF THE RAILWAY

A bronze plaque in the garden of Union station, Los Angeles, commemorates its opening in 1939: 'Through the portals of this historic edifice,' it says, 'have passed the great and the near-great of the world.'

I love that 'near-great'. It is so uncharacteristically modest.

In those days, shortly before the United States turned its back on railroads in favour of jetliners and automobiles, Union station had fifty-two acres of land, more than a thousand employees and an average of fifty-six trains a day. It oozed casual southern Californian glamour.

Thanks to a recent restoration, which has smoothed away the wrinkles and made good the years of neglect, sentinel palms once again grace the pale, curvaceous exterior. The gardens burst with jacaranda and frangipani. Inside, fluted wooden armchairs with leather the colour of French mustard stand islanded in light.

Waiting for the Southwest Chief, which was to take us the first 2,265 miles to Chicago, we – the passengers – rather let the side down. Jeans for the young, slacks for the old, luggage wheeled and rarely matching. None of us would have dreamt of eating at Traxx, the chic station restaurant. Traxx diners are on expenses and are the sort of people who would go to Chicago by plane.

Or would have, until 9/11, as the Americans refer to the day the terrorists struck, when domestic air passengers were forced to seek alternatives. For the first few days, Amtrak, the company that runs American passenger trains, honoured air tickets. Its website and phone lines were jammed. Tragedy apart, it was presented with an unprecedented chance to welcome new passengers.

It was now a month later. I was standing beneath a towering silver double-decker Superliner, waiting to go coast to coast during one of the strangest periods in America's history. The last smokers sucked at their cigarettes. Larry, our attendant, rounded up any strays. We slid out, unfanfared, stopped to pick up mail, and then started in earnest. Ahead were Arizona, New Mexico, Colorado, Kansas, Iowa, the old Santa Fe Trail and, for some of the way, Route 66.

I found myself fantastically excited. It was dark and the butt-end of LA was easing past the window – the city river, unloved in its culvert, truck yards and factories, security lights probing puddles of shadow, the odd gabled fast-food joint, like a child's farm building plonked down in an adult world. Someone's radio was playing distant, sibilant jazz. It was like watching the opening frames of a film noir.

The reverie was shattered by a disembodied voice. 'Last call for dinner, ladies and gennelmen!' Last call? When was the first? 'First *and* last,' explained Larry. 'We don't have much time tonight.' He flattened himself against the wall as a scrum of senior citizens came cantering down the corridor and I was swept away to the dining car.

There was no messing with the dining car. If you missed the first sitting, you gave your name to be called later. My memories of the New Mexican mesas and the wind-pumps of Kansas have a backing track of 'Tracy, party of one. Randy, party of three. To the dining car, please.'

The train whistle, or rather moan, seeped into the landscape like the call of the last species on earth. It was the loneliest sound. Rita, opposite me at dinner, had been a railroad child. She couldn't wait for bed, to be lulled to sleep by the familiar creaks and clankings. She was going to Kansas City for a wedding, and was ignoring the terrorism, even though Kansas is stuffed full of nuclear bunkers.

Three of us chatted. The fourth declined to introduce himself, ordered two chicken dinners at once and shot the loquacious Rita glances of such murderous dislike that I was quite fascinated.

In my sleeper, Larry had put down the top bunk. During the day, two seats faced each other; at night, there were two bunks. The sleeper had a tall, thin wardrobe, a small table and a big window. Time stood still. I would sit, book unread, letters unwritten, as the United States sailed past the window. I felt what one railroad writer called 'a separation from ordinary life, which the motor car lacks'.

At night, when the little houses too near the tracks were lit up, we could see into their lives and they could see into ours. We eased over the southernmost dribble of the Sierra Nevada to Flagstaff and woke up to snow-dusted hills and scrubby plateaux veined with ravines. Pieces of machinery left to die in the fields were carefully ploughed around. Telegraph poles rose and fell, with rows of green glass conductors like tea lights. Outside Albuquerque, as we left the mountains, two teenagers in baggy jeans waited until the train had nearly passed before jabbing up the middle fingers of both hands.

The scale was immense. On one famous curving haul, up to the top of the Continental Divide (about 7,000ft), I could see both ends of the train. Four locomotives. Fuel and baggage cars. Coach accommodation. Observation car. Dining car. Us. And stretching out behind, another twenty mail and freight cars.

Amtrak trains are not tourist trains. Except on the high-speed Washington-Boston route, they share tracks, at a price, with the more lucrative freight trains (railroad companies were on the verge of dumping passengers altogether when Amtrak was incorporated in 1970). The stops are workmanlike – five minutes or so – and the food is controversial. I liked it, but then I had been at boarding school.

One night I ate with three thirty-somethings. In a country where vacations average two weeks, long-distance passengers tend to be retired, with a smattering of teachers and students. The events of 9/11 had caused this younger group to try rail travel for the first time. They were impressed.

Bobbi, a federal prosecutor from DC, was on business. 'For five years I've been putting up with flying, but not enjoying it. Then this happened and I was downright scared. So I thought I'd try the train – and I love it.' Matt and Melissa were on vacation and had upgraded to a sleeper. They had a job for me. 'Have you seen the Amish?' I had. Two couples had boarded at Albuquerque, the men in blue shirts and straw hats, the women in dark dresses and white bonnets.

'Well, they quack.' What? 'They've got some sort of cell phone, and it quacks. You're a journalist. You ask.'

Later, in the observation car, wilderness had long since given way to farmland. We left Kansas City – the old jumping-off point for the wagon trails west – and crossed the Missouri, moaning fit to bust. The mighty Mississippi was next. Yellow and orange leaves splashed the trees and wooden churches appeared. So did the Amish, who seated themselves next to me.

One of the women asked where I was from. 'England.' She looked blank. 'Europe,' I added. 'Is that near Mexico?' she said. I looked at her hard, wondering if this was an Amish joke, and asked about the quacking. For an awful moment her eyes widened in surprise – and then filled with laughter. 'It's a toy, a gift,' she said. 'It went off in his pocket and he was too embarrassed to explain.' I said we thought it was an Amish cell phone. They were still laughing, in Pennsylvania Dutch, when I left.

In the heyday of rail, you could go from California to New York in one sleeper; these days you have to switch trains. Reboarding after a few days in Chicago, this time a single-decker Viewliner, called the Lakeshore Limited, I could see the strain that Amtrak was under. The north-east is the busiest region in the country, and the train was packed. It was unseasonally hot and the station's Metropolitan Lounge – for sleeper passengers only – was bursting with querulous travellers.

At dinner, I sat next to Dale, an ex-beatnik (his description) on his way home to Hoboken, New Jersey, who said that he had always liked the train. 'How else am I gonna meet my fellow Americans?' he smiled. The conservative couple opposite smiled gamely. That night nobody mentioned terrorism or anthrax. It depended on your table – some people wanted to talk about it all the time.

Back in my sleeper, things had changed. It felt like a tiny airline cabin, with new upholstery, a video monitor, cunning storage, a better table. Gone was the easy old west. This felt like the brisk, businesslike east.

Outside my window the next day, the scenery, too, had pulled itself together. A billion trees marched in fall livery. The houses had narrowed their shoulders, observing the proprieties. Wide verandas gave way to small square porches and church spires poked skywards.

I could not find the lavatory. I looked up and down the corridor. I asked the man next door. 'It's in your room,' he said, and showed me. Under my suitcase was a loo that I had mistaken for a bedside table. Above it, an ingenious sink. No walls, no curtain. No way. I'm afraid I peed in coach.

A day later, as the distressed industrial towns of New York state appeared, with their red bricks and roads that wiggled instead of following grids, I realised I was homesick. The blue hills in the distance made me think of Dartmoor. The train moaned sympathetically; a last mating call before the fleshpots of New York. 'Sophie, party of one,' intoned the dining car, primly.

At lunch I got talking to two organ pipe-makers from Worcester, Massachusetts, about terrorism and war. It was my last Amtrak meal, roast chicken with garlic mash, and I stopped feeling homesick and felt nostalgic instead.

The train split at Albany and the pipe-makers went off to Boston. We turned down the Hudson River valley, en route to Manhattan and its ruptured skyline. The valley, gorgeous in its massed foliage, lifted its skirts every so often to reveal an immaculate lawn sweeping down to the river-bank, a trim boathouse, or the colonnades of a grand mansion.

'West Point Academy,' announced the driver, who had barely spoken before. There was a pause, as we stared at a collection of concrete buildings on a bluff. 'God bless America!' he added, and switched off the mike.

TRACKS DEVOTED TO THE RAILWAYS

THE SMITH QUARTET'S NEW RECORDING WILL BE LAUNCHED IN A TRAIN CARRIAGE.
IVAN HEWETT EXPLAINS

A first-class train lounge isn't an obvious choice of venue for launching a CD. But it seemed just right for the Smith Quartet's new CD of Steve Reich's 1988 classic *Different Trains*, released next Monday on the Signum label. It's a piece that mingles the sound of string quartets (live and pre-recorded) with the sound of trains, though not the prosaic sounds we hear these days: they're the richly evocative whistles and horns and harsh metallic scrapes of American and European trains from the 1930s and 1940s. Reich's piece is an evocation of a vanished era, but it's much more than that. It's also connected with his own disrupted childhood, and the sinister uses of trains during the war in eastern Europe.

But none of this was on his mind when he started. 'What got me going was technology. I'd made tape pieces out of little bits of speech in the 1960s, treating them almost as if they were musical phrases which could be repeated. Then in 1988 I first came across a digital sampler, which really excited me because it gave me a way of repeating phrases at intervals in a precisely timed way. I didn't know what to do with this idea, until I got a request from the American patroness Betty Freeman for a new string quartet to be performed by the Kronos Quartet. So I thought, why not create a piece where the quartet would pick up and develop the melodies hidden in verbal phrases.'

It's a wonderfully simple, even naive idea, which Reich has since combined with images in his 'video opera-documentaries' such as *Three Tales*. But progress to begin with was slow, because Reich didn't at first know what speech material to use. At first he thought of using archive recordings of the Hungarian composer Béla Bartók, one of Reich's heroes and composer of the greatest quartets of the 20th century, but he abandoned it ('I realised you don't want him sitting on your shoulder when you're writing a string quartet.')

Then one day the idea of trains and the reminiscences of people who travelled in them came 'like a light bulb' into his head. 'I'd spent a lot of time travelling on trains across the US between my parents, who had divided custody of me after they divorced. I used to make these trips with my nursemaid, Victoria, and as she was still alive I started by recording her. Then I discovered one or two very old retired stewards of the old Pullman trains, and they were happy to talk about the old days.'

But what about the European connection? Was that a later thought? 'No, it came straight away, because when I imagined myself travelling across the US I thought of those other little Jewish boys forced to travel by train at the same time, who never came back from their journey. I was told of a recorded archive of Holocaust survivors.'

The fleeting voices of those survivors can be heard in the second movement of Reich's piece: 'Lots of cattle wagons there – they shaved us – they tattooed a number on our arms.' It's a dark and compelling piece, but there's a hint of radiance at the end, where one survivor remembers: 'They loved to listen to the singing, the Germans.' When she stopped singing they said, 'More, more.'

But it's only a hint, as you'd expect from this most honest and least sentimental of composers. 'Yes, the oppressors are touched by music, but only for a minute. Afterwards they go back to their killing. If there's one thing we learned from the war, it's that artistic sensitivity doesn't make anybody into a finer human being.'

SILVER BULLET, GOLDEN DISTANCE

CROSSING CANADA ON THE CANADIAN GAVE **GAVIN BELL**
A WELCOME OPPORTUNITY TO WATCH THE WORLD GO BY,
WHILE DAYDREAMING ABOUT BOTH PAST AND FUTURE

For hours there had been no signs of human life. Pine forests and silent lakes glittering in the sun stretched to far horizons, a pristine wilderness without so much as a dirt track to signal that man had ventured here.

Then I saw a lone figure clothed in deerskin, moving stealthily from the cover of the woods. By the banks of a river an elk was grazing, unaware of the danger. Slowly the Iroquois hunter raised his bow, an arrow flashed in the sunlight, and the elk staggered and fell in the shallows. In the forest a grey wolf, cheated of its prey, loped away.

A mobile phone rang. The image faded, and reality returned with an attendant announcing that lunch was being served in the dining car. Daydreams come easy on long-distance trains. Especially when they traverse landscapes where bears and wolves outnumber people. The Canadian hurtles for three days and nights across the second-largest country in the world (after Russia), between Toronto and Vancouver. It is not only an instant geography lesson, it is a journey into history.

The vision of the Iroquois hunter came as we were crossing French River, part of an old fur trade route that linked Montreal and Lake Superior. The first Europeans to see it in the early 17th century were the French explorers Samuel de Champlain and Etienne Brule, and it has hardly changed since they turned up with their beaver hats and long rifles.

After reading of their exploits, it doesn't take much to imagine them hacking and paddling through the untamed land the Iroquois called Ontario, meaning 'shining waters'. It is an apt description since it contains a quarter of the world's fresh water, much of it visible from the train. In the long, long intervals between towns, the unfolding panorama of nature is interrupted only by an occasional log cabin, looking as if Brule has just left it on a hunting trip.

It is not only what you see that fires the imagination, of course; it is how you see it from the windows of a train. From the comfortable solitude of a private compartment, or from a companionable lounge, you gaze on a moving tapestry. Here an unseasonal flurry of snow deep in a pine forest, there a lonely farmhouse on endless plains where Cree and buffalo roamed, ahead the serrated peaks and glaciers of the Rockies glimmering like a mirage. Hours and miles fly by in quiet contemplation of the rugged beauty of nature. The traveller can muse on the hardships faced by pioneers, and then stroll to a lounge for tea.

Robert Louis Stevenson, who crossed America by train in 1879, was an early railways enthusiast: ' … while the body is borne forward in the flying chain of carriages, the thoughts alight, as the humour moves them, at unfrequented stations; they make haste up the popular alley that leads towards town; they are left behind with the signalman as, shading his eyes with his hand, he watches the long train sweep away into the golden distance.'

Six years after Stevenson's American adventure, the last spike in the 2,800-mile Canadian Pacific line was driven at Craigellachie, high in the mountains of British Columbia. When the first transcontinental passenger train steamed west a few months later, it was greeted along the way by bonfires, fireworks, artillery salutes and a solemn Crowfoot, chief of the Blackfoot tribe, in full regalia. First-class passengers viewed the celebrations from the comfort of a sleeping car equipped with a full-sized bathtub, and from an equally opulent dining car serving delicacies such as prairie hens and antelope steaks.

The bathtubs and the magnificent steam engines sporting cowcatchers – and in one case the jaunty figure of a Scottish highlander holding a Union Jack – are long gone. But refurbished 1950s rolling stock with glass-domed 'skyliner' cars now hauled by 3,000-horsepower diesels are a fitting complement to one of the world's great railways.

They seemed to fill the massive hall of Union station, Toronto, when I arrived for an early morning departure, struggling against a tide of commuters. The train was so long – with thirty carriages and three engines – that it had been split on to two platforms. At first sight, the Canadian rekindles the romance of travel. A caravan of shining silver and blue bullets, poised to hurtle across a continent, it stands imperiously apart from local trains like a prince among paupers.

Keith, a health worker from Stafford, had waited a long time to see it. 'When I was a boy we used to have Empire Day, and it always made me think of Canada and the train with viewing platforms on top that ran across it,' he said. 'It's an image that has stayed with me. I've always wanted to ride this train.' So now he was stepping aboard with his wife, Barbara, and for good measure they were continuing to Alaska on a cruise from Vancouver.

The train seemed to be filled with people visiting relatives, with a sprinkling of enthusiasts who would not consider travelling any other way. Florabelle and her husband from California were old campaigners who had done this run four times before. They had also taken trains from London to Hong Kong, but annoyingly had to skirt Afghanistan by bus owing to difficulties involving the Taliban. 'We're retired, so we're in no hurry to go anywhere,' she confided. 'The train takes as long as it takes. When you fly you don't see anything.'

We didn't see much of Toronto from the train, either, because the city was shrouded in mist. The soaring column of the CN Tower, the tallest free-standing structure in the world (1,815ft), was reduced to a decapitated pole by surreal gloom that swirled around skyscrapers and deadened sounds, so it seemed we were riding out of the city on a ghost train.

This gave us all time to walk up and down the corridors, exploring berths and lounges, and bumping into each other with apologies in half a dozen languages. I noted with some concern that my carriage was called Blair Manor, but was reassured that it had been named after a premier of New Brunswick rather than New Labour. My compartment in the 'Silver and Blue' class was perfect, a cosy cabin furnished with a couple of armchairs, two fold-down beds and washbasin and WC. On request I was given a folda-way table, which meant I could sit in comfort while reading, writing, doodling and watching the world go by.

There was a shower cubicle at the end of the corridor that nobody else seemed to use, and a couple of carriages away lay a dining car tastefully decorated in soft shades of plum and green. It became apparent that this was a serious train, with none of the fanciful clutter of reproduction belle époque coaches favoured by Agatha Christie characters. Instead the decor was minimalist steel and chrome, with details of art nouveau, simple and pleasing to the eye.

Elsewhere on the Canadian, about a quarter of a mile away, were carriages with reclining seats for backpackers and others on modest budgets. For us toffs at the back of the train there were observation lounges, a bar and an amusements carriage offering wine tasting and films. The overall impression was of a time capsule from the 1950s, awaiting news of the coronation of young Elizabeth.

In fact the train has carried royalty of a kind, in the form of Marilyn

Monroe. The thought that my compartment might have been occupied by a goddess of the silver screen is the stuff that dreams are made of.

So is the rich farmland north-west of Toronto that drew generations of immigrants from crowded Europe seeking new horizons and lives. Their successors live in a green and pleasant land of meadows and hedgerows, Dutch barns and grain silos, and quiet country roads. There are hamlets of clapboard houses with wooden porches and big lawns, and dirt roads winding into woods that you want to follow to see where they lead. From the train they look like a succession of toy towns, an illusion occasionally heightened by a house with a flag saying 'Home sweet home'.

Look away for an hour or two and the scene has changed. We are in a country of wild woods and fast-flowing rivers, and maps bearing the names of the first Europeans who saw them – McKee's Camp, Copelands Landing, Savant Lake. To watch endless wilderness speed by, and compare our snail-like progress on a map, is to understand the vastness of Canada. Ontario is almost as big as France, Germany and Italy combined, with a northern coast higher than the Alaskan panhandle and a southern boundary on the same latitude as Rome. People here live in a world of their own.

After nine hours we make our first stop at Capreol (population: 3,600), a quiet, nondescript town of timber-frame houses. There is time to stroll down Main Street, and catch up on the latest news. It seems not much is happening, judging by an overheard conversation: 'Pity you didn't go down to the river today: three geese hatched some goslings.'

I ask a woman in a grocery store what people do in Capreol. Not much, she says. Most of the bars have closed because of anti-smoking laws, but there are plans to open a mine nearby. 'Hopefully that'll bring people in. We need 'em,' she says. At the station, train attendants are calling: 'All aboard'. Our silver caravan resumes its journey, and soon Capreol is lost from view.

When we leave Ontario, we find there is nothing on the other side. It is called Saskatchewan. If we are visited by hostile aliens I hope they land in the monotonous, mercilessly flat prairies of the Canadian mid-west. After wandering around aimlessly for a while, they will no doubt lose interest and go somewhere else.

Out here folks say that if your dog runs away and keeps running you can see him three days later. My guidebook says tactfully that tourism is not a major industry in Saskatchewan but that many people pass through. Some even like it, and pick up local sayings such as: 'The Rocky Mountains are nice but they get in the way of the view.'

I prefer the Rockies. They appear in the far distance like an illustration in a fairy tale, a shimmering of snow-capped peaks above a dark belt of trees. We cross Sundance Creek, snake up through wooded foothills, and then we are in the realm of native gods, and great shaggy monsters of mountains glowering at us through dark clouds and swirling mists. The weather brings drama, changing the characters of the mountains: one moment benign in a shaft of sunlight and the next mysterious and menacing behind curtains of rain. Above us, like emblems of freedom, eagles fly.

At Jasper there is a brief halt and time to admire a grand old railway pioneer. Canadian National Steam Locomotive 6015, mountain type class U-1-A, stands in a railroad yard in as fine shape as the last time she hauled wagons through the Rockies half a century ago. Gleaming black with wheels as tall as a man, she boasts a cowcatcher, a huge light up front and an impressive brass bell on top of her boiler – a genuine iron horse in all her power and glory. No wonder Crowfoot was impressed.

The best views of the journey come last. Champagne is served in the 'skyliner' as we speed through Yellowhead Pass, along the shores of emerald lakes reflecting the loftiest peaks in the west. Rival railroad construction gangs once traded shots across these tranquil waters; now the only ripples are from a lone sailing boat moored improbably 5,000ft above sea level.

I missed hurtling through the gates of Hell into Deadman Valley, because I was asleep. The fearsome stretches of the Fraser River canyon passed by in the moonlight, and by the time I awoke the Fraser was a broad, peaceful estuary dotted with logs and tugboats.

In the distance rose the glass and concrete spires of Vancouver, a blessed city with its feet in the Pacific, its head in the Rockies and its backside on a bar stool. After almost three thousand miles of time travel, we had come back to the future.

But memories of great railways linger, real and imagined, and sometimes they are hard to tell apart. When you cross French River, keep your eyes peeled for the Iroquois hunter.

ALL ABOARD THE VODKA EXPRESS

SOPHIE CAMPBELL AND FRIENDS JOIN A BAND OF ECCENTRIC RUSSIANS ON AN EPIC JOURNEY FROM MOSCOW TO PEKING

Even on the coldest winter nights in north-east Moscow, the underpass below Young Communists' Square is lined with people. They stand there hour after hour, shoulder to shoulder, each selling a single item: a coat, a puppy, a pair of trainers.

Above them, at Yaroslavsky station, the Trans-Siberian trains pull in after their six-day journey from Peking or Vladivostok, disgorging traders laden with cheap Chinese clothes, shoes and electrical goods that seep into Moscow's private enterprise system via the corridors and underpasses of the Metro, or the flea market at Lenin Central Stadium.

As a handful of westerners about to begin the 5,500-mile ride across Siberia and Manchuria, we were obviously the only people boarding this train for fun. In the ticket hall, babushki sat guarding nylon bags and holdalls on flimsy trolleys. Men with bundles stood on the dark platform pooling clouds of breath and waiting for the train doors to open. Our Russian guide whispered a word for these traders: Torgashki – 'people who will do anything for money'.

This made it even more surprising that Train 20 was a picture of domestic bliss. A roller-towel ran the length of the narrow corridor, to protect the carpet. Fake flowers hung above a glass-framed train timetable. The berths (four to a second-class compartment) were of fat orange leatherette and the curtains were freshly laundered. Zena and Mikhail, our carriage attendants, wore smart black coats, thick boots and fur hats, and kept the train as cosy as an airing cupboard.

Adroit negotiating by Russian passengers ensured all the Anglichanki (actually two English, three New Zealanders and two Scots) were together. This was a blow, but the Russians next door didn't flinch when I produced *Getting By in Russian*, so I still anticipated conversation – there were 250 other passengers on the train. My companions, Stuart and Simon, worked for the tour operator Bridge the World, which arranged our trip.

In the morning, we woke to find that a slight sense of depression is a feature of your first day on the Trans-Siberian. It settled like a cloud as if, after all the excitement of departure, we had realised the magnitude of the journey ahead. We had crossed the Urals in the night and were trundling towards Ekaterinburg, where Tsar Nicholas and his family were shot in 1918. Nicholas had dug the first spadeful on the railway twenty-seven years earlier, opening Siberia to an empire hungry for minerals, furs and timber. Freed serfs and exiles poured over the Urals, settling in towns beside the track. Communism brought heavy industry in its wake.

For most of us, this involved some mental adjustment. Forget Dr Zhivago, sleigh bells and Julie Christie in a fur hat. Think factories, power plants and slag heaps.

The friend who told me there was a shower on the train was wrong. There were steel compartments at each end of the carriage with corner basins and lavatories opening straight onto the track. Windows were sealed for winter and smoking permitted only between carriages. Outside, the scenery was as flat as a blini and the rivers frozen caviar-black. Dean, a New Zealander on his way home after two years of travelling, woke up and looked around. 'Jeez,' he said, 'there's shet-all to do around here!'

In a sense he was right – there is nothing to do. But there is a seductive rhythm to life on wheels. Mornings began with Mikhail priming the coal boiler that heated the carriage and the samovar. Zena, wearing a spotted pinny, worked her way down the carriage with the vacuum cleaner. We sat in each other's compartments and played games, read or slept. Dima and Alexei from next door struggled to teach me Russian, talking about their lives and pointing out famous towns and rivers.

At every stop, Zena held up chubby fingers to indicate how many minutes we had. Stalls sold pirozhki (sausage rolls), sunflower seeds and cigarettes with names such as Hollywood and Apollo-Soyuz. Ice creams, bizarrely, sold like hot cakes. It was two-way traffic; the passengers did brisk trade in anoraks and leggings from Moscow.

The Russians never ate in the restaurant car, which was filled with mysterious boxes draped in bedspreads. Every so often one would fall off, revealing a crate of Crimean champagne or a water melon. Some of my best memories of the Trans-Siberian are of this twilight zone: frankfurters and fried chicken, slurred toasts, getting trapped behind a table by Vladimir the chef – who spent his life tricking unwary westerners into vodka-drinking competitions – and having to run for it, slamming doors behind me all the way down the train. Vladimir was a direct descendant of the yamschiki, the sled-drivers on the Great Post Road, which preceded the railway; when drunk, they would tip their fares into rivers.

Outside in Siberia, the temperature was dropping. Asian faces, framed in fur, began to appear on the platforms. Names went by: Omsk ... Novosibirsk ... Krasnoyarsk ... We saw real countryside for the first time: hills fringed with acres of silver birch and fir and wooden villages surrounded by tiny dachas. The train shrugged off snow crystals as it cornered. People fished in ice holes on the rivers. Inside, in the tropical heat, our precarious collection of friendships and courtesies rumbled towards some sort of climax.

As we passed through one time zone after another – seven, altogether – half the train stuck to Moscow time while the other half tried to adjust as it went along. I like to think this is why we all started drinking. I became blind drunk on vodka and pickled cabbage and spent the night with my head in the lavatory bowl, sobbing. Michael and Rory from down the corridor drank a litre and a half of Stolichnaya with Vladimir and had to be put to bed. We slept through Irkutsk, the Paris of Siberia ('You didn't mess much,' said Dean, 'it was all groimy and grotty like everywhere else'), and only just managed to sprint down to Lake Baikal and back before the train left.

At the border with China, officials stalked the train. Narrow-gauge wheels were fitted and Vladimir was shunted off and replaced with the long-awaited Chinese dining-car. Alexei, full of over-the-border bonhomie and good cheer, bought a bottle of Chinese vodka and began the toasts: 'SPARTAK MUSKVA! GLASGOW RANGERRRS! DEMOCRACY! FRIENDSHIP!' Then Stuart beat him at chess.

'Safie! He horse move two!' said Alexei, pale and indignant. It was a queen, said Stuart, not a horse. Alexei drew himself up, went next door and reappeared holding a full bottle of vodka. He peeled off the cap. 'You've got to be bloody joking!' said Stuart. 'I Russki,' said Alexei with deadly intent. 'You drink this [a toothmugful]. I drink this [the rest of the bottle].' I went to get Dima, who shrugged and said: 'He does it all the time.'

Rory arrived with more vodka, in a glass made from the bottom of a plastic bottle, to say that Dean was arguing with Michael. Down the corridor Stuart could be heard roaring: 'Checkmate in four bloody moves and the bastard cheats like a Russian!'

Simon had had enough. 'SLEEPSKI!' he said firmly, propelling Alexei out of the door. It opened immediately. 'Sorry,' said a woebegone figure, 'Sorry, sorry, sorry.' Simon shut the door. It opened again. 'Vodka I can drink mnogi [much],' said Alexei, 'so sorry,' and he lurched off, spilling a bottle of Peking beer into Michael's berth on his way to bed.

In the morning the Manchurian sun slid over our bedside table. *Getting By in Russian* and a half-eaten bowl of pot noodles lay in a pool of vodka. Empty bottles rolled around on a carpet that was now 45 per cent proof and flammable. A strand of cabbage stuck to the front of my notebook. Through the windows, grain silos, wheat fields and horses and carts floated by. This was China. We were nearly there.

Instantly the irritations of the night before evaporated at the thought of having to get off and leave Zena and Mikhail behind. Pride at completing a journey so big that you could almost feel the curve of the earth was mixed with sadness at saying goodbye to our new friends.

We gave Alexei – chirpy as a cricket – the dollars we had smuggled over the border, swapped fragments of Chinese and wished each other luck. Coats were unfolded. Bags were packed. The train pulled in after six days, five-and-a-half-thousand miles and two continents, just ten minutes late. Westerners to the last, we clutched maps marked with the Great Wall, the Forbidden City and Peking McDonald's. Everyone else was going shopping.

ACROSS THE PLANET BY RAIL

STARTING FROM WICK IN SCOTLAND, **PETER HUGHES** SET OFF FOR VLADIVOSTOK AND THE SEA OF JAPAN ON THE LONGEST CONTINUOUS RAIL JOURNEY IN THE WORLD. IT MEANT GOING THROUGH SEVEN COUNTRIES AND TEN TIME ZONES – BUT WAS HE ON THE RIGHT TRACK ... OR EVEN THE RIGHT TRAIN?

In a fractional way, it was my Captain Scott moment – the one when Scott realised that Amundsen had reached the South Pole first. 'The worst has happened, or nearly the worst,' Scott wrote in his diary. Without the frost-bite or the peril, I still had an inkling of what he felt.

My 'pole' was to make the longest continuous rail journey from Britain, from Wick in the north of Scotland to Vladivostok on the Russian shore of the Sea of Japan. Now, after more than three weeks of travelling and within hours of my goal, I was confronted by the equivalent of Amundsen's tent. I was on the wrong train.

I was having dinner on the Trans-Siberian Express. My companion was Dieter Hauss, a German rail buff. To describe him as an enthusiast is like saying Leonardo da Vinci was an odd-job man. I explained my project and how it had brought me from within whistling distance of John O'Groats to Khabarovsk, just north of the Chinese border, twenty hours from Vladivostok. Tomorrow it would be complete. 'But there is a journey longer,' he said. The train gave a lurch. Or was it the Uzbek kebabs of the farewell dinner doing a reverse-one-and-a-half-somersault-pike-with-half-twist in a synchronised dive with my ego?

Dieter, who was making his seventh Trans-Siberian journey, has an apartment in Frankfurt station and was travelling with two model steam locomotives he had commissioned from a maker in Moscow. Dieter, whose rail travel is planned up to 2006, would be right. He was already elaborating: 'Now you can go through Siberia to Mongolia and China to Vietnam all the way to Ho Chi Minh City.' What was it Scott also wrote? 'All the daydreams must go; it will be a wearisome return.'

But to begin at the beginning, ten time zones, six countries and eight thousand miles earlier, at Wick in the county of Caithness ...

THE 16.17 TO INVERNESS

When the Far North Line from Inverness was completed in 1874, there was a fleet of about a thousand fishing boats operating out of Wick. The town had three hundred coopers turning out barrels for salted herrings. By 1930 the industry was all but gone. The fleet was reduced to about thirty boats, pretty much the size it is now. 'Really, it's the tourists who keep the line open in summer these days,' a ScotRail man told me.

Like most people, I went to Wick only to leave it. Unlike anyone else, I immediately headed south again. Usually visitors continue another seventeen miles north to John O'Groats, drawn by the abstruse magnetism of extremities. Then they head south, perhaps for that other extremity, Land's End, 874 miles away in Cornwall.

The 16.17 to Inverness set off at a canter, its two-tone horn creaking like a gate in need of oil. In 18 days I should be in Vladivostok, 8,457 miles to the east. The low, green hills of the Ord of Caithness were daubed with sunlight.

Big pastures gave way to moorland, cattle to sheep. In this open-plan landscape each homestead can see about six neighbours. Habitation dwindled and disappeared and the country became wilder and marshier. Companies of Forestry Commission evergreens stood in disciplined squares. A herd of deer grazed by a small loch. The hills grew bigger. Little stations had grassy platforms.

The station at Dunrobin Castle seems to be disguised as a shooting lodge, half-timbered and up to its eaves in rhododendrons. It serves the castle, seat of the Dukes of Sutherland, the third of whom was a fervent railway supporter and encouraged the building of the line, not least perhaps because he owned the coalmine at Brora. He parked his private locomotive and carriage in his own siding at Dunrobin.

The first duke is commemorated, wearing a toga, by a monstrous statue built on the top of Ben Bhraggie, right on the skyline above the village of Golspie. Ten years ago there was a campaign to have it removed, not because it was an eyesore but because the duke was held to be one of the arch villains of the Highland Clearances. Reputedly the richest man in Britain, he was one of the landowners involved at the end of the 18th century in the ruthless depopulating of the north of Scotland in which thousands of crofters were thrown off the land.

At Ardgay we reached the Dornoch Firth. The train waded through bracken, its wheels tapping out the rhythm of impatient fingers on a side drum. We rattled through Fearn. I started. Fearn! This was where my mother spent her childhood summers, wistfully remembered for the rest of her life. I had always thought it was the name of her uncle's house, not a place. But here it was, Fearn, a tiny railway halt in Ross-shire. I tried to imagine my mother in her teens between the wars. She would have alighted on this platform, dressed like Jenny Agutter in the film *The Railway Children*, and been met by a pony and trap.

We didn't stop. Fearn flickered by as I was still struggling with my memory of the 'bright young things' disporting themselves in a family photograph album. Now the 21st century was back at the window. Six drilling platforms were squatting on their colonnaded legs in the Cromarty Firth awaiting maintenance at Invergordon.

Across a threshold of pebbledash bungalows and larch-lap fencing, tool sheds and washing lines, we arrived at Inverness, or Inbhir Nis, as the station signs have it. Because of 'a wee signalling problem' the train pulled into the station ten minutes late. Stage one was complete.

THE 07.55 INVERNESS TO LONDON

The Scots like their trains to have names. The 07.55 Inbhir Nis to King's Cross is the *Highland Chieftain*, which follows the route of the *Flying Scotsman*. It says so on the side of every carriage. 'Och it's a nice train, that,' a train driver in Wick had said. 'A bit springy, mind.'

Today it wears the navy and tangerine livery of G.N.E.R. and has amenities undreamt of in *Flying Scotsman* days — a customer service manager, for a start. His name was Craig. Coach D, he announced, was a 'quiet coach' where no mobiles, laptops or personal stereos were to be used. There were also smoking compartments. It was the no-smoking compartments you had to look for in the old days.

But it is not what happens inside the *Highland Chieftain* that matters so much as what goes on outside. For the first two-and-a-half hours it provides the best seat in the house for a performance of some of the most sublime scenery in the world. Long views down the banks of the Moray Firth, across fields green with young corn in early summer and yellow with oilseed rape, are followed by the Highlands. It's a massive landscape in which the train feels insignificant, beetling out of the view as if it is trying to avoid being noticed. Huge, bare, humpback hills are textured like tweed, patched by shadow and darned with heather. By Falkirk it's over.

A grand lady, in an expensive twin-set, and her deferential companion had boarded at Inverness. At Pitlochry, Derek and Norma sat with them. They were on their way home to Essex from holiday. Derek began a conversation about the Duke of Atholl, which he pronounced like a coral island. 'Atholl,' the lady in tweed corrected . 'You pronounce the "h".' And they all looked out of the window.

Edinburgh passed, and the border at Berwick. South of Newcastle you can see what happens when farming is neglected. It will not be bramble or coarse grasses that overrun the countryside but the houses and industrial estates already massing at the headlands. To the rapacious eye of a Prescott, nothing looks more enticing than once-immaculate acres of agriculture driven to dereliction.

The East Coast Line left the east coast, the grey sea and discoloured breakers, and made the long haul south through middle England – flat, ordered and, today, wet. We got to London five minutes ahead of our scheduled four o'clock arrival.

THE 07.43 EUROSTAR TO BRUSSELS

European railways are like a complex root system where the trains of one country penetrate, without interference, deep into the territory of another. Eurostar is a foreign train; it tends to speak English with an accent, reverting with relief to its native French as soon as it is east of the Channel. Euroland starts in London SE1. It would have puzzled the Duke of Wellington, but passports are checked by a French policeman at Waterloo; you can buy breakfast in euros, the trains have numbers, not names, and the coaches are in order to come from the Continent. Coach No 1 is at the front of the trains from France.

The 07.43 to Brussels (Train No. 9112) left on time, ambled through the back gardens of south London – Penge East and Bromley South – hit the high-speed section of the English track outside Maidstone ... and stopped.

The technical term was 'stalled'. There had been a signal failure. We edged forward as the signals permitted but did not have the momentum to cross the 'neutral' section of overhead cable where the UK power supply ends before French electricity takes over. Like Paula Radcliffe in Athens, we sat just outside the Channel Tunnel, head metaphorically in hands.

Except we sat there for fifty-seven minutes. That meant I would have sixteen minutes in Brussels to find my train to Cologne. The Eurostar made up time and in Brussels a 'fast exit' was opened to the platform from where the German expresses left. And there was no identity check. The glance the

French policeman had given to my passport in London would see me all the way to Poland. The only borders one is aware of crossing in Europe these days are between the territories of the different mobile phone servers, though even they don't welcome you to France or Germany, but to F Bouyg and D Interkom.

And in the end I reached the platform before the German Railways Inter City Express (ICE).

THE 12.16 ICE BRUSSELS TO COLOGNE

There it was, waiting in the wings, a droop-snooted phallus the colour of skimmed milk – newer and more spacious than Eurostar, with bigger windows.

It was like entering a corporate headquarters: all hissing glass doors, grey-striped carpet, chrome and charcoal faux-leather seats. The seat-back televisions were showing a film of men welding. I had the same seat number as on Eurostar – seventy-one; on a German train it is a sitzplatz.

The front of the ICE is just anorak Nirvana. Beyond a glass bulkhead, in full view of the carriage behind him, is the driver. You never see his face. He sits, silhouetted against his windscreen, the line ahead tapering to infinity at speeds of up to 150mph.

His is a spacious, hi-tech compartment, more control room than driving cab, still less footplate.

THE 15.48 ICE COLOGNE TO BERLIN

Cologne has the biggest cathedral in Germany and one of its most important railway stations. The two are built almost on top of each other. A lot more urgency was given to providing a place for trains than for faith. The cathedral, started in 1248, was not completed until 1880; the station opened twenty-one years earlier.

My train, older than the one from Brussels, skirted the Harz Mountains and aspirated through Hagen, Hamm and Hanover. It flirted with the countryside but, for all the occasional forest and farmland, never quite shook off habitation and industry. Small redbrick houses sheltered under roofs that came down to their ankles; pylons strode across the landscape and slow-turning wind generators stood around chewing the breeze.

I broke the journey with two nights in Berlin. I was brought up with a fragment of wartime loot from the city. My father was among the first British troops to reach Berlin in 1945. In the Reichstag he hacked off a corner of the stair carpet. It was pink with a maroon border and, woven for the jackboot, extremely hard wearing. At home it was consigned to the lavatory, in my father's opinion the only place for it. We were urged to spend our time there contemplating all those whose footsteps had preceded ours. 'Hitler's stair carpet' eventually disintegrated at the end of the 1980s.

Berlin is a city odd among capitals in its dearth of monuments. It has one to Frederick the Great, and the Siegessäule column celebrates Prussia's military triumphs. The Russians built a memorial to their Second World War dead, and crosses wired to a park railing near the Reichstag commemorate the East Berliners who died trying to get over the wall there. There's a preserved section of the wall, though it is apparently rotting; a dotted line of cobbles traces the course of the rest of it. Near the Brandenburg Gate – itself a monument, if with discomforting connotations of Nazi rallies – a huge memorial to the victims of the Holocaust is about to be inaugurated.

In one respect East Berlin is better off than west. Its ironwork may be rusting and its concrete cracked but, particularly in the side streets, it has parades of handsome 19th-century buildings, the like of which in the west were carried away on tides of subsidy and redevelopment. The basements of these old buildings are now occupied by cellar bars and nightclubs, their ground-floor windows full of fashion, food and electronics.

There is still plenty of the former GDR's architectural severity. Karl-Marx-Allee, the huge boulevard where the communists strutted their military stuff, contains a mixture of prefabricated apartment blocks and Stalinist offices adorned with heroic effigies of workers with clenched jaws and flat caps. No shortage of idols here.

For me Karl-Marx-Allee led to Lichtenberg station, the sleeper train to Moscow and the Trans-Siberian Express, the big daddy of all the world's great railway journeys.

PART 2: BERLIN TO NOVOSIBIRSK

The Moscow Express, Train No. 247 from Berlin, entered the Republic of Belarus, part of the old Soviet Union, to a sullen protocol that could have been choreographed by John Le Carré.

At midnight the immigration officials came banging on the doors. The train was still so you could hear them coming. For an hour and a half the carriages were infested with uniforms: Polish, Belarus and Russian passport officers in green and Belarus customs inspectors in blue and without hats. Three countries' border formalities completed in darkness in a single, surly bureaufest of inkpads and suspicion.

At 3 a.m., with a series of resounding jolts, we were shunted into a dimly lit shed for one of the most eccentric frontier procedures in the world. Because the gauge of Russian railways is 89mm wider than the standard gauge used in the rest of Europe, the wheels of the entire train have to be changed. Each carriage, passengers and all, is jacked up and adapted for the rails of Mother Russia. Nobody has ever invaded her by train.

I had wanted to take photographs, but by the time I reached the carriage door we were already 15ft off the ground with a gang of men working quickly and efficiently by floodlights to remove one set of bogies and roll in the next.

The Moscow Express is a Russian train, the first of three that would eventually take me across Siberia. It has smart scarlet and royal blue livery and small green compartments. Everything is green: walls, ceiling, towels and sheets. For one person it is cosy; for three – the compartment's capacity – it would be like travelling in a pea pod: the same colour, space and configuration because the passengers sit side by side.

The sun, which had set on Poland, rose on Belarus: identical landscape, farmland and forest; different houses and level of prosperity. In Poland they had new German combine harvesters and Massey-Ferguson tractors; in Belarus less of the land was cultivated and the implements were antiquated – a horse and cart in one case. Old women in headscarves hacked away at allotment strips beside the track.

It was twelve years since I had been in Moscow. Then I hated it. The man who had met me at the airport carried his windscreen wipers in his breast pocket. He had removed them from his Lada, knowing they would be stolen if he didn't. In those days everything was broken; nothing really worked. It was drab, repressed and threatening.

Now Moscow is a truly exotic city, glistening with affluence. From the moment I left my hotel room to find two black-suited bodyguards posted in the corridor outside my neighbour's door I knew it was different. Buildings have been restored, church towers dazzlingly regilded, streets repaved, façades repainted. The refurbished St Basil's wears its gaudy domes like party hats.

Communism is now a tourist curiosity, always a sign that something is finished, as with coalmines and battlefields. Lenin lookalikes, along with doppelgängers of Marx and Rasputin, hover round the edges of Red Square to have their photographs taken with giggling trippers from Smolensk. There is a humour in the streets and pickpockets working scams on unwary tourists. And there are old party members. I saw them muster outside the

Historical Museum and march behind the hammer and sickle to patriotic Soviet anthems crackling from a battered ghetto-blaster carried on the shoulder of an old woman.

In Moscow I joined the Trans-Siberian Express. Historically there was never a train of that name: there is now. This is a private train run by a British company that takes a leisurely twelve days to cover the 10,405km (6,503 miles) from Moscow to Vladivostok via St Petersburg.

The group I joined was 105-strong — British, Australians, South Africans and Americans who were all exceptionally well travelled. They had been dog-sledging in Greenland, around the world by cargo ship, to the Galapagos and to Antarctica. One, a New York psychologist, had descended to the *Titanic* by bathysphere: evidence, if it were needed, that crossing Siberia is a prize item in any collection of global journeys.

And there was Dieter, a German train buff who was making his seventh Siberian crossing. Last year he toured Brazil by rail; next year it would be South Africa. He was sixty-nine, had short cropped hair, heavy-framed spectacles and, whatever the temperature, wore a heavy brown leather jacket. His head protruded from the collar like a tortoise appearing from its shell. Several of the passengers on the Trans-Siberian Express were going on to Seoul or Tokyo; Dieter was returning to Moscow on the train.

My first-class (standard) cabin was just like the one on the Moscow Express, but older. Two bench seats were laid with bedding. More green sheets, this time under a dark tapestry cover with an abstract pattern. It looked vaguely ecclesiastical. Storage was on two plastic hangers and in bins beneath the beds. Fine for one; two people would have to organise their lives by roster. By the time we reached St Petersburg after one night's travel there were few not wondering how we were going to manage for the next twelve days or, more to the point, nights.

The Trans-Siberian railway was built at the end of the 19th century. It was a formidable project, providing a physical contact — a band of steel — connecting Moscow with the eastern reaches of this vast country. There is still a reverence for the railway. The stations are frequently the most distinguished buildings in town: the one in Irkutsk looks like the Winter Palace in St Petersburg. The railway authority usually occupies the second most imposing offices: the politicians have the most imposing. Under Communism, all fifteen Politburo members had their own private carriages, four of which are now used by the Trans-Siberian Express as four-berth VIP cars. They have their own showers, as do the new, purpose-built deluxe carriages, which have four double berths. The sixteen passengers in the first-class carriages have to stagger to a shower car wrapped in white bath-robes like patients in a clinic.

On the first morning out of St Petersburg I reached the showers at 7.20 a.m.. They were closed. 'Seven o'clock,' said the attendant. 'But it's 7.20 now,' I protested. 'Moscow time,' came the rejoinder. The entire Russian railway runs to Moscow time. Even in Vladivostok, where there is a difference of seven hours, the station clocks and timetables all give the time in the capital.

We had put our clocks forward two hours and crossed from Europe into Asia when we reached Yekaterinburg. It loiters on the eastern slope of the Urals on a stagnant river, khaki with pollution. Boris Yeltsin, born nearby, was once the regional governor. 'He didn't do much,' said the guide. 'But he liked women's volleyball.' Yekaterinburg has one of the best teams in Russia.

The city used to be Sverdlovsk, named after one of Lenin's hatchet-men. It was he who authorised the murder of the Russian royal family in the cellar of the merchant Ipatyev's house. No tourist train would stop here otherwise. The house was demolished long ago and a blancmange-shaped church is on the site. Apparently the local guides consider it a place of shame and would much prefer to conduct tours of a machine-tool factory. Like the old days.

Siberia begins just beyond the city at the trackside post showing 2,102km (1,313 miles) from Moscow. The boundary used to be marked by a square brick pillar beside the Old Post Road. It was there, a century before the labour camps of Stalin's Gulag, that thousands of exiles who disappeared into Siberia's terrible void bade bitter farewells to their families.

Seven time zones is one measurement of Siberia's size. There are others: if it were independent it would be the largest country on earth. It comprises one third of the northern hemisphere, a twelfth of the world's land mass, and it could contain all of western Europe and the United States, Alaska included, without their touching the sides. But the truest Siberian dimension is time: from the life sentence in a labour camp to the months the early exiles took to walk into their imprisonment and the eight days it takes to cross in a tourist train.

The train swam through an endless parting of fir trees pierced by flashes of birch – the taiga. Enter the forest here and you could walk in a straight line for a thousand miles before re-emerging. Occasionally there were clumps of small wooden houses with ridged tin roofs and unpainted picket fences. Then, after a night of bumping and clanking, the forest receded. We were on the Baraba Steppe, a huge grass plateau racing away to a rim of birch trees on the horizon. There were signs of human activity – mounds of hay, muddy tracks, an occasional line of pylons tramping over the view – but few humans.

Novosibirsk is the geographical centre of Russia, which is not the same as its heart. The city spills across the steppe in an eight-storey grey stain. It is characterised only by statistics: the biggest city in Siberia, the third biggest in Russia, possessed of the country's largest opera house. Novosibirsk was created by the railway, built at the point where the line crosses the Ob, one of the great rivers of Russia and – need you ask? – the fourth longest in the world. In the windy expanse of Lenin Square, where the figure of Vladimir Ilyich has sensibly been provided with a heavy greatcoat, I asked the guide how long these huge statues would continue to dominate Russian city centres. 'It doesn't dominate,' he replied testily. 'The traffic dominates.'

The gesticulating Lenin, still found in every town, looks like just one more lonely old man in the square. He's a bit confused, tends to wave his arms around and talks to himself. But he's harmless. The guides right across Russia have a reprise: 'It's our history and we can't do anything about it.' One put it more pithily: 'We don't notice the Soviet symbolism now. We haven't for years.'

I left the Trans-Siberian Express there to experience a public train. It was nearly my undoing. But 'Whispering Natasha' saved my bacon in Novosibirsk … only for Dieter, the railway buff, to cook my goose in Khabarovsk.

PART 3: NOVOSIBIRSK TO VLADIVOSTOK

The railway station at Novosibirsk has the vaulted halls, chandeliers and chocolate-coloured marble of a grandiose Victorian city hall. Like everything else in Novosibirsk, it is the biggest of its kind in Siberia, except for the apartments Khrushchev built in the 1960s. These are so small the locals call them 'louse holes'. However vast Siberia is, everything still comes down to the size of your living quarters, or in my case the compartment and corridors of a train.

Having arrived in Novosibirsk on the Trans-Siberian Express, I wanted to experience the Rossiya, the famous express that every other day makes the classic week-long journey between Moscow and Vladivostok. My plan was to rejoin the T-SE two days later in Irkutsk. Simple enough, because the faster Rossiya would arrive half an hour before the tourist train. First, though, I had to catch it. If I did not, there was not another for two days and I should not see the group again before Vladivostok.

The T-SE, with its guides and comfortable routines, pulled out of the station and I waved goodbye to my companions and most of my luggage. I was left with an overnight bag, a useless phrase book and a station official in an army-style forage cap and shapeless raincoat. She told me the Rossiya would probably leave from platform two. Platform numbers are announced only five minutes before the trains arrive, but as the indicator board for eastbound trains was broken that was academic. 'Vladivostok?' I asked a family on platform two. 'Nyet. Tri [three],' I was told. That exchange exhausted my conversational Russian.

The Rossiya was scheduled to stop for seventeen minutes. My reserved seat was in the last carriage. I presented my ticket. The attendant shook her head and passed it to a colleague, who fiddled with her torch. Time and adrenaline were now running fast. She too shook her head and said something in Russian. 'English,' I said uselessly. 'Sem,' she said, holding up seven fingers. So that was it. Wrong carriage.

I hastened back along the platform. I had ten minutes. At coach seven I showed my ticket again. More head-shaking. Then the conductor materialised. He was a small, elderly man with an expressionless, grey Slav face. Something was wrong with the ticket. He led me to an office where a woman at a desk was snacking from a heap of sunflower seeds. There were five minutes before the Rossiya was due to leave. The woman took a handful of pips and reached for a phone. Almost instantaneously the official in the forage cap arrived and, I assume, provided me with a bona fide.

'Dollari?' asked the conductor. 'You pay?' 'Yes, yes, dollars,' I said. 'I pay.' With one minute to go he motioned me out of the office and on to the train. I was shown to a first-class two-berth compartment in which was sprawled a thickset man in an Adidas tracksuit with all the sunshine in his soul of a party boss at a May Day parade. He clearly thought he had the place to himself. He crunched his face into a scowl and moved his things off the empty berth.

For thirty-one hours we travelled in our own little Cold War capsule, uncommunicating, unsmiling. After the banter on the T-SE it seemed very lonely. Only when I left the train at Irkutsk did I discover there had been a couple of English backpackers two compartments up the corridor.

Soon after the train started, the conductor beckoned me into his compartment. A jolly-looking woman in baby-blue flannel pyjamas was awaiting us. She was Natasha, a guide accompanying a group of German tourists, and the conductor had roused her from her bunk because she spoke English. Actually, she didn't so much speak as whisper. 'The director wants to know why you were so late,' she breathed.

'I wasn't late,' I breathed back.

'Your train was this afternoon.'

In this strange, susurrant tête-à-tête, my problem at Novosibirsk was unravelled. The travel agency in Moscow had issued the wrong tickets. They had confused Train No. 2 – the eastbound Rossiya (Train No. 1 runs west) – for No. 222, a local train that had left much earlier in the day. And the dollars? The kindly conductor charged me the difference between the two tickets – $40 – without a cent for himself.

There was a dining car on the Rossiya, though most passengers bought food from the station kiosks when the train stopped to change locomotives. The food was not the least of the reasons to be glad to be back on the T-SE. There we ate three ample meals a day, typically porridge for breakfast, perch for lunch, braised beef for dinner and, on a couple of occasions, caviar and blinis. Beer and wine were complimentary with meals, otherwise there was the bar. There Alexander Block, a shy, black-tied concert pianist, performed complete works by Scriabin and Prokofiev in what had to be the world's most cultural cocktail hour. Sometimes he stooped to Tchaikovsky, once or twice to Gershwin, but mostly it was Glinka and Rimsky-Korsakov.

On the days when we did not leave the train there were talks. Alexander Block gave one on Russian music; the chef gave one on Russian food. Coached by the staff, some of the passengers put on a play in Russian. There were also reminiscences from the guides of the Soviet era. Marina Linke, the tour director, told the most extraordinary story.

She was born in 1967 in Rostov-on-Don in the Caucasus. Her father's family was German; her grandfather served in the German army in the Second World War. In 1942 he was captured by the Russians. When the war ended the family village came under Russian control as part of Poland; Germans were given twenty-four hours to leave. All did, except Marina's grandmother and her two boys, Marina's father and uncle. While the rest of the village headed west and emigrated to Canada, Marina's family went east. Her grandmother asked to be reunited with her husband in his Russian prison camp. The Soviets duly imprisoned her – in a different camp.

Marina's grandmother and the boys spent seventeen years in prison. Her father was thirty-two on their release. Homeless and stateless, Marina's grandmother renewed her search for her husband. After three more years she found him. He had remarried and had a child.

Marina's story was one of thousands of similar stories of separation and imprisonment that hang like silence in the Siberian air.

Irkutsk was a frontier town. It had a garrison and a goldrush and labour camps going back to the tsars. Once it was known as the Paris of Siberia. It still has several folksy wooden houses with delicate fretwork around their eaves and decorative window frames. Much grander is the blue and white timber mansion built by Maria Volkonskaya. Her husband, Prince Volkonsky, was banished by Tsar Nicholas I for his part in the failed Decembrist coup of 1825. His wife, like Marina's grandmother, voluntarily followed him into exile. In Irkutsk she created a cell of St Petersburg society. The T-SE people arranged a candlelit concert in the drawing room of the house, recreating one of Maria's soirées. It was introduced by a small bald tenor in a dinner jacket who was exactly the shape of a Russian doll.

The Trans-Siberian Railway was constructed simultaneously from east and west. The lines met at Irkutsk in 1900. It was another four years before trains could steam round Lake Baikal. Until then, passengers made the crossing by ferry. The T-SE makes a detour, tiptoeing up the south-west shore beside the satin-surfaced water on a little-used spur line.

It is a weird place. The lake is one of the biggest in the world, easily the oldest and the deepest – it is more than a mile to the bottom. It holds a fifth of the fresh water on the planet, enough, someone calculated, to meet the globe's demands for forty years. The water is highly oxygenated and well over half the species that inhabit it are unique. Among them are freshwater seals and a type of crab that devours everything organic, which accounts for the lake's vodka clarity. Who knows? The crabs may even have eaten the locomotive that fell into Lake Baikal during the 1904-05 Russo-Japanese War when tracks were laid across the ice.

One night further east is Ulan Ude, close to the Mongolian border and capital of the Buryat Republic, home to the largest of Siberia's ethnic groups. This is a land so remote it makes New Zealand seem like a metropolis. Within it are two atolls of religion, one Buddhist, one Christian, both survivors of years of ruthless intolerance. The Datsan monastery at Ivolginsk is the only one left of scores that were once dotted across the steppe. Built in 1946, its lemon pagodas rise, with curling eaves, from an immense cow pasture. For those who associate Buddhism with the tropics there are incongruities. Monks in magenta robes scurry from Russian cottages; prayer flags flutter from fir trees and grinning statues of Siberian tigers guard the temple. Inside, the scarlet silks and gilded serpents are scented by smouldering juniper wood and illuminated by butter candles.

That afternoon came the Christians. A choir of Old Believers, bundled into the high necks and long sleeves of their richly coloured traditional costume, sang hymns for us in sinewed harmony. We had been taken by bus to the village of Tarbagatay, where the ancestors of these Christian dissenters fetched up in the 18th century. Expelled by Catherine the Great, they trekked the 3,500 miles from Moscow.

Their apostasy was to ignore a new Orthodox liturgy. Nearly two hundred years later, under Stalin, their persecution began all over again. Churches were destroyed and their worship driven underground. Older villagers remember only ever praying in the dark. Today the Old Believers are among some twenty groups, and the only one from Russia listed by Unesco under the category 'Living Human Treasures'.

On the penultimate morning in the train I went for my shower. Outside there was permafrost – Siberian winter temperatures fall below –60°C – but the shower was hot. I soaped and lathered my hair and then turned on the tap again to rinse. Nothing. Only by squatting in the corner of the cabinet could I coax the system to deliver a few drips of icy water. On day two that would have been morale-testing; on day eleven it made a good story at breakfast.

Jan, one of the Americans, did not share my forbearance. 'Five thousand dollars is an awful lot to pay to be uncomfortable,' she said. 'Why does the train lurch? I haven't shaved my legs for ten days in case I end up sprawled on the cabin floor.' Most of my fellow passengers, though, thought they had got more than their money's worth, not least from the camaraderie.

The interminable forest had again withdrawn to the horizon. On either side grassland rolled away to infinity. That night, near Khabarovsk, I had dinner with Dieter Hauss, the German rail enthusiast. I told him of my wheeze in starting my trip from Wick to make the longest continuous rail journey from Britain. 'But there is a journey longer!' he exclaimed. It had taken more than three weeks to get this far. I was a day away from my goal, Vladivostok, and now Dieter was telling me I could have made a much longer journey if I had gone to Ho Chi Minh City. Too bad. At this stage no train was wrong, least of all one that had shown me Moscow, St Petersburg and Siberia and still had Vladivostok up its sleeve.

We had travelled to Russia's Far East region, within a few hundred miles of Japan, closer still to North Korea and China, yet we arrived in a totally European city, more western by far than Moscow. It was as if all those miles and banging nights had been an illusion. Vladivostok city centre, packed with elegant turn-of-the-century buildings, is regularly used as a European backdrop by oriental film-makers. The previous week, for a Chinese movie, it had been 1940s Hamburg.

There was a zest about the place not shared by the Siberian cities. Pop music jangled from open windows; there were ice-cream sellers on the pavements, outdoor cafés and trees shading pedestrian streets. But tour guides march to an incessant drum. They neither wander nor sit. And in Vladivostok, which until 1990 was closed to foreigners, they seemed unsure about what exactly they should be showing.

At the city's main museum we did two floors of indigenous people and stuffed fauna but not the third, which is devoted to the Communist years. 'Let's go down,' said the guide. 'The Soviet period is not so interesting.' We saw the Pacific Fleet from a distance and the memorial to the thousands of its members who lost their lives in the Second World War. We filed through a submarine – another museum – and drove past Yul Brynner's birthplace. His family business was the Far Eastern Shipping Company on Aleutskaya Street.

And then it was over. At the airport a policeman looked suspiciously at our one-way tickets for the nine-hour flight back to Moscow. 'How did you come here?' he asked. 'By train,' said someone.

'By luck more than judgement,' I thought. He shrugged and let us through.

CHAPTER 6
CLOSE TO HOME

---

12 DECEMBER 1960

DELIGHTS OF RAIL TRAVEL,
TIME FOR REFLECTION

Sir — Your correspondent who complains of his expensive fourteen-hour journey from London to Glasgow has, with all respect, missed the whole point of rail travel.

The purpose of railways is not to convey people as quickly as possible from A to B, but rather to recall modern man from his headlong rush to nowhere by providing him with a time opportunity to consider whether his journey from cradle to shroud is worthwhile. As Mr T.S. Eliot has observed:

'You are not the same people who left that station

Or who will arrive at any terminus.'

The railways are one of the few remaining English institutions that provide such an opportunity for reflection — and who would begrudge an extra pound for such an invaluable public service?

Yours faithfully,

Kenneth M. Boyd, Sheffield

ALL THE WAY

CHRISTOPHER MIDDLETON TRAVELS THE LENGTH OF
BRITAIN ON THE CORNISHMAN, A TRAIN THAT 'COMBINES
MUNDANE PRACTICALITY WITH A LITTLE MAGIC'

Daybreak in Dundee, and as the dawn air fills with the smoke of departing diesel train, a lone stationmaster gives a solemn farewell wave. It's 6.40 a.m. on a wet Scottish morning, and the start of the United Kingdom's most epic daytime rail journey.

Forget the Orient Express, forget the Trans-Siberian. Every weekday a train departs from Scotland's third city and follows a route that is the equivalent of these more illustrious journeys – at least in terms of sheer human drama and diversity of scenery. Welcome aboard the Cornishman, a service that starts at Dundee, ends 704 miles later in Penzance, stops at 33 different stations and (in theory) takes exactly 12 hours and 12 minutes to do so.

In a world of trimmed-down timetables and cut-to-the-bone cost-effectiveness, it does seem strangely anomalous that a train exists that caters for that fairly limited number of people who want to travel from the east of Scotland to a small seaside resort in Cornwall. There again, that is to underestimate the pulling power of the Cornishman, a train that somehow combines mundane practicality with a little bit of magic.

No more than two minutes into the journey, the train trundles onto the River Tay rail bridge – whereupon it seems to take off into the sky. All right, so maybe this is just an optical illusion brought about by the grey mists coming up from the river merging with the grey clouds coming down from the sky; but as the opening act of a twelve-hour drama, it's a pretty attention-grabbing special effect.

Sadly, there are just twenty-six souls on board to witness this phenomenon, and most of these are cross-looking young men with fists punched into shiny, black bomber jackets. For me, this is a romantic trans-Britain rail adventure; for them it's the morning commute into Edinburgh. Over the course of the next twenty-five minutes, we stop at no fewer than five stations. Crowds of schoolchildren pile on carrying hockey sticks and making rude words out of dinosaur names. 'You pratosaur, Colin,' 'You're a totalwasteosaurus, Kenny.' Jostling with them are scores of office workers from Standard Life and the Scottish Office. One young woman goes up and down the train collecting colleagues' signatures on a get-well card – 'It's for Marjorie in Systems,' she explains. 'She's a wee bit poorly at present.'

Two stops before Edinburgh and it's standing room only. 'You wonder if anyone ever takes this thing all the way to Penzance,' says one cramped commuter to his friend. 'They'd have to be mad,' comes the reply. Somewhat more tactfully phrased confirmation of this comes from Henry Gibson, a Royal Navy officer turned train manager. 'We don't get many Dundees-to-Penzances. But I've got a couple of Berwicks-to-Truros getting on later.'

First, though, it's time for a temporary closure of the buffet bar – 'for stocktaking and change of staff'. This, it emerges, is not because the crowd from the Scottish Office have drunk the train dry in the brief hour it's been running - but because it's time for the original buffet steward to go off duty. 'The lad will have brought the train out empty from Edinburgh to Dundee at 4.30 this morning,' confides his replacement, Jim Bastick. 'He's prepped [stocked up] the buffet, brought it here, and now he's got another train to prep. I'm only on 'til Derby; after me, there'll be two more buffet stewards.'

As it turns out, the various staff changeovers are altogether more notice-able milestones than the stations themselves. Each new arrival brings his own individual style on board; whereas Henry has been all granite-jawed dependability, his younger successor, Steve Payne, brings an air of game-show host to the whole thing. 'Are you sure this is really yours?' he asks one elderly lady, scrutinising her ticket in a twinkle-eyed way. 'I'm afraid you don't look nearly old enough for a senior citizen's railcard.'

Walking up and down the train with Steve is a bit like being with a Butlin's Redcoat, an impression heightened by his crimson Virgin uniform. His train manager's cubby hole has the feel not so much of a guard's van as of a backstage dressing room. 'It's a nice train, this one,' he says, in the same way a comedian might talk about a matinee audience. 'Lots of pensioners, lots of students, not too many businessmen fussed about time. I used to work the East Coast Main Line with G.N.E.R. and, I can tell you, some of those execu-tives can get very aggressive if there are delays. On the Dundee-Penzance, though, you get a more laid-back sort of crowd. You'd be surprised how many little old Scottish grannies have relatives in the south-west.'

A stroll through the carriages bears out what he says. A party of four from Dundee are on their way to a funeral in Weymouth, there's a grandmother and her granddaughter travelling to a wedding in Liskeard, and a retired father is going from Birmingham to St Austell to see the son with whom he is shortly to live. 'Hope it won't be as dramatic as last time,' he says. 'No sooner had I got there than my pacemaker packed up.'

Even Jim, the buffet steward, has his story to tell, having moved on to sandwich duty after being diagnosed with diabetes. 'Twenty-one years on the railways, but when you have to start giving yourself insulin injections you can't be a guard any more – public safety at stake,' he says. 'That said, though, there's quite a bit of skill involved in this job – especially now we've started offering hot drinks to first-class passengers at their seats. You soon get to know the stretches of track where you don't want to be pouring out coffee; there's this bit just outside Berwick that's really bumpy, plus a couple of steep inclines – one into Lockerbie, the other between Penrith and Oxenholme. Can be very nasty if you're caught unawares.'

As the miles mount up, and the train turns right at York and heads down towards Sheffield and Birmingham, so it emerges that Jim is a real veteran of the Dundee-to-Penzance line. 'For years, I used to do the journey from start to finish, and spend the night at the Queen's Hotel in Penzance. Made a lot of friends there, in my time. Some passengers used to make the day go a bit faster with the odd drink or two. I once sold £50 worth of John Smith's bitter by 9 a.m. And there's many a sweet, little old lady who would come up and order a double vodka before eight in the morning.'

No hardened drinkers on the train today, though, apart from a lady called Pat, in the smoking carriage; as well as grumbling about the forth-coming cigarette ban on Virgin trains, she has plenty to say about the on-board beverages. 'Always bring my own cup,' she declares, brandishing a black china coffee mug. 'Can't stand the taste of plastic cups.'

But even she can't complain about the view after Exeter, when the same windows that have offered rain-swept Leeds and Birmingham New Street suddenly fill with glorious coastal seascapes, in which the waves are practi-cally breaking on the rails. All of a sudden, the trees turn from suburban elms to tropical palms, and the walls from urban concrete to biscuity sand-stone cliffs.

Ten hours previously, the train was alive with Lowland brogue, but now there's not a Scottish accent to be heard, and even the Yorkshire and Lancashire voices are giving way to West Country burrs. At Truro, a group of cheeky local teenagers is thrown out of first class by Alan, the fourth and final train manager of the day. Their getting-off at Redruth coincides with the disembarking of nearly all the remaining passengers. At peak occupation point, somewhere around Bristol, the train was carrying 250 people, but for the final run-in to Penzance, we're back down to 37. It's as if the train has lost its whole motivation, and the engine seems to roll the last few seaside miles in listless fashion.

Within ninety seconds of pulling up at the grimy old hangar that is Penzance station, the train is empty. Only clusters of old banana skins and hollow sandwich packaging serve as reminders of passengers who have been and gone. Over the course of the journey, most seats have been occupied at least four or five times. Mine is the only one to have had someone stay with it the whole way.

The train's day is not over, however. Having travelled 704 miles in 732 minutes, and arrived precisely on schedule at 6.52 p.m., the Dundee-to-Penzance must now transform itself from long-distance stallion into short-haul workhorse, and become the 7.09 Penzance-to-Plymouth.

As the dark sea mists form overhead, locomotive No. 43160 once more takes a deep breath, expels the diesel smoke from its spout and heads off on the last journey of its long day. I stand at the end of the platform and watch it pulling out, like an old friend leaving home for good. There's no station-master watching it go, though. This time, it's just me who's doing the waving.

DEPARTURE OF THE QUEEN FOR SCOTLAND

Her Majesty the Queen left Windsor Castle for Balmoral yesterday evening, shortly before 7 p.m., accompanied by their Royal Highnesses Princess Louise and Beatrice, and Prince Leopold, and attended by General Grey, Lord Charles Fitzroy, Dr Hoffmeister, Mr Sahl, Mr Duckworth and others. The royal party was driven to the Great Western Railway station at Windsor, and was received by the officers of the court and the railway company.

At seven, the special train started on its long way… The carriages for the entire route were provided by the [London & North-Western Railway], and they are as luxurious as can be imagined, being fitted with every requisite for night travelling. They have been furnished by Messrs John Maple and Co., the cabinet makers and upholsterers, of Tottenham Court Road, and their completeness of elegant comfort leaves nothing to be desired.

The royal train consisted of twelve carriages, a truck for Her Majesty's fourgon, and a break at each end. The first three carriages contained the pages, servants, dressers, and ladies' maids. A double saloon carriage which came next was intended for the Prince and Princess Christian, but their Royal Highnesses were detained at Frogmore by the sudden indisposition of the Princess. The next saloon was occupied by Princess Beatrice, her governess and maid; and a similar carriage was provided for the personal attendants of the Queen. The saloon appointed for Her Majesty and Princess Louise was in the middle of the train, and was connected to the preceding carriage by an expanding passage, permitting ready communication.

The day saloon is furnished with blue moiré antique and inlaid satin wood; and the sleeping chamber has two beds and gilt chairs covered with white moiré antique, the walls being hung with padded Turkey chintz. The ceilings are also padded and covered with white silk…

Very strict injunctions were laid down by the railway authorities yesterday for the prevention of cheering or other demonstrations, the object being that Her Majesty should be perfectly undisturbed.

MORE B&Q THAN ORIENT EXPRESS

Caroline Davies

For years Buckingham Palace officials have insisted that the Royal Train is not the 'palace on wheels' we all imagine. Yesterday they proved it, allowing selected journalists to snoop round its sleeping, dining and working quarters.

Only the Queen and Prince Philip's 'hers 'n' his' private saloons were out of bounds. But if, as we have been assured, they resemble the rest of it, the Royal Train is more B&Q and Homebase than Orient Express.

'It's not very glitzy. It's not lavish,' said Group Captain Tim Hewlett, who is in charge of royal travel. 'There are no chandeliers or carved oak panels. It's comfy, but there are no gold taps.'

Sir Michael Peat, the keeper of the privy purse, describes it as 'Formica and aluminium, like first class in the 1960s and 1970s'. Which is exactly what it is, the royal saloons having been presented to the Queen as a Silver Jubilee gift by British Rail in 1977.

The Prince of Wales's lounge – a cacophony of blue and white swirls on the sofa and chair – is decorated with watercolours from his private collection. In fact, the only personal touches evident on the train are the paintings, etchings and prints from the royal collection that decorate the corridors and executive bedrooms. One exception is Prince Philip's 'senior citizen railcard', a mock-up dated June 1987 and framed for display.

In the compact office from which the Queen's private secretary works, the red boxes containing official documents sit atop a Formica desk, next to a fax machine and a copy of *Who's Who*.

The Queen's senior staff have 10ft by 6ft single-bed cabins with small en-suite bathrooms, plastic see-through shower curtains, wood-effect laminate walls and pink Pears soaps. And, yes, the taps are chrome. Junior staff are confined to tiny cabins, some just big enough for a short single bed or bunk beds and a sink.

The staff dining room resembles any first-class dining car, apart from the bullet hole in one of the tables caused when a detective, stretching in the chair, accidentally discharged his handgun, waking the Queen at 5.30 a.m. in a Gwent siding.

During the three-month Golden Jubilee tour, two Class 47 locomotives – the Prince William and the Prince Henry, thirty-seven years old but renamed in 1995 – will pull the nine-carriage train. Between eight and nine drivers will be at the controls during each trip, chosen for their experience and expert parking – to align Her Majesty's carriage within six inches of the red carpet or waiting dignitaries.

The latest it has ever been is thirty-five minutes, owing to flooding in Scotland. It has never crashed, although there was one suicide, when someone leapt in front of it at Chester while Prince Philip was on board.

The Queen leases the train. It is owned by Railtrack and operated by the English, Welsh & Scottish Railway. Others can lease it but the only one to do so recently was Cherie Blair, who ferried Hillary Clinton and other leading ladies from Birmingham to Chequers during the G8 Summit in 1998.

At an average £35,000 per journey, the train is the costliest form of royal transport. But Sir Michael Peat has argued before MPs that it is 'an invaluable asset' during the Golden Jubilee tour. With the axe hanging over it, its future will be decided in the autumn.

TRAINS OF THOUGHT

TWENTY-ONE YEARS AGO, BRITISH RAIL INVENTED THE
CONCEPT OF INTERCITY. WAS THIS THE END OF THE LINE
FOR RAIL BUFFS? **MICHAEL PALIN** THINKS NOT

There is InterCity and inter-city, and the two are not necessarily the same, as I discovered when I travelled recently on the route between Glasgow, Sheffield and London, which used to be linked by the Thames-Clyde Express. When I was a train-spotter, the Thames-Clyde seemed the epitome of inter-city travel, bringing to the humble environs of Sheffield Midland an intoxicating whiff of places far away: Carlisle, Skipton, Dumfries and Kilmarnock. It was never a very fast train. Its heyday, if you can call it that, was just before the Second World War, when it wound its way down from Glasgow to London in eight-and-a-half hours. By the early 1960s it had slowed down by an hour and ten minutes, and it was given the kiss of death pretty soon after inter-city became InterCity in 1966.

One of the most successful and durable brand names of recent times, InterCity stands now for a hard-nosed commercial enterprise. It's an independent sector within the overall railway business, with its own budget, investment plans, operating targets and 125mph trains. But will it still get me from Glasgow to London via Carlisle, Sheffield and Leeds in 1987? The answer is no.

I enjoy railway timetables and, as I plan my homage to my favourite express, a sort of Thames-Clyde revisited, I find myself cross-referencing with a vengeance. Indeed, there are still trains connecting Glasgow and Carlisle with Leeds and Sheffield and London, but there is no longer one of them. The minimum needed today is four.

The Thames-Clyde used to have a distinctly hagiological flavour, bringing together, as it did, St Enoch and St Pancras; but St Enoch has since been re-stationed and London-bound services from Glasgow now leave from Central station. I am pleasantly surprised, almost shocked, by what I see and hear as I step out of the cab at Glasgow Central at 8.30 on a middling morning in February. White floor tiles stretch across the concourse, almost dazzling me. The theme from *Exodus* fills the station and resounds off the huge electronic arrivals and departures board, packed with information about Crossmyloof and Pollokshaws East, but still with room enough for 'Welcome to Glasgow' in three languages. As the music hurls itself into repeated inspirational surges I half expect to see St Enoch himself descend and bless the rush hour. I note, with pleasure, that the 9.10 a.m. InterCity departure for Carlisle and London is still called the *Royal Scot*.

InterCity in the 1970s went through a grey period which reflected the pervasive influence of functionalism. Lately, I'm happy to say, they have discovered that anonymity may keep costs down but doesn't bring revenue up, hence renewed naming of trains and also the remarkable turnaround in the fortunes of the distinctive Pullman services – all set to disappear only seven years ago, now revived on five routes and planned for Sheffield and Birmingham later this year.

The reawakening of the long dormant search for the happy passenger is responsible too, I presume, for all the tie shops, pancake parlours and decorative plants which seem to have replaced porters on so many stations. Today I am even offered tea or coffee before the train has pulled out.

The *Royal Scot* travels on an electrified route all the way to London and the journey time is five hours. It might have been a lot quicker but for one of the great failures of the InterCity years – the development of the advanced passenger train.

This train, chiefly renowned for its tilting mechanism, left egg on a lot of faces before it was finally scrapped in the early 1980s. I have a certain sympathy for the engineers who worked on it. If they had been given as much research and development money as was spent on one tip of Concorde's wing, they might have come up with a design success comparable to Concorde. And of course it would have been of far more use to far more people.

The issue of tilting, dormant as a discussion topic since the Middle Ages, suddenly seems all too relevant as our train weaves and snakes its way through the Tweedsmuir hills, setting up an arhythmic chorus of sliding coffee cups punctuated by the odd 'Oh, blast!', as someone gets a lapful. The coffee is of the filter cup variety and very nice too, though served with an almost Hitchcockian sense of tension, with cups issued at Glasgow, filters placed on them at Motherwell, and hot water appearing just after Carstairs.

We arrive at Carlisle five minutes early. Here I have to leave the InterCity network, which no longer sees it as any of its business to connect the cities of Carlisle and Leeds, and change to a four-coach train comprising old, damaged, draughty stock with no provision for refreshment of any kind on a journey of two hours and forty minutes. Believe it or not, British Rail wanted at one time to supply even less than this. No lines at all. But such was local and national feeling that, with the help of Cumbria Council and others, British Rail agreed to give a temporary reprieve to what is now one of the best-known stretches of railway in the whole country: the Settle and Carlisle line.

In my view, the Settle and Carlisle line should be declared a national monument. It is longer than Nelson's Column, and much more useful. Between the trackside rubbish tips of Carlisle and Leeds lies a visual feast that would probably have given Wordsworth terminal euphoria.

Proceeding quite briskly among the gentle irregular hills of the Eden Valley, the Thames-Clyde spectacular stops at stout and satisfying market towns like Appleby, then suddenly takes on the Pennines, sometimes slowing to little more than cycling pace as it heaves us up and over the mountains to Settle. A series of tunnels adds excitement and unpredictability. We enter one in bright sunshine and emerge half a mile later in swirling cloud and rain. Dark slabs of mountainside drop away to be replaced by treeless moorland wilderness, in turn replaced by rocky tree-covered defiles, which at last give way to wide inviting dales. It's not just the showpiece landscape, but the fact that you are viewing it from a railway carriage, that makes the experience unique. This train is also unique in that there is no other that will take you all the way from the Scottish borders to the centre of Leeds.

Today Sheffield and Leeds are another two cities with no InterCity link, so I am obliged to change to a two-coach diesel, which is clean, modern and comfortable but which sets me down in Sheffield just eight minutes late for the connection to London. Fifty-two minutes later I am at last on a high-speed train, and the gentle amble across the north of England has turned into a frenzied dash for the south.

There are plenty of remarkable statistics about the high-speed trains, with which British Rail will happily supply you. Many of them travel more than a thousand miles a day. In their first ten years they have clocked up the equivalent of five hundred trips to the moon. But the danger of using such statistics is that they lead you into such speculations as how far into the galaxy all the bacon rolls served on trains over the past twenty-one years would stretch if laid end to end.

What is true is that at a stroke they improved journey times between

Sheffield and St Pancras by almost a third. Prices to pay for their effortless celerity include windows set just a little too high for a good view, no room for bikes, a nasty smell whenever the brakes are applied, hard seats and boring locomotives. Among the pluses are the automatic sliding doors, which we now take for granted. It would be a salutary experience to go back to the old doors, with which you needed to be a combination of Arnold Schwarzenegger and Olga Korbut to be able to bring two coffees back from the buffet.

The buffet car on the 4 p.m. Sheffield to St Pancras train today is a distinct improvement on its counterpart of twenty years ago, for various reasons. One is that it's there at all. Another is the comparative enthusiasm of its staff. They now tell you that the buffet is open with the sort of relish which used to be reserved for telling you that it was closed.

There are few sensations in life, apart from a really successful orgy, more enjoyable than hurtling across the surface of our green and pleasant land while slowly attending to a half-bottle of Muscadet. So it is today. Even stopping at Leicester doesn't wholly detract from my present happiness. Of course I would rather be travelling behind a locomotive called *Galatea* or *The Seychelles* than *BBC Look North*, but the old steam engines would hardly have clattered into Kettering by the time we pull into the great railway cathedral of St Pancras, a blessed three minutes early.

From what I have seen of it there is no doubt that the InterCity network of 1987 is faster, cleaner and more efficient than ever before. It is also smaller. The range of express services, of which the old Thames-Clyde was one, has passed into history. InterCity 1987 has electrification, VDU screens, credit-card ticketing, bright new stations and piped music. But inter-city 1939 had a train that connected Glasgow, Carlisle, Leeds, Sheffield and London. In one hour less than it took me today.

THE TRACKS OF MEMORY

ON ITS 150TH ANNIVERSARY, **P.J. KAVANAGH** PAYS
TRIBUTE TO THE GREAT WESTERN RAILWAY
AND THE MAN WHO MADE IT

Travelling on a high-speed InterCity train from Paddington to Bristol some time ago, my small boy companion remarked disappointedly that we did not seem to be going very fast. A passing guard paused, took out his watch, ducked slightly to check our position through the window and said, with Great Western hauteur, 'One hundred and twenty-five miles an hour at this point,' and went on his way.

I hoped the boy was impressed (he had the kindness to pretend to be), but I could hardly see the point in travelling so fast with no sensation of speed. You arrived at your destination more quickly (other things being equal), but I wondered if in after years he would have, as I suddenly had, any sense-memories of the mysteries and strangeness of the journey itself, of train interiors, smells, rhythms. I was invaded by a picture, by the feel, of a leather window-strap, punched with regular holes, which you used to pull towards you to open the window and hook on to a brass stud to keep the window at the required height; I remembered luggage racks, with sagging string mesh, and the coloured pictures of holiday resorts below them. Like most people, I had for years used cars more frequently than trains and now I realised how much had changed while I was not looking, and had gone for good.

I also remembered that because of the places we lived in during the war most of my memories were of this line, which used to be called the G.W.R., and that its carriages were painted a special cream and brown, and the green and black engines had curved nameplates on their sides (if they were grand engines) with fine brass lettering, and how snug and secret the old compartments had been. Would a memory of this plastic and open-plan interior, with its walls almost entirely of glass, one day afflict this boy with nostalgia, as I had just been afflicted? Possibly it would, but there seemed fewer differences, fewer details, for memory to hook itself on to.

I was surprised I remembered so much, and so vividly, for I was unaware of being interested in trains. There were changes, of course, which I had noted and (equally, of course) lamented. Until quite recently you could get a delicious cooked breakfast on the down train from Swindon to Paddington, seated in splendour. I used to board the train on a branch line at what is still my station, Kemble, and – did I dream it? – I seem to remember the attendant pausing in his breakfast-laying duties to greet regular commuters – 'Morning, Sir George … Mr Folkes-Trumpington' – and presenting them unasked with their customary gin and tonics. Not before breakfast, surely? But now, in an era of waxen paper cups, that is how I recall it.

It was the ghost of the old G.W.R. reputation for service still lurking: between the wars you could drink G.W.R. whisky while eating G.W.R. biscuits and, perhaps, reading a G.W.R. book ('For boys of all ages'). The G.W.R. was conscious of its special image before the word had even been used in that sense.

All this I knew, but what I did not know was that the quarter-mile of tunnel you go into after Kemble is only there because the squire of Kemble insisted there should be no sight of the new railway from his house; neither did I realise how much the main line from Paddington to Bristol is intricately mixed into the mercantile history of 19th-century England, or that the whole of it was laid down 150 years ago by a very remarkable man indeed, Isambard Kingdom Brunel.

He was the sort of engineer who, when he swallowed half a guinea while trying to amuse some children and it stuck in his windpipe, could devise a machine (while almost suffocating) that might remove it. First, foolish fellow, he called in an eminent surgeon, who operated and left him with a hole in his windpipe and the coin still firmly in place. So, with time running out, he bethought himself of centrifugal force and devised a board which would spin him round and tip him up and down; he had himself strapped to this, spun and tipped, nearly close to death and, then, 'At four I was safely and comfortably delivered of my little coin … expect to be at Bristol by the end of the week'. A man, and an engineer, to be reckoned with.

He was not due at Bristol to talk about the railway – that came later – but to design the Clifton Suspension Bridge. As a preliminary he had an enormous iron bar wrought, 1,000ft long, and slung across the gorge. He went over first in a bucket on a pulley. When the bucket stuck halfway he shinned up the rope and freed the roller. To such a man the laying of a railway from London to Bristol, through virgin territory, would present few difficulties. Yet his biographer, L.T.C. Rolt, states baldly: 'History holds no previous records of engineering venture upon so heroic a scale.'

This was the line I had ignorantly chuffed up and down as a boy, to home, to school, and was now travelling at more than 100mph with another small boy, my son. Perhaps it owes its distinctiveness to the fact that it was from the outset the conception of one man.

He built it because the other great English port, Liverpool, already had a rail connection, and Bristol had to have one to London if it was to retain its pre-eminence. He had to start more or less from scratch (existing railways had been built piecemeal), funding new tools, new men, and it was at this stage he met the great locomotive engineer Daniel Gooch. The two were friends and colleagues for the rest of Brunel's life, but in the first decision they took they were eventually to be defeated. They decided that the new railway should be broad gauge.

The other railways then in existence, like George Stephenson's Stockton & Darlington, had a gauge of 4ft, 8½in, for no better reason than that was the width of the old coal wagons on Tyneside. Both Gooch and Brunel favoured 7ft, because it would give greater wagon capacity, a more balanced ride and greater speed (which was proved to be true when the two gauges were compared in practice). This inaugurated the 'gauge war'. There was no reason why the narrower gauge should prevail, except for the significant one that by 1846 there were 1,001 miles of it, compared with the broad gauge's 274. But the change of freight from one gauge to the other caused endless difficulties when a national network began to shape itself; so almost straight after his death, Brunel's gauge was scrapped. I should have liked a ride in one of his broad-bosomed trains.

What is attractive is that, when they wanted to convince doubtful directors how good their broad engine was, Daniel Gooch drove it himself, often with Brunel on the footplate. When they were not happy with an engine's performance they examined it on their own. You can imagine them clambering over it at night, like schoolboys, discussing a change here, an adjustment there, which would be put into effect the next morning and usually do the trick.

There is an atmosphere of daring and inventiveness about the inception of God's Wonderful Railway – and of fun, though they both worked tirelessly. The whole vast enterprise was completed in five-and-a-half years, despite appalling weather, doubting directors, the constant sniping of competitors, and the scale of sheer inventiveness which was daily required.

Brunel went back to first principles, as there was no precedent for much that he did. People said his railway bridge across the Thames at Maidenhead would never stand. It still does, little altered. They said his Box Tunnel outside

Bath would suffocate passengers, or drive them mad. He built it, we still breathe and remain reasonably sane: and it was the longest railway tunnel ever attempted, nearly two miles. It is lined – the statistic is irresistible – with 30 million bricks specially baked for the purpose. Not only that: the entrances are fine architecture, in Bath stone, the eastern one a worthy classical gateway to the beautiful city. He always tried to use appropriate materials.

Brunel saw to the design of everything: signals (those semaphore signals are his), platforms, waiting rooms – even catering. The first licensee of the first refreshment room (at Swindon) received the following blast from Brunel: 'Dear Sir, I assure you Mr Player was wrong in supposing that I thought you purchased inferior coffee. I thought I said to him I was surprised you should buy such bad roasted corn. I did not believe you had such a thing as coffee in the place; I am certain I have never tasted any.'

Do the directors of British Rail ever write to their employees, or concessionaires, like that?

It was a time of individualism, and individuals. Brunel always insisted on being solely in charge; he disliked committees and loathed bureaucracy. To some extent he has been made a hero of the Industrial Revolution and of dynamic Victorianism – think of that famous photograph of him, muddy, top-hatted, cigar in mouth, against a background of enormous chains. It was in fact taken at a time of great difficulty and he wanted to be photographed with others; it was chance, as he said, that he alone was 'hung in chains'. Nevertheless, that photograph has done much to promote an heroic image of 19th-century thrustful capitalism, even though Brunel made no fortune for himself as a working engineer and despised the later 'railway mania'.

Whether he concerned himself with the huge changes his work made to the life of England is uncertain; perhaps his hand would have shaken a little if he had. Nevertheless, his individual handprint is on his railway to this day, which is why we are marking its 150th anniversary with special affection.

For a while, after nationalisation, the regions were allowed to go more or less their own way and the old G.W.R. seized the opportunity with zest. It retained the cream-and-chocolate livery of its carriages, its distinctively green engines. When diesels came in, Western Region favoured its own special type. Eventually standardisation triumphed, but 'his' railway is still distinct, still the 'holiday' railway, for it had quickly fingered its way into the West Country and into Wales. Many of the resorts it still visits came into existence as holiday places because of it. Indeed, at one time it visited so many such places it was known as the Great Way Round.

But that was not enough for him. When people first worried about the enormous length of the line he was surveying, from London to Bristol, he replied, 'Why not make it longer, and have a steam boat go from Bristol to New York and call it *Great Western*?' In time it was, and it did, and he built it.

Then he built a bigger boat, the *Great Britain*, which became the pattern for all steamers built after it and still remains so, now replaced in the dock Brunel built for it in Bristol.

We now face the other way, not towards America but eastwards to Europe. Bristol flourishes, but not as a port. Yet Brunel's legacy remains. I can never now travel his line without looking out of the window and thinking of him tirelessly surveying, exhorting, contriving, up and down every inch of it. Also I think of the navvies cutting through Sonning Hill, 60ft deep, and the many who died making the Box Tunnel. We take too much for granted; railways have not always been there – ask the squire of Kemble. Men made them, individual men.

His palatial Paddington, that he designed with M. Digby Wyatt, survives. I cannot look up at the decorated iron girders there without thinking of him. He cared for such detail, supervised everything, even the type of grass sown on the embankments. It occurs to me that rolling stock lasts a long time and much of it was old when I travelled it as a boy. Perhaps he was responsible for the leather window strap, the mesh of the luggage rack?

TEA IN TRAINS

Owing to the difficulty of obtaining crockery the service of cups of tea in trains in Britain may have to be stopped.

THE RISE AND FALL OF RAIL REFECTION

FROM VICTORIAN FIVE-COURSE LUNCHES TO RANCID SCOTCH EGGS, **TOM BRUCE-GARDYNE** TRACKS THE HISTORY OF BRITISH TRAIN FOOD

Scrambled eggs on the slow train to La Paz were divine – I can almost taste them now. I remember the cook with his back to the track poking a blackened pan, occasionally lifting it off the flame. The comforting bubble and spit from the cooking mingled with the rattle and creak of the ancient wooden dining car. This was the last carriage on the train and you felt you could spend all day just watching the cook and the man in a crumpled suit opposite being plied with drink by a pair of mysterious women.

As somewhere to while away the time it was perfect – which was just as well since the train was barely making a dent on the bleak moonscape of Bolivia's Altiplano.

Travelling on trains brings on a nostalgia and with it a sense that things were always better in the past. But something has dogged food on trains since Trollope first savaged the railway sandwich in 1868, describing it as 'that white sepulchre … so meagre, poor and spiritless within'. It has been a remarkably durable prejudice and people treasure their tales of the bad days of British Rail catering as they do airport nightmares.

My own worst memory was of a Scotch egg on a West Country train in the early 1980s. I bit and spat almost simultaneously – the yolk was pea green. When I asked for my money back (I was broke at the time), the buffet-car attendant refused, saying there was nothing wrong with it.

And to prove the point, to my total amazement, he gobbled the entire Scotch egg in one go. If a wave of nausea did sweep through his body, it never showed on his face, but he grudgingly handed back my 20p.

Rail catering got off to a bad start in Britain as I discovered while traipsing round the National Railway Museum in York. One early scam was to serve coffee and soup from the platform that was so hot passengers could barely manage a sip before the guard blew the whistle for everyone to rejoin the train. At which point the mugs were tipped back into the pot to be reheated for the next batch of passengers.

The first dining car ran from King's Cross to Leeds in 1879. Despite teething problems, such as soot blowing on to the food whenever the train went through a tunnel, the idea quickly caught on – though not within the royal family. Queen Victoria found the notion distinctly unnerving, insisting that her train, already restricted to 40mph by day and 30mph by night, come to a complete stop whenever meals were served. The journey to Balmoral must have taken weeks.

Contemporary journalists, meanwhile, waxed lyrical about 'gliding through the suburbs of the metropolis … the crockery enticingly a-jingle' as waiters appeared with coffee, toast, eggs, bacon, fish and cutlets.

Lunch would have been a five-course affair with such Victorian staples as grilled turbot, roast sirloin and bread-and-butter pudding. The cost in 1898 was 2s 6d – about £7 at today's prices.

The effect was to cloak everything through the train's steamed-up windows in a post-prandial glow: 'Even the smoke pall over Crewe,' declared one Manchester paper, 'has a romantic appearance in the blurring half-light.'

Third class soon had its own dining car, too, a vision of polished mahogany, to judge by the carriage at York's museum, though it rather paled beside the plush set of Pullmans also on display. By the mid-1920s, the *Flying Scotsman* offered first-class passengers a cocktail bar and hairdressing salon on the non-stop service from King's Cross to Edinburgh.

A key issue soon arose as to how to feed the masses at their seats. At one stage you could order a hamper to pick up at the station and leave farther down the track when you got off. These included the Kingussie Breakfast Basket, the Aristocrat, which included chicken and a pint of claret, and the Democrat – a cold pie and a bottle of stout. Efforts to introduce trolleys were tripped up by narrow corridors and demarcation disputes until 1980.

Buffet cars came in with the Depression, some with bar counters the length of the carriage and bar stools upholstered in buffalo hide. But the fallout from nationalisation in 1948, coupled with post-war austerity, conspired to rob the railways of what glamour they once possessed. Rationing saw gravy browning used to darken coffee and washing soda sprinkled in teapots to extract maximum flavour from the leaves. Railway food was soon back there with the mother-in-law as the nation's oldest joke.

Since privatisation, the pace of change has been driven by the desire to pander to business passengers. Trains have never been classless, but today the contrast in service seems starker than ever, with those in first class left in peace, while those in standard class are subjected to an unending mantra from the buffet car exhorting them to queue for tea and toasted sandwiches alongside the bulging bin liners.

A restaurant car on a train effectively allows you to travel in first for the price of a standard ticket, though not on Virgin (except on Sundays), or Midland Mainline unless you pay through the nose. When I travelled, passengers with a standard open return from London to Sheffield would have paid £35 for an upgrade plus £13 to have breakfast. As the company admitted, 'not many do'.

Today, restaurant car menus are likely to offer such exotica as 'red pepper and polenta gateau' (Virgin) and 'marinated pork loin with Asian spices' (G.N.E.R.), yet somehow the old jibes refuse to die. Aware of this, the PR folk at G.N.E.R. put their last ever burger box on display at the National Railway Museum last summer. And for all the modern-sounding menus, something of the old B.R. lives on. A friend, back from a year in France, was greeted with blank stares when she asked for a croissant at Waverley station in Edinburgh. Finally the penny dropped. 'Och, you mean a crescent roll.'

MACRO-CHIPS

Peterborough

Sir Peter Parker may be interested to hear about the distinctly crude technology employed by some of the staff on his sophisticated 125 trains.

Surprised to be approached on my way to London from the West Country by a ticket collector carrying a large potato who asked me for a rubber band rather than my ticket, I asked what he was up to. 'Well,' he said, 'these trains have a fine internal tannoy system, but we've twenty-three passengers on board who want to stop at Reading and I need to tell the signalmen that we'll be making a special stop. So I tie a message round this here potato and lob it out the window.'

This he duly did. Unfortunately his aim was none too good and a man standing on the end of the platform we were flying past got the shock of his life to see a potato hit the wall above his head and land in soggy pieces on his copy of the *Daily Telegraph*.

A RHINO'S DEATH

Sir – Peter Simple's story of the rhinoceros that expired after eating the contents of a British Railways packed lunch has caused considerable concern to British Transport Catering Services and their suppliers.

His anecdotes are well appreciated by a wide public, but by describing deliberately the packed lunch as one prepared by British Transport he is quite unfair to them and their suppliers.

In my experience they buy high-quality products from firms of national repute and this fact would be well known to any users of railway station catering facilities.

Yours faithfully,

R.E. Doubleday,
Managing director, R.E. Doubleday & Co. Ltd
London, SW2

AUTRE TEMPS ...

Peterborough

Peter Simple's nonsense story of the rhinoceros that died from eating a British Railways packed lunch has drawn a letter of protest from a caterer. In the usually less-sensitive middle of last century the *Daily Telegraph* had to pay £25 damages and costs for libelling the soup sold at Peterborough station.

Sir – Mr R.E. Doubleday's concern about Peter Simple's story of the rhinoceros that expired after eating a British Railways packed lunch is appreciated. I assume from his letter that his firm's products were not to blame.

He is apparently acting as spokesman for the British Transport Commission's catering services, for he states that the story has caused concern in official circles. It is surprising that an official statement has not been issued on the subject, for the B.T.C. usually defends its services with the utmost vigour.

Let there be a public inquiry on this subject which Mr Doubleday takes so seriously. I would suggest Peter Simple as its chairman. The Royal College of Veterinary Surgeons should be asked for an autopsy, and Mr Doubleday should be called on to watch the interests of rhinos that rely on British Railways' catering facilities.

But where is the dead rhino? Lying in the lost property department of a station on a closed branch line?

Yours faithfully,

H. Leech
London, EC3

THIS IS THE NIGHT TRAIN

(WITH APOLOGIES TO W.H. AUDEN)

Craig Brown

This is the Night Train crossing the border,
Air-conditioning out of order
Windows sealed, atmosphere muggy,
Outside breezy, inside fuggy
Seats for the rich, straps for the poor
Everyone else stuffed up by the door
'We apologise for the sudden halt
We'd like to remind you it's Railtrack's fault.'
This is the Night Train recrossing the border
Forward lever out of order.
'Ladies and Gentlemen, no cause for concern
In eighteen miles' time, we'll attempt to turn;
So why not try a microwaved pasty
Or our new Spongiburger, naughty but nasty'
Coffee for the rich, crisps for the poor
With a sudden lurch, they're all over the floor.
Hissing noisily, horribly crammed
Oh dear! The sliding doors have jammed.
This is the Night Train re-recrossing the border
Toilets temporarily out of order
'Ladies are requested to cross their legs
Gentlemen advised to purchase pegs'
Lurching wildly, the Night Train passes
Silent miles of terrified grasses
'Customers are requested to remain at ease
If you still feel desperate, cross your knees'
Trees groaning as she approaches
Thankful they're not in those coaches
Leaves busy growing, dreaming of the day

They can fall on the line causing major delay
Cows staring at passengers all asleep
Think to themselves, 'They're just like sheep'.
This is the Night Train re-re-recrossing the border
Signals and points all out of order
'No time of arrival billed as yet –
Why not try our new filled baguette?'
Groans of defiance, sighs of despair
Hands clenched in anger or pulling out hair,
Passengers demanding information
On times of arrival at their destination
Executives bursting with curses and moans
Fishing in pockets for mobile phones
Calls to the secretary: 'Cancel that meeting!'
Calls to the conference: 'Rearrange that seating!'
Calls to the PA: 'Reschedule my life!'
Calls to the colleagues and calls to the wife,
Calls to the operator; I demand compensation!'
Calls to the mistress in a huff at the station.
Moans from the oldies ('Disgraceful, innit?')
Threats to the kiddies ('Stop that this minute!')
Abuse from hooligans, harrumphs from commuters
Tapping out grievances on personal computers:
'Never again… prepared to do battle …
Absolute outrage… herded like cattle'
At last! The conductor, braving the squeeze
'When will we get there?' 'Don't ask!
Tickets please!'
This is the Night Train, re-re-re-recrossing the border
Overhead lighting out of order
Arrival delayed 'til 15.22
So why not try our pizza vindaloo?
Or a tasty masala, buy-two-get-one-free –
Or a piping hot beverage, spilt straight on your knee?
This is the Night Train, re-re-re-re-recrossing the border
Whoops! Clean off the rails!
Apologies in order!
Owing to derailment, we suggest you alight
And if you run fast, you'll be home Monday night.

WALES, WITH NO REASON TO HURRY

A LOT OF WELSH BRANCH LINES WERE SHUT IN THE 1960S, BUT **JIM PERRIN** KNOWS THE ONES THAT ESCAPED

Even Phileas Fogg would have been put on his mettle had he been required to get from end to end of Wales in a day with no help but that afforded by the National Rail Timetable.

It is theoretically possible to set off from Llandudno on the north coast before eight in the morning and, travelling all the way by train, with a brief digression on to the English side of the border, arrive in Swansea a little before pub closing time. A much longer digression into England, and it's possible to make the journey in an afternoon, but that's to miss the point entirely.

Wales is a gorgeous country and its railways — the few that remain after Dr Beeching's savagery forty years ago — enable you to see a substantial part of the best of it.

I had a plan: I'd take three days over the trip. That would reduce the anxieties every rail traveller feels these days around connections and timetabling. Also, I'd invite a comedian to accompany me, because Wales has a reputation in England for being a melancholy nation skulking under a pall of rain clouds and chapels and slate tips, its collective breast swelling only at the sound of the first organ chords. I knew this to be untrue, but it's best to guard against stereotypes. I asked Mike Harding along.

Now I'd been with Mike in Llandudno on two previous occasions, both marked by insobriety. To meet there early in the day was to tempt providence. Also, comedians are generally of depressive or choleric disposition. Think Lenny Bruce. Think Max Wall. I couldn't imagine Mike's temper being improved by Llandudno. For my part, I like it.

It's the most unspoilt of all the great Victorian seaside resorts, its setting between cliff-tiered headlands as dramatic as any in Britain. Half the population of Liverpool was conceived here, though that wouldn't raise it in Mike's estimation. I took a train of two carriages and clacked down the little spur to arrive at Llandudno Junction on the Euston-to-Holyhead line.

A minute later, Mike jumped down off the Manchester train. You could tell it was from somewhere important. It had three carriages. He was in a bad temper, just back from Barcelona, where all his belongings had been stolen.

'Travel light,' I'd told him, 'steep hills, small trains.' He had four bags. I ended up carrying five – two of my own (the National Rail Timetable took up one by itself), and three of his. He leapt and I staggered on to the train for Blaenau Ffestiniog at the end of the Conwy Valley Line.

How this line survived Beeching was one of the miracles of the 20th century. There was a reason, of course. There always is when the government of the day appears to have made an oversight. Out of the terminus at Blaenau a track twists south for five or six miles to the nuclear power station at Trawsfynydd. The map would have you believe it's disused. It was built to carry radioactive waste away. So the branch line's survival is one of the few reasons to feel grateful to the nuclear power industry.

This route is astonishingly lovely, running at first by the side of the River Conwy, simple old churches set against a backdrop of the Carneddau mountains. Beyond Betws-y-Coed, by means of viaducts and brief blinks of tunnels it slips into the gorge of the Afon Lledr, old oak woodland crowding the track, the river fuming and frothing beneath, salmon lazing in its pools, Snowdon itself briefly visible, before a long tunnel suddenly debouches into the ruined industrial grandeur of Blaenau.

In this epicentre of one of Britain's dead industries, grey terraces of quarrymen's houses cluster together in glaciated hollows of the mountains, and down upon them from every angle spill slopes of slate waste and spoil.

The local roofs these days are repaired with tiles from Spain. Heritage tourism is the industry here now. Crowds come up from the coast on the narrow-gauge railway. They flock on to underground tramways the miners once used. They see how things used to be.

We passed on that, installed ourselves in a first-class carriage of the Ffestiniog Railway and, drawn by a sturdy, double-headed steam locomotive, chuffed downline instead. Mike was positively beatific, imagining himself descending from some hill station of the Raj.

Stewards brought coffee. The rocky, wooded rhododendron landscape we travelled through was a delight, the view to Snowdon from the last embankment before Porthmadog's harbour station as sublime as when Shelley had proclaimed it the finest in Europe. We took refuge in a pub and consulted the National Rail Timetable.

This formidable volume is set in six-point type and printed on the equivalent of what used to be called fine India paper, 2,272 pages of it, very few of them relating to Wales and those few widely dispersed. After an hour with the magnifying glass we deduced that a train would shortly convey us onwards if we were to hurry to Porthmadog's other station, serving the Cambrian Coast Line, a mile across town. We caught it. Timing is everything.

Its departure coincided with the daily parole of schoolchildren. They caught it too. Three stations down the line a rival horde had been released. We got off. You think soccer hooligans are bad? Here's where they start out.

Fortuitously, we alighted at Harlech, which has a tearoom with the best view in creation. It's at the top of an exceedingly steep hill and is called the Hotel Plas. To keep Mike from thinking about muggers in Barcelona or the schoolchildren of Porthmadog, I recited a medieval Welsh story on the way up to it, full of giants wading to Ireland, speaking starlings, decapitated talking heads, wronged wives and other such wonders. And all set here. By the time we sat over tea on sunlit lawns, with the great Edwardian castle at our elbow, Snowdon hanging over its battlements and a bay of pure cerulean beneath, his mood had improved.

It stayed that way when we resumed the coast-hugging journey. Ruskin thought there was only one finer walk than from Dolgellau to Barmouth, and that was the walk from Barmouth to Dolgellau. Crossing the Mawddach estuary bridge on a sun-flooded evening with the sculpted long ridge of Cadair Idris thrown into sumptuous relief, it's difficult to disagree, and the quality of scenery diminishes hardly at all between here and Machynlleth, where we spent the night in the 18th-century Wynnstay Arms.

Charles Dark, the proprietor, regaled us with the best food – all of it locally caught and grown – that I've eaten in Wales. Fish, fowl and flesh punctuated by tiny, delicious sorbets and culminating in fine port and a magnificent, parochial cheeseboard. There was the conversation of locals late into the night, too.

Charles left a bottle of Irish whiskey on the table and went to bed. The comedian likes hotels like this. Except for the headaches, a day, a week, a decade here would slip imperceptibly by. It is the most charming and inter-esting of small Welsh towns. It has museums, art galleries, bookshops, eccentric cafés, nearby beaches, bird reserves, a street market, a concert hall in a mellow wood-galleried old chapel, and the inspirational, endlessly fascinating Centre for Alternative Technology.

But we had a train to catch. It goes to Shrewsbury, and beyond that with surprising regularity to Birmingham. It passes through a score of Adlestrops, each of which tempt you to stop. This is Montgomeryshire – a quiet county of scattered farms, dog rose and elder in the hedgerows, cows grazing. By way of decorative, brick-built Caersws, where a famous and still popular Welsh poet of the century before last was station master, and Newtown, where Robert Owen was born, and Welshpool, where hearsay has it Hilda Murrell was held in a safe house before her murder, you dawdle through green valleys out of Wales, into the Marches with England, and down to Shrewsbury, which is the most perfectly medieval of England's cities.

We allowed ourselves a couple of hours there, looking for – and finding – green men (an obsession of Mike's) in the roof of St Mary's church, before boarding the single carriage that runs four times a day up and down the one-hundred-and-twenty miles of the Heart of Wales Line.

There are three great rail routes in Britain: from Settle to Carlisle through the northern Pennines; the West Highland Line from Glasgow to Mallaig; and the Heart of Wales Line from Shrewsbury to Swansea. The last is the least celebrated, the least used, and the most consistently beautiful. You could alight at a dozen whitewashed and flower-potted station platforms for small towns and villages along its route, and end up staying forever.

We chose Llandrindod Wells, where most of the population looked as though they had done just that. The station bore a plaque commemorating its 're-Victorianisation' in 1990. Its bookstall sold manuals for Austin A40 Somersets and the nearby garage still advertised 'Commer, Hillman, Humber and Sunbeam'. We sat among the purple-rinsed in a café by the lake – round which, attended by a stooping man in a beige raincoat, for lap upon lap waddled a plump Cardigan corgi – and watched the rain hiss down. Mike descanted on comely waitresses with smiley faces.

Chris Burton, a retired police inspector from Bristol who runs a farm guesthouse 1,200ft up in the nearby hills with his wife Pauline, collected us in an immaculate, elderly Volvo and drove us, with a brief visit to Disserth's exquisite, bat-adorned 13th-century church, into curlew-haunted moorland. We woke to a valley filigreed with mist, slipping away between bosomy hills patched with cloud-filtered sun. There were yellowhammers on the bird table, red kites quartering the pasture and ravens calling from the trees behind.

If Wales in general is beautiful, Radnorshire is quietly transcendent. When we reboarded the train, that ravishing mood of landscape prevailed down to Llandeilo at least, if not quite to Swansea itself.

In Llanwrtyd Wells the guard strolled though the carriage announcing that the up train was ten minutes late, being packed with golfing types for some tournament along the line and hence struggling. So if we cared to go for a stroll round and get a cup of tea, he'd count us out and count us back in again.

You can count me in for a journey like this any day – there's none lovelier in Britain. I'll take a week over it next time – or maybe a month, Mike thought, muttering to himself of green men and Machynlleth and opportunities missed.

IN THE DARKNESS, THEY CREEP LIKE GHOSTS TOWARDS BRITAIN

DAVID GRAVES WITNESSES THE NIGHTLY ASSAULT OF ASYLUM SEEKERS ON EUROTUNNEL

As nightfall descends over Sangatte, the first groups of asylum seekers emerge from the gates of a cavernous blue warehouse. Some groups are only three or four, others fifty strong. They shuffle off towards Coquelles, past the cornfields rippling in the wind, and prepare for their nightly battle with Eurotunnel to get to Britain.

Caught in the headlights of passing cars, they tread a well-worn route. Past the neat houses on the outskirts of Coquelles, where most of the local people are preparing for bed, and onward past the village post office towards the Calais-Boulogne motorway. Under a fence, across the motorway and towards the Cité Europe shopping centre.

Beside the lights of the shopping centre, where tens of thousands of Britons shop for cheap wine, the asylum seekers start to fan out across rutted fields and through deep culverts towards a clump of small pine trees, in which they take cover. There is an odd shout or whistle, but otherwise silence, apart from the rustling wind.

It is here that the final dash to the Eurotunnel terminal, half a mile away, is planned. Kamal, an Iraqi Kurd, tells his friends of a breach in the 22 miles of razor wire around the 1,250-acre compound. It is a small hole under the perimeter fence, just big enough to wriggle under. There is a shout in the distance. Kamal, twenty-four, who has been travelling through Europe to the Channel for three months, whispers: 'It's the police.' Everyone stays quiet for half an hour until it is time to move again. By now it is pitch black.

Moving as silently as possible towards the perimeter fence, the asylum seekers ghost through the night towards the hole. It has not been discovered by Eurotunnel's security guards patrolling the compound. One by one, the refugees slip under the coils of razor wire. Ahead of them are the railway lines and trains they hope will take them to Britain.

Kamal is travelling with three friends. They are all Kurds from Kirkuk in northern Iraq. They have suffered years of persecution from Saddam Hussein and Turkish forces. Their desperate families have raised thousands of pounds to enable their sons to start a better life in Britain. First, though, they have to get to Folkestone to claim asylum.

The plan is to wait for a slow-moving European freight train. As it approaches the entrance to the Channel Tunnel, Kamal and his friends will attempt to jump on one of the wagons. They fan out towards the tracks, trying to avoid the floodlighting Eurotunnel has installed.

An hour or so later, they return. They had been unable to board a train, because none was moving slowly enough. It is the fifth successive night Kamal has failed in his quest to reach Britain. 'It is only twenty-five minutes away, but it could be another world,' he says in near-perfect English.

As dawn starts to break over Coquelles, they begin to walk two miles back to the warehouse in Sangatte, an International Red Cross holding centre funded by the French government. 'We will try again tonight. Everyone will. We have nothing to lose,' says Kamal. As he trudges back towards the warehouse, there are other groups retracing their steps to the holding centre. No one will know who made it to Britain until the morning, when a familiar face may no longer be there.

'Everyone hopes it will be him,' says Kamal. He prepares to spend most of the day in bed, resting for his next attempt.

SIX-HUNDRED-MILE TRIP FOR 2d

While seeing a blind friend off in the *Royal Scot* Express from Euston yesterday morning, Mrs Wornell, of Addiscombe Avenue, Croydon, accidentally remained in the train when it pulled out. The *Royal Scot* made a special stop at Carlisle and Mrs Wornell returned in another express. Her 600-mile journey cost her 2d, the price of a platform ticket.

RICKETY, TICKETY-BOO

PUNCTUAL, CHARMING AND WITH VINTAGE EQUIPMENT,
TWO RAIL SERVICES ON THE ISLE OF WIGHT PROVE
IRRESISTIBLE TO **CHRISTOPHER MIDDLETON**

It's a very *Alice in Wonderland* moment. One minute you're sitting on a perfectly normal London Underground train, the next you're looking out through the window, not at tunnel walls and your own reflection but at open seas and swirling waves, just a few feet below your wheels.

The strangeness of the sensation catches both adults and children by surprise. It's as if your tube carriage has suddenly been transported into one of those great big holiday posters that line the sides of stations. Only this particular advertisement isn't for Mauritius or the Maldives, but for the Isle of Wight.

We are at Ryde harbour, to be precise, travelling on one of the two extraordinary and, in many ways, quite wonderful pier railways that still operate in the Solent. The other (at Hythe) can claim the older engines, but this one (the Island Line) has by far the longer track. Once its trains have traversed the 700 rickety yards between Ryde Pier Head (i.e. the ferry terminal) and Ryde esplanade (dry land), they have another 8 miles to go until they reach the terminus at Shanklin (via Smallbrook Junction, Brading, Sandown and Lake).

At first sight, the pier does not inspire confidence. In addition to its skeletal, see-through look, it has the rusting and rather unnerving remains of an old tramway running alongside it (opened 1864, closed 1969). However, Andy Naylor, the Island Line general manager, is full of assurances about the structure's safety, except in the choppiest weather.

'Very occasionally, when the wind's in the wrong direction, we do get the waves starting to come over the tracks,' he says. 'It doesn't happen often, but when it does, we have to shut down the pier stretch. Basically, water and electric rails don't mix.'

The trains themselves are not in the first flush of youth, either; the carriages were built in 1938 and already had fifty years' hard labour on the

Northern Line behind them when they were shipped across to the island in 1989. As a result, they have not just a driver on board but a guard, who doubles as fare collector and ticket inspector, and has to move between the two carriages during the journey.

Far from enjoying a leisurely retirement, the carriages still have to work as hard as ever. Starting at 5.30 in the morning, and finishing at 11 every night, each train has to travel the length of the line at least 29 times a day. And although four of the six carriages are decked out in dinosaur theme-park colours, the Island Line operates not to a Mickey Mouse timetable but to a grown-up schedule laid down by the owner, Stagecoach (the Island Line is part of the South West Trains franchise).

At every station, there are notices testifying to the trains' punctuality (99.7 per cent on time at the last count). In fact, the line's claim to being the country's most reliable rail service is challenged only by its rival across the water, at the Hythe Ferry pier train.

Confirmed by *The Guinness Book of Records* as being the world's oldest continually running pier train (since July 1922), the Hythe train trundles back and forth twice an hour every day, departing at fifteen and forty-five minutes past. It is not just a pleasure ride, either; each service is timed to deliver departing passengers to the Hythe Ferry (twelve minutes across the water to Southampton), as well as receiving arriving passengers off it. And whereas the carriages on the Island Line are merely retro, Hythe's highly polished wooden compartments are positively antique.

'They were built for much smaller people than we are now,' says Jerry Barton, a former welder who has been a driver on the pier railway for sixteen years. 'Sometimes when passengers are jumping in, they don't take into account how narrow the doors are. Every now and again I look in my rear-view mirror and see arms and legs sticking out from the sides of the carriages.'

Not that it is a high-speed experience. Whereas maximum speed on the Island line is 45mph, the Hythe train rarely gets above 10mph in the course of its 700-yard journey, especially if it is carrying a full load of passengers (48). 'Joggers go faster than we do,' says Lloyd Lay, one of the directors of White Horse Ferries, the company that took over the operation in 1993.

That's hardly surprising, given that the engine is a strange little green-painted locomotive that started its working life during the Second World War, at a factory making mustard gas for the trenches. It also saw active service at that time, continuing to work the line despite the frequent air raids on Southampton.

'The train used to travel a bit faster in those days,' says Barton. 'People didn't want to hang around out there in the middle of the pier when the enemy bombers were coming in low.'

So warmly do local people feel towards the pier that 500 of them have paid to sponsor new (Cameroonian hardwood) planks along its walkway (from £30 to £90 a time). Go by foot rather than train and you can see their engraved messages ('From Joyce and Grumpy', or 'The Jolly Boys at Fawley Power Station'). On the long list of famous passengers from the past are to be found the names of King George VI and Lawrence of Arabia.

Despite a dip in passenger numbers during the 1990s (and a brief lull in 2003 when a dredger ploughed through the pier), the Hythe train-and-boat operation now carries 430,000 people a year. For commuters, the journey represents a convenient alternative to the twenty-five-mile trip they would have to make into Southampton by car.

But it's not just business people who ride the Hythe rails. 'The reason we're still going is that we don't just depend on one group of people,' says Barton. 'As well as our rush-hour regulars, we've got tourists, we've got school parties, we've got pensioners, we've got shoppers, we've got people who want to ride on the ferry and look at the ships, and we've got people who want to go into town for a night out (at weekends, the last ferry back to Hythe leaves at 11.10pm).

'I once sat down and worked out that, since it started, this little train has travelled a total of 80,000 miles. That's three times round the world – and all without leaving Hampshire.'

RAIL, RHYTHM AND BLUES

STRANGE THINGS ARE HAPPENING ON BRITAIN'S BRANCH
LINES. **JOSIE BARNARD** SEES MUSICIANS PULLING IN THE
PASSENGERS BETWEEN HUDDERSFIELD AND SHEFFIELD

'I'd choose "Hoochie-Coochie Man" on the Meadowhall Sprinter over
bingo every time,' Doreen White says as she waits in the queue to the ticket
window.

Blues and trains have been linked from the start. If bluesmen weren't
building the railroads in the American Deep South, they were trying to
hitch rides on them. But when King Solomon Hill sang: 'Mmm, mmm, I
wanna ride your train,' he wasn't referring to the Huddersfield-Sheffield
return.

'The line was under threat of closure,' explains Paul Salveson, chairman of
the Penistone Line Partnership. 'It's a spectacular rural route. It goes over the
150-year-old Lockwood Viaduct, through the Pennine hills. But it just wasn't
attracting enough users. So four years ago we persuaded Regional Railways to
schedule in a few live music nights, and we haven't looked back.'

It's 8 p.m. I'm waiting on a very wintry platform one. They say that to
really sing the blues, you need to feel blue yourself. 'No trouble there,' says
Jimmy Bergin. 'Huddersfield station'll do that for you every time.' He
improvises a wailing harmonica sound with his hand and sneezes. 'I'm
perishing.'

A white-haired fifty-something, Jimmy is head 'boy' of the Beale Street
Boys, tonight's local band. 'I need to start playing to get my circulation
going,' he declares. 'Where's that train?'

The Sprinter pulls in. I'd had romantic images of an old timbered steam
engine. The 8.15 p.m. to Sheffield, via Barnsley, is a standard Metro train
circa 1970, very brightly lit. The promised 'real-ale bar' is a couple of crates
of beer being loaded on at the far end. Sixteen people are huddled, keen to
board, and that's already two hundred per cent more than was usual for a
Monday evening. 'Numbers were sparse,' Paul Salveson admits. 'Now, for
the Blues Night alone, we get between forty and a hundred people.'

News got round largely by word of mouth. Dave Crowther saw advertisements in his own shop, the High Burton Co-op. 'I wasn't a blues fan, actually, but I like to support local enterprise.' He and his pals Jack Walker and Alan Dearnley have been regulars for two years. As they wait on the cold station, their eyes sparkle beneath their woolly hats.

The train doors hiss open. The Beale Street Boys rush on. As he heaves a couple of speakers after him, Keith, the keyboard player, says, 'Not much time.' The train runs to a normal timetable. The band has only minutes to set up. They pull out two central seats, pile the drum kit on one side of the aisle and shove amp, mikes and guitar on the other. Craig, the guitarist, tunes up under a no-smoking sign.

Dave, Jack and Alan stake out front-row territory with polystyrene dishes and Coke bottles. 'We like to make a party of it,' says Jack. He runs a fish and chippie, so he's brought smoked salmon. Alan's contributed fizzy pop laced with Jack Daniel's and Bacardi.

A moustachioed man moves his briefcase to make space for me. We're on first-name terms immediately. 'Bill, university lecturer,' he introduces himself. 'I always make sure to stay late so I can commute home on the Blues Train.'

Doreen sits opposite and, holding her friend's hand, tells us, 'Jean here's disabled. She's mad about trains, and I love the music, so we kill two birds with one stone, all for a standard £3.80 return ticket.' She presents a Tupperware box filled with meat-paste sandwiches. 'Want one?'

'Hello, good evening,' yells Jimmy Bergin from behind his mike, as we enter a tunnel. His first song is "Every Day I Have the Blues". I know this only because Dave shouts the title in my ear.

A Metro train presents logistical problems. Everything's run off batteries, so the sound quality's rough and ready. It takes a while to get attuned to the music over the carriages' rattling. But there are advantages. For one, the seats all face the band. And the atmosphere's spot on. It's winter, so the windows have steamed up already. We could be travelling into the Mississippi Delta instead of past Denby Dale and Silkstone Common. As the train builds up speed, the rocking motion gets feet tapping and bodies swaying.

'The ride can get wild and woolly at times,' says Paul. 'I've had smoother trips on a rollercoaster,' says Pete, who'd thought this was the train to Marsden and is rather pleased about his mistake.

The train lurches. Valerie Hirst, a lively blonde, gulps her real ale down to prevent spillage. 'It beats the pub, doesn't it? And I don't have to worry about drinking and driving.' Her village is one of the stops. 'I come for the dancing.' She's jiggling her elbows in anticipation.

There's not much room to move, let alone boogie. It's so crowded that a two-person seat's got a whole family in it, complete with toddler. Their buggy and four bags of shopping bulge into the aisle. 'It's the only way to get your baby to sleep of a night,' says the mum, Linda. 'Ssssh,' says her husband, Desmond. 'This one's my favourite.' The band mellows into "Stormy Monday". Most people are here specifically for the music. A few shoppers are surprised, but soon let go of their umbrellas and Argos bags and start humming along.

At Sheffield, there's a short turnaround. More beer is loaded on. The conductor pokes his head out, looks up and down the platform. The sound of the whistle has a Pavlovian effect. We're on our way back. There's a time limit on the amount of pleasure remaining. Suddenly everyone's mojos are working nineteen to the dozen. Valerie, unable to restrain herself a moment longer, grabs an MTL transport manager and starts jiving energetically, creating a bit more space with every twist and twirl. The drummer, Geoff, goes free with his sticks and uses the luggage rack to create an overhead washboard sound.

Already most of their way through a supply of Beaujolais and Twiglets, students from a local design course decide it would be a laugh to use photographs of the band in their wallpaper-motif project. Cameras flash. Some lads get on at Berry Brow, go straight to the middle and start jamming. Keith, over by the toilets, displaced from his job on keyboards, reflects cheerfully, 'Anything goes on the Blues Train.' A green-mohicaned youth serenades us with "Hey Jude" to riotous applause.

This amount of jollity at 11 p.m. on a Metro train outside Wombwell is a bit of a shock to the system. I go for a breather at the far end. The conductor, Dave, due for retirement, is sanguine. 'It livens up my job,' he says. 'I didn't know I liked the blues. But I do. And it keeps the passengers happy.'

When we arrive back in Huddersfield to the romping sounds of "Dust My Broom", there's a sense of elation. Only Jack Walker feels he can get near describing the pleasure. 'I used to fly model planes. The Blues Train gives me the same adrenaline high.' Alighting passengers nod their heads. Any who weren't committed regulars will be from now on.

What started as a way of saving an underused rural route has become a much-loved alternative night out.

AND HERE, DEEP IN THE SUSSEX COMMUTER BELT, RARELY SEEN IN THE WILD, IS A VETUS MACHINA LAVANS

ARMED WITH A HANDY LEAFLET, BINOCULARS AND INSECT REPELLENT, **JEREMY CLARKE** TRIES OUT THE 'NATURE TRAILS' THAT HAVE BEEN LAUNCHED ON TEN OF BRITAIN'S BUSIEST RAIL ROUTES

'As the train pulls out of Victoria and you cross the Thames, look out for the statuesque grey heron standing motionless at the edge of the water waiting for an unsuspecting fish to pass by.' A typical sentence, this, from *Tracking Wild Britain*, a handy new leaflet, jointly compiled by the RSPB and Mammals Trust UK, highlighting which birds and mammals the weary commuter can expect to see on ten of the busiest rail routes if he troubles to look out of the window.

Unlikely as it may seem, the London-to-Brighton run, according to the leaflet, is teeming with wildlife. Once he's got the statuesque heron (and maybe even the unsuspecting fish) under his belt, and if he keeps his eyes peeled, the commuter might also see cormorants, foxes, squirrels, rabbits, muntjac deer, roe deer and peregrine falcons. And that's not all. 'Encircling central London,' the leaflet goes on excitedly, 'are populations of moles, which tend to be found in low-lying land, rarely coming to the surface, but remaining in their tunnels and conspicuous by their tunnels' excavated earth — molehills.' Armed with leaflet, binoculars and insect repellent, I joined the scrum for the 5.15.

Sadly, the statuesque heron was not at his post when we crossed the river, and the besieging army of moles were remaining in their tunnels, as we were in ours, soon after departure for quite some time. As we started moving again and headed out into open country, however, I kept an especial eye out for muntjac deer (muntiacus reevesi), not having knowingly seen one before. To help me identify these small and secretive animals, the leaflet had a helpful colour photograph with a caption telling me that the muntjac is also known as the barking deer.

After three-quarters of an hour, however, we were already at Haywards Heath and I hadn't seen a thing. Well, I'd seen a few cows, and a pair of magpies, an old washing machine (vetus machina lavans), an orange hoarding advertising a travel website, and a man ambling along with a shotgun under his arm, but there was no sign of any of the exciting mammals and birds detailed in the London-Brighton page. Perhaps the man with the gun had shot them all.

At Burgess Hill, a uniformed lady came through the carriage holding open a large polythene bag and inviting passengers to lob their rubbish into it. I showed her the relevant page in *Tracking Wild Britain*. If anyone could vouch for the claim that if one paid attention the London-to-Brighton service was like an east African safari, it would be this woman, Angelina, who went there and back all day, like a yo-yo. 'Have you, in all the time you've been working on this service, ever seen any of these animals?' I said. She wrinkled her nose and studied the text and the photographs on the opposite page, then shook her head doubtfully. 'Not even a rabbit?' I pleaded. About rabbits she was definite. 'No,' she said. 'Never.'

'Do horses count?' said Brigitte, seated opposite, helpfully. 'Were they wild ones?' I said, hopes soaring. She rather thought not. Alex, the Polish refreshments trolley lady, had not only never seen a muntjac deer, she also had no conception of what one was. She knew what a rabbit was, though, but said she had yet to see one from an English train.

I went back on watch. Another claim made by the leaflet is that 'rail routes can provide green corridors for wildlife'. But the embankments had been denuded of vegetation by fire, chainsaws, and mechanical flails, and sprayed with weedkiller. Every day, 3 million people in 20,000 trains hurtle through them at speeds of up to 125mph. Surely, no shy, secretive muntjac deer in his right mind would make a leisurely migration along one of these corridors.

It was only as the train pulled into Brighton station that I spotted one of the creatures highlighted in *Tracking Wild Britain* – a seagull. What sort of gull remained a mystery. For although seagulls get a mention in the guide, no individual species is identified; they are airily dismissed by the catch-all phrase 'various gulls'.

Bitterly disappointed, I took another train, to see what wildlife the Exeter-to-Penzance line had to offer. The route to Exeter was not included in the guide so I didn't look out of the window. From Exeter onwards the guide promised wildlife a-go-go, including ducks, geese and swans; herds of 'elegant fallow deer, easily distinguished by their fluffy white-undersided tail'; the 'elegant' little egret; 'buzzards circling on raised wings or perhaps sitting on posts at the side of the railway'; plus, incredibly, bottlenose dolphins, which 'travel in groups of up to twenty-five and delight people lucky enough to see their playful behaviour'.

I got off to a flying start as we sped along beside the River Exe – three sacks of winkles, the day's harvest of a man wading about in the mud. I know my winkles. I once collected a sackful during a morning's work from an estuary in Cornwall, but neglected to tie up the end of the sack. When I came back in the afternoon to pick it up they'd all escaped and were nowhere to be seen.

Winkles aren't mentioned in the guide, but seconds later I spotted an 'elegant' fallow deer, then another, then a herd of perhaps 200 of them, assiduously grazing in the grounds of Powderham Castle, their fluffy white under-sided tails glowing orange in the late afternoon sun. They weren't wild ones, but a wonderful sight all the same. 'Look!' I said to the chap sitting across the aisle absorbed in his broadsheet. He looked, saw, cocked his eyebrows and returned to his paper.

Unfazed and on a roll now, I eagerly scanned the sea at Teignmouth for pods of cavorting bottlenose dolphins. But that was it as far as Hayle in Cornwall – where I saw a bewildered-looking Canada goose standing alone in a meadow. Maybe I was sitting on the wrong side of the train or just plain unlucky. Anybody want to buy a pair of binoculars?

A WALLABY SEEN FROM A TRAIN

I fear that Jeremy Clarke was merely unfortunate in not spotting more wildlife from the train when he tried the new railway nature trails (Focus, 24 April). As a frequent train user I can assure him that over the years I have seen a wallaby, several adders, grass snakes, herons and a scorpion (I don't know how it got to Ashdown Forest).

Perhaps Mr Clarke should travel on one of the slow trains as they do not appear to startle the wildlife. It is to be regretted that the new guide does not mention that the last dragon in England was spotted at Faygate (which is on the railway line to Horsham). Unfortunately this was before the railway.

Niall Mitchell
Crawley, West Sussex

CHAPTER 7
WORKADAY JOURNEYS

---

29 JANUARY 2005

CRUSH HOUR

SUKETU MEHTA CELEBRATES THE 'CHOREOGRAPHY
OF COMMUTING' IN ONE OF THE WORLD'S
MOST CROWDED CITIES

Bombay is a fast-paced, even hectic city, but it is not, in the end, a competitive city.

Anyone who has a 'reservation' on an Indian train is familiar with this word: adjust. You might be sitting there on your seat, the prescribed three people along it, and a fourth and a fifth person will loom over you and say, 'Psst. Adjust.' You move over.

You adjust.

It is a crowded city, used to living with crowds. In our building in Manhattan, people found it strange when my wife's parents came to live with us for six months in our one-bedroom apartment. Our landlady withheld part of our security deposit for 'excess wear and tear' caused by the presence of two more adults. Nobody in Bombay asked us how many people were going to live with us in our apartment; it was taken for granted that we would have relatives, friends, and friends of friends coming to stay, and how we would put them up was our problem.

A recent magazine advertisement for an Ambassador car, the sturdy workhorse of the Indian roads, illustrates what I mean. The car, an unadorned version of a 1950s Morris Oxford, is trundling along a rain-drenched street. The ad copy doesn't devote the usual lascivious attention to leather seat covers, digital dashboards, electronic fuel injection or the trim lines of the car's design. The Ambassador is actively ugly but lovable in the way elephants are, with a jaunty visor and a wide grin. Instead, there is a snatch of dialogue from within the car. Three people can be seen squashed together on the front bench seat. A man crosses in front of the ungainly pachyderm, holding a briefcase over his head to ward off the downpour.

'Arrey ... isn't that Joshi?'

'Yes. Let's take him also.'

'But we are so many.'

'Have a heart, we can always adjust.'

Car ads in most countries usually focus on the luxurious cocoon that awaits you, the driver, once you step inside. At most, there might be space for the attractive woman you'll pick up once you're spotted driving the flash set of wheels. The Ambassador ad isn't really touting the virtues of space. It's not saying, like a station wagon ad, that it has lots of spare room. It's saying that the kind of people likely to drive an Ambassador will always make more room. It is really advocating a reduction of personal physical space and an expansion of the collective space. In a crowded city, the citizens of Bombay have no option but to adjust.

I am on the Virar fast train during the evening rush hour, possibly the most crowded of the locals. I am clutching the strip at the top of the open door with both hands, my only other connection the front half of my feet. Most of my body is hanging substantially outside the speeding train. There is a crush of passengers. I am afraid I may be pushed out by their pressure, but I am reassured. 'Don't worry, if they push you out they also pull you in.'

Someone says: 'This is a cattle shed.'

Girish [a computer programmer and shanty dweller who acts as the author's 'sherpa'] once drew for me on a piece of paper a diagram of the dance, the choreography of the commuter trains. The Bombay Central contingent stands in the centre of the train from Borivali to Churchgate. The people around them move clockwise around the BC contingent like this: first are the Jogeshwari batch, then Bandra, then Dadar. If you are new to the Bombay trains, when you get on and are planning to get off at, let's say, Dadar, you must ask, 'Dadar? Dadar?' And you will be directed to the precise spot where you must stand to be able to disembark successfully at your station.

The platforms are on different sides of the train. There are no doors, just two enormous openings on either side of the compartment. So on arrival in the station, you must be in position to spring off, well before the train has come to a complete stop, because if you wait until it's stopped, you will be swept back inside by the people rushing in.

In the mornings, by the time the train gets to Borivali, the first stop, it is always chock-full. 'To get a seat?' I ask. Girish looks at me, wondering if I'm stupid. 'No. To get in.' This is because the train in from Dadar has started filling up from Malad, two stops ahead, with people willing to loop back.

It doesn't help to travel in first class, which is only marginally less crowded during rush hours. Girish's brother Dharmendra has a first-class season pass. But when the train is really crowded, he'll go for the second-class coaches. 'In second class they are more flexible. First class, you'll have some Nepean Sea Road type. He won't move; he'll stand where he is.'

I mention to Girish a statistic I'd read, about the 'super-dense crush load' of the trains being ten people per square metre. He stretches out his arm, says, 'One metre,' and makes a calculation. 'More,' he says. 'More. In peak time, if I lower my arm like this, I won't be able to raise it.'

Many movements in the trains are involuntary. You just get carried along; if you're light, you might not even have to move your legs. In 1990, according to the government, the number of passengers carried in a nine-car train during the rush hour in Bombay was 3,408. By the end of the century, it had risen to 4,500.

According to a letter to the *The Times of India* by G.D. Patwardhan: 'This is a mockery of our statutes, which lay down the precise number of live animals – cows, buffaloes, goats, donkeys and so forth – that can be carried in a wagon of specified dimensions. Any breach of such rules is an offence punishable under the railways' own disciplinary action procedures and also under the Prevention of Cruelty to Animals legislation. But no such rules and legislation govern the transportation of human beings.'

When I ask people how they can bear to travel in such conditions, they shrug. You get 'habituated'. You get 'used to it'.

The commuters travel in groups. Girish travels with a group of some fifteen people who take the same train from stations farther down the line. When he gets on, they make space on their laps for him and have a pot-luck breakfast together; each of them brings some delicacy from home – the Gujaratis batata paua, the Telugus upma, the Bhaiyyas alu-poori – and they unwrap their contribution in the cramped space of the compartment.

They pass the hour agreeably, telling jokes, playing cards or singing, sometimes with castanets on their fingers. Girish knows where the best singers are on each train. There is a group on the 8.15 that sings nationalistic and anti-Muslim songs very well. There are others who specialise in bhajans, and in call-and-response chanting. Thus the journey is made bearable for those who get a seat, and diverting for those standing. When Girish worked for Kamal right there in Mira Road, he continued taking the train to Bombay Central once a week, just for the pleasure of breakfast with his train group.

The trains are a hive of industry. Women sell underwear in the ladies' compartment, huge abdomen-high knickers that are passed around and inspected, the money passed back through many hands for those bought. Women chop vegetables for the family dinner they are going to cook immediately on reaching home. The ads on the Bombay locals are the same as the ads in the New York subway, dealing with indescribably private subjects: haemorrhoids, impotence, foot odour. In this safely anonymous mass, these ads can be perused; there is comfort in knowing that these afflictions of the body are universal, shared by the flesh pressing all around. They too need these pills and potions, this minor surgery.

The western branch of the train terminates in beauty, the eastern branch in horror. On the Churchgate train, past Charni Road station as it sees the sea, past the gymkhanas – Islamic, Catholic, Hindu, Parsi – as the shacks fade away, Bombay becomes a different city, an earlier city, a beautiful city. All of a sudden there is the blue sky and the clear water of Marine Drive, and everybody looks towards the bay and starts breathing.

The eastern branch, the Harbour Line, towards its end passes slowly through people's bedrooms: in stretches the shacks of the poor are less than a metre away from the tracks. They can roll out of bed and into the path of the train. Their little children come out and go wandering over the tracks.

Trains kill more than a thousand slum dwellers a year. Others, who are on the train, are killed by electricity poles placed too close to the tracks as they hang on to the train from the outside by the windows. One such pole kills about ten commuters a month as the train comes rushing around a curve.

One of Girish's friends on the 9.05 from Jogeshwari was killed when he was hanging from the window and a pole loomed up, too close, too fast. Just the previous year another of that group, playing the daredevil by riding on top of the moving train, was hit by an arch and survived. Girish muses on the injustice of the two accidents. The show-off survived and the shy window-hanger, to whom Girish had only minutes before offered a place inside the train, died.

Paresh Nathvani, a kite dealer from Kandivili, performs a singular social service: he provides free shrouds for those killed in train accidents. About a decade ago, the kite merchant saw a man run over by a train at Grant Road. The railway workers tore down an advertising banner to cover the body. 'Every religion dictates that the dead be covered with a piece of fresh white cloth,' he realised. So every Thursday, Nathvani visits four railway stations and supplies them with fresh shrouds, two metres each. The biggest station, Andheri, gets ten shrouds a week. The stationmaster initials a ledger that Nathvani maintains and stamps it with his seal. He runs through 650m of cloth a year. But it's not enough; it's a long way from enough. The trains of Bombay kill four thousand people yearly.

The manager of Bombay's suburban railway system was recently asked when the system would improve to a point where it could carry its six million daily passengers in comfort. 'Not in my lifetime,' he answered. Certainly, if you commute into Bombay, you are made aware of the precise temperature of the human body as it curls around you on all sides, adjusting itself to every curve of your own. A lover's embrace was never so close.

Asad bin Saif works in an institute for secularism, moving tirelessly among the slums, cataloguing numberless communal flare-ups and riots, seeing first hand the slow destruction of the social fabric of the city. Asad is from Bhagalpur, in Bihar, site not only of some of the worst communal rioting in the nation but also of a gory incident where the police blinded a group of petty criminals with knitting needles and acid. Asad, of all people, has seen humanity at its worst. I asked him if he feels pessimistic about the human race.

'Not at all,' he responded. 'Look at the hands from the trains.'

If you are late for work in the morning in Bombay, and you reach the station just as the train is leaving, you can run up to the packed compartments and find many hands stretching out to grab you on board, unfolding outwards from the train like petals. As you run alongside the train, you will be picked up and some tiny space will be made for your feet on the edge of the open doorway. The rest is up to you. You will probably have to hang on to the door frame with your fingertips, being careful not to lean out too far lest you get decapitated by a pole placed too close to the tracks.

But consider what has happened. Your fellow passengers, already packed tighter than cattle are legally allowed to be, their shirts already drenched in sweat in the badly ventilated compartment, having stood like this for hours, retain an empathy for you, know that your boss might yell at you or cut your pay if you miss this train, and will make space where none exists to take one more person with them.

And at the moment of contact, they do not know if the hand that is reaching for theirs belongs to a Hindu or Muslim or Christian or Brahmin or untouchable, or whether you were born in this city or arrived only this morning, or whether you live in Malabar Hill or New York or Jogeshwari; whether you're from Bombay or New York.

All they know is that you're trying to get to the city of gold, and that's enough. Come on board, they say. We'll adjust.

342-MILES-A-DAY TRAVELLER WINS COMMUTER AWARD

Godfrey Barker

The 'Commuter of the Year' award was presented yesterday to a structural engineer who travels 342 miles a day and describes himself as 'going rapidly round the twist'. Mr Barry Haddow's journey begins at 6.20am in the Welsh mountains and ends at 9.20am in his Marylebone office.

He was met on his arrival at Paddington yesterday morning by Tony Brandon, the BBC's early-morning disc jockey. Mr Brandon handed over the prize – an AA atlas – to a bleary-eyed Mr Haddow, forty-four, who had written in to claim the title as the person commuting furthest by any form of transport on a daily basis.

Later Mr Haddow explained his conditions for maximum comfort on British Rail: a back-to-the-engine seat (to avoid the rising and setting sun), in the centre of the carriage (not over the wheels), and the *Daily Telegraph*.

Mr Haddow spends £1,200 a year in rail fares and about £500 on taxis. It's all made worthwhile by the five-figure salary he earns from various oil companies. 'London's where the work is, I'm afraid,' he said.

Mr Haddow, 'a creature of habit at 5.50 in the morning', paid British Rail's high-speed train service from Newport the compliment of being 'pretty good'. It takes one-and-a-half hours each way. But before he gets to Newport station he has a 14-mile drive through the Welsh countryside, watching balefully for slow-moving sheep. He usually gets home by 7.15 p.m.

'I think you've got to be pretty philosophical about it. Maybe the *Telegraph* will advertise the right job in South Wales,' he added.

RIDING OUT HOMELESSNESS ON A TURIN TRAIN

Alison Clements

An Italian pensioner who was unable to pay his rent has slept each night for the past year on a train from Turin to Savona and back.

Signor Giovanni Spinoglio, sixty-two, said he was unable to face 'living like a tramp' in Turin hostels, so he spends his occasional earnings as a car-park attendant on a £50 monthly ticket to make the seven-hour round trip twice a day. 'The carriages are heated and there are essential hygiene services,' he said. 'On a train the hours fly by and I can get off when I like and have a chat with the railwaymen.'

Signor Spinoglio, whose difficulties began when he was thrown out of his lodgings because he could not afford the rent, insists he is not a tramp. On some trains in Italy, unlike those in Britain, it is possible to get a good night's sleep without paying for a sleeper compartment. Seats that remain upright during the day can be pulled down on both sides to form beds, and ticket inspectors rarely disturb travellers.

Signor Spinoglio says he needs only 5,000 lire (about £2.50) a day – for cigarettes and coffee – and the price of his ticket, because he is fed by charities. His night journey begins at 1 a.m. in Turin where he boards the train for Savona. His alarm wakes him at 4 a.m. when the train arrives and he gets off and awaits the return train, arriving back in Turin at 8 a.m.. He takes breakfast with the San Vincenzo religious community, lunches in a hostel for the poor, and by 2 p.m. is back on a train for Savona.

Signor Spinoglio is one of many, according to an information officer at Turin station: 'The ticket inspectors on the 3.20 a.m. from Savona say the train is full of people, many of them questionable types, who are obviously on board for a bed.'

A HORSE IS A SAFER BET THAN THE TRAINS

BORIS JOHNSON, TRYING TO TRAVEL FROM LONDON TO NOTTINGHAM, FINDS HIMSELF 'IN A CRAPSHOOT WITH THE DEVIL'

At moments of supreme stress a little John McEnroe voice comes on in my head, shrieking against the injustices of fate. Out of good manners, I try to bottle him up, but the other day he was beside himself. 'You cannot be serious!' he shouted silently, as the man from Midland Mainline gave his latest bulletin on the health of the signals ahead.

I closed my eyes, sank back on the bubblegummed seat, and tried to control the raging homunculus within. For a moment or two, by chewing my tie and digging my nails into my palms, I was able to subdue him. But then there was another wretched apology over the loudspeaker, and my internal McEnroe lost it altogether.

'No!' wailed the voice in my skull. 'I just do not believe it! You,' said Mac, directing his wrath at the goon from Midland Mainline, 'are the pits of the earth!' And as the minutes swirled into the gutter of history, and as the entire carriage babbled around me into their mobiles, I found myself twitching and barely restraining the McEnroe bawlings in my skull. I faced a national humiliation, worse than appearing on any comedic quiz show.

I was about not to appear on television. Across the country, thousands of people - well, hundreds; oh all right, call it a few dozen; at any rate, a handful of friends and family - were staying up to watch me on *Question Time*.

And what would they see? What would the producers put in my place? A tub of lard, no doubt, or some amusing straw-topped effigy. A train that was meant to be going to Nottingham had spent two hours going nowhere, and as I conferred with the BBC producer on the mobile, his voice started to rise in pitch so that soon it resembled the aero-engine howl of the demented intracranial McEnroe. Bedford, as the poet Edward Thomas might have said, yes, I remember Bedford, because one afternoon, the 5.40 from London stopped unwontedly for a quite unconscionable time. It was late June.

I say all this because later that night the BBC was to broadcast that I, the Tory representative, had let the side down by 'missing the train', an allegation silkily repeated by Sandi Toksvig, the Liberal Democrat.

Ladies and gentlemen of the jury, I did not 'miss the train'. I caught the train I intended to catch – the 5.40 – because in my doubtless naive way I believed the promise of Midland Mainline that it would deliver me to Nottingham shortly before eight and in good time to record the show.

I forgot that these days catching a train from London to Nottingham is like going from Delhi to Rawalpindi. I forgot that we have now – in the succinct view of Peter Hain – 'the worst railways in Europe'. I forgot that to rely on a train, in Blair's Britain, is to engage in a crapshoot with the devil.

In the sense that I forgot this dismal reality, I suppose I am to blame. But who do I really blame for this intergalactic cock-up? I don't blame David Dimbleby: the show must go on. I don't even blame Skandi Tostbread, the achingly correct Liberal Democrat, though I wouldn't be surprised if she had a hand in it somewhere. I blame the government. I blame this hopeless and incompetent Blair ministry, because if Edward Thomas were alive today, and he were to be inspired to write a poem about a train conking out in late June, there is one word he would not use, and that is 'unwontedly'. To be stuck on a train, imprisoned in some inexplicable siding, forced to stare at the same dusty buddleia, must be about the most wonted experience that can befall the modern British passenger.

Indeed, a glance at the figures will show you that conking trains have become more and more wonted by the year. Get away with you, all you who reflexively blame 'privatisation'. In the six years of Railtrack, from 1996 to 2002, trains were delayed by an average of 6.5 million minutes through failings in track and signals. That figure has now more than doubled, to 14.7 million minutes per year.

Do you really think the government has improved timekeeping, by smashing Railtrack? Has it made our lives better by pouring gigabucks into a not-for-profit morass called Network Rail, a leaderless, directionless, state-owned invertebrate, run with all the panache and market sensitivity of a gumboot factory in communist Bulgaria? Of course not. In those derided days of Railtrack, do you know what percentage of passenger trains arrived on time? It was 91 per cent. Today that has fallen to 77 per cent, which by my maths means that I would have had a 10 per cent better chance of being disgorged in Nottingham on time than I do under the shambles produced by Prescott, Byers and Darling.

Yes, there were problems with the method of privatisation. But the answer was not to destroy Railtrack, simultaneously defrauding its share-holders and depriving the railways of the means of raising capital on the markets. Yes, there were accidents, as, alas, there always will be. But 1998 was the first year since 1902 not to produce a railway fatality; safety actually improved under privatisation; and it was just crazy to respond to the Hatfield disaster by digging up miles of blemishless track, and imposing such exacting safety requirements that the trains of Britain crawl across the landscape like wounded worms. And all the while, Network Rail is so desperately inefficient that it is soaking up more than double the subsidy – £6 billion against £2.4 billion – that Railtrack received, and delivering a service that is twice as bad.

What is Labour's legislative priority, while the people suffer? It is banning foxhunting. It seems particularly brutal and unreasonable not just to take away an ancient liberty, but to stamp out the skill of cutting across country by horse. The way things are going on the roads and rail, horse might be our only sure-fire way of getting from A to B.

MY ROUND, SAYS DRIVER, AS TRAIN IS STRANDED

Michael Fleet

Wales

A train driver took eighty passengers for a drink when a tree blocked the line, stranding them in the country.

As rescuers worked for more than an hour to clear the tracks, Richard Mayrick, fifty-nine, led the way to a nearby public house. Then he bought £100-worth of drinks for the delighted commuters and earned a pat on the back from British Rail for his initiative.

His Manchester-to-Cardiff train was forced to stop at Wem, near Shrewsbury, Shropshire, when gales brought down a tree. 'I was told it could take some time to clear the track, so rather than just leave everyone sitting there I decided to take them to the pub,' said Mr Mayrick.

'I checked with my local manager that it would be all right. I told the passengers to have whatever they wanted, and although a lot were a bit hesitant at first they soon got into the swing of things.'

The Albion had been having a quiet night. Mrs Joyce Chapman, the landlady, said it turned into the busiest she can remember. 'I had to ask two of my regulars to help me behind the bar.'

Mr Keith Farr, a British Rail spokesman, said Mr Mayrick, from Merthyr Tydfil, Mid Glamorgan, had shown great initiative and confirmed that British Rail would foot the bill. 'We like to think we have greater awareness of our passengers' needs these days and the driver did the right thing,' he said.

Mr Mayrick insisted it was all in the line of duty. 'I had a few drinks waved under my nose, but I had to drive the train later.'

LIVES ON THE LINE

ANDREW EAMES MEETS THE GANG THAT WALKS ONE OF THE LONELIEST RAILWAYS

Donald Mackay is a peeway man in a place where working on the peeway (permanent way) is a pretty permanent way of life. With his pipe and fish-plate spanner he has been walking the line from Inverness to Wick and Thurso for twenty-three years and his uncle trod the same stretch before him.

The rest of the gang of five based at Rogart station are pretty permanent too: on average they have served seventeen years each, have walked their thirty miles of track nearly a thousand times and no one – they're all under fifty – looks like giving up for many years to come, health and privatisation permitting.

Jobs in this area of Sutherland have never been easy to come by. The last advertised vacancy for a trackman received a flood of applicants. Despite a basic salary of just £146 a week, the Rogart gang are grateful to be there.

And the job requirements? 'Big feet, strong back, weak brain,' comes the chorus from around the table, where the conversation more often than not centres on the quality of sheep rather than sleepers. Four of the Rogart five are crofters with livestock. 'There's more to talk about with sheep,' ventures one. 'That's a matter of opinion,' chides the one who isn't. 'I'd rather talk about women and football.'

Conversation pieces or not, the sheep certainly benefit from the track-walking crofters, particularly during lambing. 'If I saw a ewe in trouble, I'd jump the fence and lamb her straight away,' says Donald. 'Of course,' he adds, thoughtfully, 'I'd have to catch her first.'

Despite only three trains a day in each direction, this remote line receives the same amount of attention as the national average: every week every yard of the nation's 23,000 miles of permanent way is walked at least once by one of 20,000 trackmen, no matter how hard it is to reach.

Track-walking from Rogart was once a solitary and risky business. Now it is just solitary. Until ten years ago, teams of three men were allotted to long stretches of lonely line, which they had to reach by whatever method they could (bicycles, says Donald) and walk in their own time, watching their own backs and carrying their food with them. When the weather deteriorated they took refuge in little trackside bothies in the middle of nowhere and, in the old days of steam engines, would signal to the passing driver to drop off lumps of coal to keep the bothy fires burning. Many a long story would be told waiting for the weather to lift.

It was during those more hazardous years that Donald's uncle died while walking the track alone. The alarm was raised when he failed to return to the station in the evening. The gang set out in pairs to look for him and it was Donald and a colleague who found him. He'd suffered a heart attack. 'By good luck he just fell by the side,' says Donald. 'The two midday trains passed him. If he'd fallen over the rail, it would have been nasty.'

This is not the place to get into difficulties. Donald prods the horizon with his pipe. 'That way is a fair bit before you come to anything,' he says, with typical understatement. And the other side? 'That way too.'

Rogart may be remote, but the area to the north is about as remote as you get on British Rail, miles from any road. For maintenance, the track gang has to wait until the day's trains are finished before travelling out by night on a motorised trolley.

The track-walkers have the track to themselves. Radio signalling operated from Inverness has dispensed with isolated local signal boxes and has improved safety standards. When a train has passed, the peeway men are given complete control of their sector of the track via a radio set in their lorry and can start their solitary walking safe in the knowledge that nothing can enter their sector and run them down.

There have been incidents. Derailments have carved their signatures in the wooden sleepers ('Coal wagon, 1978,' grunts Donald, identifying a set of scars), but today's most frequent casualties are the deer, with several carcasses a week. Removing them can be a deeply unpleasant task.

However, all agree that maggots in the ballast are better than midges. When the wind drops these little tormentors rise from the tracks in clouds and the track-walkers have nowhere to run. 'At times it's enough to make you sick,' says Donald. Each walker is provided with a protective mesh hood but these tend to make the wearer sweat and the midges more frenzied than ever.

This day, Donald has found nothing untoward on his stretch and nor has anyone else. In this job, finding nothing is good news. A few 'keys' had popped out between sleeper and rail, and a couple of fishplate bolts needed tightening. Birds were singing in the birch, the roe deer were being stand-offish and the lambs were approaching mutton. We met no one and came across nothing unpleasant deposited by passing trains.

When they're not walking the line alone, the gang gathers to mend fences, clear culverts or improve corners. A distant urban office decides the speeds ('Probably all done on computers,' says Donald) and sends instructions on the angle at which the corners should be banked by sweat and strong backs. Year by year the line has steadily improved and has no particular restrictions – 'but it'll be a great number of years before we see an InterCity up here'.

Undoubtedly. This year has seen a reduction in service (last year there were four trains a day in each direction during summer, now there are three) and the track-walkers' employer, retitled Infrastructure Services, has been readied for privatisation. The regulator has guaranteed another seven years of operation, but the Rogart peeway men can't help but feel that their jobs are on the line in more ways than one.

The alternatives? Going away for work, probably. Survival in Sutherland has never been easy, not even for livestock. 'Up here,' says Donald, 'one sheep is another's worst enemy.'

Meanwhile, he's content to be out walking the track.

CHAPTER 8
FELLOW TRAVELLERS

_____

SIZING UP THE COMPANY

JONATHAN ROUTH FIGURES OUT HOW TO GET HIS OWN
WAY ON THE TRANS-SIBERIAN

(Extract)

First shock, and without doubt the biggest shock of our whole trip, is to discover that Trans-Siberian No. 2 is all four-berth compartments. In ours, in the bottom two berths, are two middle-aged ladies. The sudden prospect of seven days and seven nights perched on the top berths with the lack of privacy they are going to provide is a formidable one. And what about changing into my railway pyjamas in front of them? We [he and his wife] have about fifteen minutes in which to decide whether or not to call the whole thing off. We go through the various stages of 'But there must be some mistake,' 'I'd never have come if I'd known it was going to be like this,' and 'Let's see if there isn't an empty compartment somewhere and alter the numbers on our tickets to its number.' But there is obviously no mistake, equally obviously no empty compartment. It is going to be like this if we stay.

As the train moves off we are seated opposite the two ladies – the one a nurse, the other a school teacher, both attached to an American oil company, and they are travelling this way to Japan because it is cheaper than the air trip. (Maybe, but it is also twenty times longer. The fare, incidentally, from London, inclusive of all meals and overnight stays, is £190.)

Seated opposite these two oil women we exchange mutual commiserations because they too had gained the impression from their travel agency that they would be travelling in some privacy. Grand opera is blaring out of the speakers in each compartment and corridor. A gloom as long as the Siberian winter is settling over us.

Twenty minutes later it has become a way of life. We have found the knob that controls the volume of the opera singers and turned it down to its downmost. The milkmaid has called and we have placed a standing order for two pints of soured milk to be left outside the compartment door every morning for the duration of the journey. We have found nooks and crannies in the compartment in which to conceal just enough of our luggage so that at any rate two of us may stand up at the same time.

We can now get down to first things, the first of which, if we are going to live right on top of them, is obviously to establish a relationship with the oil women. A satisfactory relationship, we reckon, will be one that bodes no complaint or argument from either of them should either of us wish the door or window open or shut, or the lights on or off. A satisfactory relationship will be one that has them asking apologetically, if not grovellingly, certainly without hope, if they want anything, but enables us to do anything we want without reference to them. The question is how to achieve this relationship.

One of the women, the more placid one, has already let slip the intelligence that she is going to miss her drop of brandy in her tea. We happen to have quite a few drops and, by sparingly prescribing it, can probably have her in our grasp. We should concentrate on finding some ways of dominating her companion who, we decide, is the sort of woman who inevitably wins, indeed sets out to win, quizzes and spelling bees. Gambling on her appetite for facts I produce the very large and rare tome I have brought on the building of the Trans-Sib. with which to tantalise her. I comment on its contents, quote interesting passages to Madam not so much for Madam's benefit as for the oil woman to overhear. The oil woman takes the bait. She starts drooling with desire to get her hands on the volume. 'I'm going out into the corridor for about four and three-quarter minutes if you'd care to have a look,' I say to her. She seizes the book rather than accepts it. So she too will now cause us no trouble. By gentle manipulation of our weapons we are going to be able to have the door, the window, the lights exactly as we want them.

THE DAY THE GROWN-UPS STOOD
UP TO THUGLETS

Janet Daley

Scenes from urban life, part 386: I am on the Tube travelling down from north London. A gang of about six young thuglets of the kind with whom we have all learnt to share our streets bursts on to the train. They are dressed in the uniform of the infant wannabe sociopath – baseball caps and hooded sweatshirts. You know the scene. They disport themselves noisily around the carriage, flinging Coke cans behind them, taking up as much space as it is physically possible for rather puny twelve- and thirteen-year-olds to occupy. (For what it is worth – since these things seem to matter so much now – they were all white.) One of them sits directly opposite me and flings himself sideways, with his legs over the dividing arm so that he can place his trainer-clad feet on the next seat. No one on the train does anything, at first.

A few days before, we had been talking at the newspaper about how intimidated respectable adults are by this phenomenon. My colleagues all exchanged their shamefaced confessions of avoiding eye contact with street gangs, crossing the street to avoid loitering louts, and generally behaving like a browbeaten captive audience to boy bravado. So I sat for only a few seconds before I thought, sod this. I am a grown woman and these are children. I leaned across, swatted the leg of the boy opposite and said, 'Get your feet down.' The effect was quite remarkable. Not on the boy himself, but on the men around us who, until this point, had apparently been deaf and blind. They were galvanised. Two of them (who I later guessed were actually London Transport employees) had been standing less than 2ft away. One of them now stood over the boy opposite me and the other one, a middle-aged West Indian man with an awe-inspiring manner of quiet authority, confronted the rest of the pack, firmly handing them back the rubbish they were strewing around the train.

From a few seats down, an older man with a patrician voice and gentle manner began admonishing the boy opposite me (who, of course, was refusing to move his feet but who looked, by this time, like a beaten puppy).

Sounding a bit like a character played by Alastair Sim, the gentleman warned him, in the good old-fashioned way, that he was heading for a life of prison or worse, and asked him how his parents would feel if they knew of his behaviour. I noticed at this point that the other boys had quietly removed their feet from the seats. A stop later and the elderly man got off. This seemed to give the boys heart and they made a show of strength.

One of them ostentatiously moved so that he could thrust a foot on to another seat. I rose and reached over toward him, intending to flick his baseball cap visor derisively. (By now the whole situation had begun to seem like an absurd – but absolutely necessary – power struggle.) When he saw me coming, he leapt to his feet in stark terror. Did he think I was going to hit him? With some real pity, I said, 'How old are you?' He replied, of course, 'None of your f---ing business'. But he, and his friends, were clearly, palpably, frightened.

Then the biggest of them – the only one who looked remotely post-pubescent, began shouting at me, 'I'll smack your mouth, you bitch,' while remaining firmly seated across the aisle. This attempted rendition of black rap patois reminded me so much of Harry Enfield's teenagers Kevin and Perry that I laughed. (Perhaps I am at an advantage here in not having led a sheltered life. For those of you who want to try this, and who may be less streetwise, let me advise: people who are seriously up to no good do not usually draw attention to themselves. Generally speaking, the more noise they make, the less dangerous they are.) At this point, needless to say, the boy who had mouthed the threat had to rise up out of his seat. He was neatly blocked in his progress by the resolute arm of the West Indian man, against which he put up no struggle at all.

The boys were taken off the train at Holborn by the two men whom I assume to be transport officials. The whole gang of them followed obediently as they were instructed. I have no idea what happened to the kids after that. For all I know, the men may have bought them ice creams. Knowing how effectual the police and the courts are about these things, I am sure they will have received nothing more from the official law-enforcement institutions than a warning.

That, after all, is only appropriate. They were not breaking the law. Their behaviour was just obnoxious, intimidatory and deliberately, but only implicitly, insulting – at least until I challenged it. What happened on the train was more significant than any official follow-up: it was the unofficial enforcement of civility and decent public behaviour which used to be commonplace between grown-ups and the young.

So unusual is it now that these boys were startled beyond comprehension or ability to cope. They were first astounded, and then afraid. This entire encounter was completely outside their experience. They had been defied by what they expected to be a cowed, passive, disparate collection of onlookers. What was most moving to me about this incident was that we who stood up to them represented a cross-cultural, cross-generational, cross-social class alliance. We were of different races, different ages, different sexes and different backgrounds, but we united, as adults, against this tyranny of children. Maybe it is fanciful to think it, but the shock of it might have been enough to put one or two of the more sensible boys off the street gang scene. Perhaps the one who held on to the arm of the kid who threatened me and told him, in a panicky voice, to 'Just calm down, just calm down'. Maybe he will be reluctant to ride the Tube again with that particular bunch of mates.

RAIL PROBLEM OF TRAVELLER
WEIGHING 50st

A short memorandum went out this week to several departmental heads of British Railways, Midland Region, giving in bald, unexcited official language the following information:

A Mr Zehe is travelling from Euston to Dublin on the Irish Mail on Saturday, 24 May. Mr Zehe is 8ft tall, 7ft 8in broad, and 50st in weight. Please make all necessary arrangements.

The 'necessary arrangements' have proved a major headache. A normal compartment, even one devoted entirely to Mr Zehe, was out of the question. For one thing the width of a compartment door is well under half that of Mr Zehe's waist measurement. [A story the following day added that Mr Zehe was the champion wrestler of Germany, and better known in the ring as 'Gargantua'.]

Railway officials studied the carriages which normally make up the Irish Mail for a place roughly 8ft by 8ft by 8ft in which a passenger could travel overnight in comfort. They found only one spot, the brake van.

No passenger is allowed to travel in the brake van, but with a 50st traveller on its hands, British Railways could scarcely adhere strictly to the letter of the railway law. The van's double doors when fully opened give a 7ft entrance, which means that 4in on either side of Mr Zehe will have to be squeezed through.

Next came the problem of a seat for Mr Zehe. In the brake van is one small seat for the guard. A normal carriage seat, in addition to being far too narrow, could hardly be expected to hold up to 700lb for several hundred miles.

The solution is now being worked out in the road vehicles department at Willesden. There, a settee is being converted into what an official described yesterday as a 'specially strong' resting place for Mr Zehe.

Railway officials at Holyhead believe that Mr Zehe will be able to get up the gangway to the ship easily – if he walks sideways. The gangway is about 3ft 6in wide, and will bear more than 50st.

A cabin has been booked for him but at present no special arrangements have been made to accommodate him in it. An official said: 'We shall get him on board even if it means using the ship's derrick.'

MR TIWARI IS MOST PLEASED TO BE OF SERVICE

THE BEST WAY TO SEE RAJASTHAN IS FROM THE PALACE ON WHEELS, SAYS **ELISABETH DE STROUMILLO**. ESPECIALLY WHEN THE TRAIN HAS SUCH A GENIAL ATTENDANT

I shall remember Saloon Captain R.S. Tiwari long after precise details of India's palaces, temples and even the Taj Mahal have blurred. For if a man can encapsulate the spirit of a train, it is Mr Tiwari. With fifteen years' experience of cosseting demanding rail travellers, he embodies the very essence of Rajasthan's Palace on Wheels.

He was probably only in his mid-forties, but so immensely dignified and upright that I couldn't possibly have asked him what his initials stood for, nor called him anything but Mr Tiwari. Solicitous but never servile, with a glint of amusement in his eyes that frequently overflowed past his luxuriant moustache into a broad smile, he attended to our needs with Jeeves-like aplomb.

From his tiny kitchen at one end of Bundi carriage, he would process proudly to the communal saloon at the other end with our breakfast, as though bearing regalia. After the first day, he never forgot who preferred tea to coffee, how we wanted our eggs cooked and which fruits each of us liked best.

He kept Bundi carriage's four cabins immaculate, of course, and produced morning and afternoon tea and mineral water on request, but he did much more besides. When my shoes got so dusty that my basic cleaning kit could no longer cope, he spirited them away and returned them gleaming – carefully held in a paper napkin to avoid leaving fingerprints.

When the bar/lounge car ran out of stamps, he walked into Chittaurgarh to buy me some – but didn't actually post my cards until we got to Jaisalmer, 'because they will go more quickly from there'.

I am sure the saloon captains of the other eleven passenger carriages were attentive, too, and certainly the stewards in the two restaurant cars and the bar were unfailingly efficient and smiling, but Mr R.S. Tiwari of Bundi carriage was something else.

Travelling as I was under the aegis of a small, specialist British company, I did my sightseeing by car rather than the buses that carried the other Palace on Wheels passengers. Most days we returned to our rolling home, having seen and done rather more than the bigger groups, slightly ahead of them, with welcome extra time to shower and change.

But on one occasion, when I reached the station forty-five minutes early, the train was still waiting to come alongside its platform and was a yawning track's width distant.

I had resigned myself to a wait when suddenly a soldierly figure in white trousers and maroon jacket appeared. Mr Tiwari had spotted me. 'Give me your things, please, and follow me,' he commanded. 'Now, wait here.' He jumped off the platform, strode over the track to the train, fetched a stool to make getting down and up again easier for me, and guided me across to Bundi with a gallantry that was nothing short of courtly.

This train succeeds the original Palace on Wheels, which had passed its prime and was in any case unable to run on Rajasthan's newly enlarged broad-gauge track. For all its wood-panelled elegance, its cool, roomy cabins with en-suite bathrooms (only the cupboard space was less than generous) and the excellent food and service, the chief joys of the Palace on Wheels were not having to pack and unpack in each new place, nor to face long exposure between them to the chaos of Indian road travel.

My fellow passengers were another plus. When the train is carrying its capacity of just more than a hundred passengers, meals are served in two sittings (with a choice of European and Indian dishes), so there is plenty of opportunity to meet people. I was part of a group that ate and chatted together, but it was a refreshingly heterogeneous one, with few members keen to discuss the relative merits of British supermarkets.

A lot of well-educated, jolly Indian families were aboard, with a sprinkle of India-based foreigners, such as the Australian couple from Bombay who bought furniture to ship to their new house in Adelaide.

There were also Indians based abroad, some visiting their land of origin for the first time. Darkly handsome Vikram, born in the US, had just graduated in classics from Harvard University; Hasan, an infant when his family emigrated, had finally, by way of Pakistan, settled in Chicago.

They were sitting at the same dinner table as Jane, an Ealing housewife who had spent much of her early life in Sri Lanka, and me, with my Indian childhood. 'If anyone were asked which of us four had lived longest in this subcontinent,' said Hasan, 'I doubt if they'd guess it was you two.'

The Hawaiian cattle rancher, making a three-month world tour with her rather younger, ponytailed doctor, had often visited India. She was now intent on buying a tea estate when they went south. 'There's just no money in cattle nowadays, honey, and it might be a cute thing to do,' she said. 'Of course I'd have my lawyers go into the deal before I bought and have a manager to run it. I'm no sucker.'

A young Japanese travel agent, checking out the train for her clients, had brought her mother along. Mother spoke minimal English but, when I gave her one of my instant-coffee sachets to cheer up a watery brew at the end of a hotel lunch (we had several of these, all very good and at extremely grand hotels), beamingly pronounced it 'deeleeceeous' and reciprocated with a Japanese cigarette.

Also good company was Lisa, a bucolic-looking widow from Bavaria. In summer, she runs a forty-bed mountain hut for long-distance walkers; in winter she moves to her house in a Corsican hamlet ('nine inhabitants, ten when I am there') to paint naif pictures. 'I have many buyers waiting for them, so in the other months I can travel: Malaysia, Madagascar, anywhere.' After the train, she planned to go to Pakistan and trek in the Karakorams.

Meeting all these people was fun, but not having to sightsee with them in impersonal busloads meant also being able to chat to local guides. Passing a score of women in luminous sarees working in a field on the outskirts of Udaipur, I asked Narpat what their menfolk did. 'Argue,' he said. 'Talk politics. Criticise someone.'

Unlike most guides, Narpat knew about plants and, when he saw I was interested, pointed out some opium fields. 'Growers are licensed by the government,' he said, 'and it buys the crops for medicinal use. If the yield is suspiciously low for the size of the field, the grower will be licensed for a smaller area next year. That way, not much gets on to the black market.'

In Jodhpur, Chittandra Singh ('call me Bobby') took pains to hunt down a pair of pukka jodhpurs for me and, in Jaisalmer, Derawa Singh, an MA in political science but also botanically literate, stopped for an unusual sight: camel-thorn bushes actually in flower (since camels seldom passed that way).

When I finally left the train, it was with real regret that I shook Mr Tiwari's hand and said goodbye. Thinking that I might send him a Christmas card, I asked whether something addressed 'c/o Bundi carriage, Palace on Wheels' would reach him. 'Of course,' he said. 'Bundi is my second home.'

DIANA RIGG AND THE RAILWAY SAHIB

THE ACTRESS AND HER BROTHER GREW UP IN INDIA. **TREVOR FISHLOCK** JOINED THEM ON A JOURNEY INTO THE PAST

(Extract)

Diana Rigg tempted me to breakfast. 'Cream cheese and Marmite,' she murmured, spreading the ambrosial goo on a fragment of toast and passing it across the swaying table. 'Isn't it bliss?' It was.

Wrapped in a thick railway blanket over her white nightdress, she ate toast and gazed from the carriage window at the unfolding camel-brown land, its scrubby trees and distant temple towers. In the early sunshine the overnight express from Delhi jogged westwards, bound for splendid Bikaner in the Great Indian Desert.

For Dame Diana and her brother, Hugh, this was a longed-for homecoming; and the journey by train perfectly appropriate. As children of the Raj they enjoyed an idyllic Indian upbringing in Rajasthan, the stalwart son and tomboy daughter of a railway superintendent, Louis Rigg, known as James. Now they were on the train to the past, searching for something of their mother and father and something of themselves.

'Dad,' said Diana, 'was a pale, skinny Yorkshire lad of twenty-two when he answered a newspaper ad and came to India in 1925.'

'After five years,' Hugh said, 'he returned to Yorkshire to find a bride and met Beryl at a tennis club. They married in Bombay cathedral in 1932 and moved into a bungalow at Bikaner. I was born in India in 1934 and mother travelled to Doncaster to have Diana four years later.'

'For us India was a wonderful adventure,' Diana recalled, 'but with some frights for my mother. She shrieked if we went out without our topis; and there were snakes everywhere, particularly in the bathrooms. The gardener showed us a snake nest and we saw the babies in their eggs.

'I spoke Hindi with my ayah and the other servants, who all spoiled me. The ayah would say "aap bahut hi badmash ladki hain" – "you're a very bad girl" – and my mother told me I talked like an Indian. She tried to keep things English and gave us the nearest thing to English food, a lot of it from tins and disgusting; although her sardine kedgeree was delicious.'

As children of the railway sahib, Diana and Hugh had enjoyed travel in a private railway carriage and now, in an echo of that luxury, they were heading for Bikaner in a private three-bedroom coach attached to the express. Two hours late, it pulled into Bikaner station. A red carpet stretched over the platform. A uniformed band banged drums and blew raucous horns. A crowd surged forward. A thousand necks craned. Diana adjusted her elegant straw hat and stepped out regally, followed by Hugh and his wife, Sue. In moments garlands engulfed them. Palms pressed together in namaste greeting.

The welcome was led by their host for the trip, Arvind Singh Mewar, the Maharana of Udaipur, seventy-sixth ruler in the world's oldest princely dynasty, a striking figure with his abundant forked white beard, his navy blazer, red trousers and yellow shirt. 'Welcome,' he boomed.

'I'm overwhelmed,' Diana said, up to her ears in marigolds.

'I know that lady,' a man in the crowd informed me. 'She is film hero.'

Another band and more garlands greeted the Riggs as they went to dinner that evening, Diana chic in a dark pinstripe trouser suit. An elderly man, Anand Singh, approached her. 'Your father,' he said, 'was a fine man, and your mother most beautiful. She taught me to dance the waltz and foxtrot.'

The next morning the Riggs drove to the engineering works their father once commanded as locomotive carriage and wagon superintendent of the Jodhpur and Bikaner State Railways. From the welcoming crowd, a jolly man stepped forward to sing a Sanskrit blessing to the children of Rigg Sahib.

'This,' they were informed as they stepped into an office, 'was your father's desk; and this the ceiling under which he worked. We have not forgotten what he did.'

'I knew you were the true son of Rigg Sahib,' a man of eighty-four told Hugh. 'You walk just like him.'

The Riggs were pied pipers as they toured the workshops. Men swarmed enthusiastically around them. 'Rigg Sahib zindabad!' they chanted. 'Long live Rigg Sahib!' The old engineer's children were visibly moved.

'I remember the smell of oil and metal,' said Diana. 'This was Dad's kingdom. He loved it so much.'

PLAYING CHESS WITH SERGEI

Martyn Harris

(Extract)

My king is a pepperpot, which falls over each time the train brakes. But all the other pieces are proper ones, apart from a pawn made from a marble and a blob of chewing gum. Sergei draws black, so I open with a dull pawn to king four, which he mimics, as he does my next three moves. I think: this is going to be a pushover.

'You like this Giuoco Piano opening?' says Sergei, and then I am not so sure.

We are strangers, sharing a sleeping car on the St Petersburg-Murmansk Express, which is tearing through the tundra at a good 7mph. He's been visiting family; I'm on my way to write about the Russian submarines in Murmansk – maybe interview a submarine officer if I am lucky. We're eight hours into the journey with twenty to go, but small talk is wearing thin. 'Ah, but I love getting back to the north,' says Sergei, and I follow his gaze to a landscape like a sheet of cartridge paper.

'Why?'

'You should see it in the summer. Four, five different kinds of wonderful berries.'

I poke a sacrificial pawn at Sergei's knight and he falls for it, giving me space for an early castle. I think: this is definitely going to be easy.

He is tall, bespectacled, with a mournful moustache. 'You do cooking and washing-up in London? My wife wants me to do these things. Also she is crazy about embroidery art. Always she wants more thread, cloth, more money. I come home, there is no soup, she says, "Fix yourself, I am working".' He pushes forward a pointless bishop's pawn.

'You have been to the Russian baths?'

'I went to the Sanduny in Moscow ... '

'Tschaa. You should go to the black baths. This is steam but also with smoke from green birch log. In Sanduny baths they beat themselves like carpets, but here in the north the beating is an art.' He borrows my scarf to demonstrate.

'On the chest you stroke the twigs. On the legs you scratch, so. And on the back, you beat with great smartness. So!' I decide he is insane but harmless, and it's only someone to pass the time with, after all. He prods another pawn vaguely into play against the gathering might of my bishop and knights. Sergei looks at his watch.

'You know in four hours' time I am free man.'

'How do you mean?'

'Tomorrow I am thirty years old, which is first date I can retire.'

'What is your job exactly?'

He moves the pointless pawn another square. 'Communications officer on atomic submarine,' he says, and I see with a sudden, sickening clarity that he has forked my bishop and knight.

BRIEF ENCOUNTER ... THE SEQUEL

FIFTEEN YEARS AGO, THE WEST INDIES CRICKET 'REBEL' **COLIN CROFT** WAS THROWN OFF A WHITES-ONLY TRAIN IN SOUTH AFRICA. ONE PASSENGER, A MIDDLE-AGED WHITE MAN, CAME TO HIS AID. LAST WEEK, THE PAIR WERE REUNITED. **PETER MITCHELL** JOINED THEM

The marketing men of South African tourism are fond of boasting that their country is a land of contrasts. Colin Croft, the West Indies fast bowler, found out just how true that is when he returned last week to Cape Town for the first time since 1983.

Fifteen years ago tomorrow, Croft made front-page news throughout South Africa when, as a member of the 'rebel' West Indies team, he was kicked off a whites-only carriage of a Cape Town train because of the colour of his skin. To add spice to the story, a white fellow-passenger remonstrated with the conductor and accompanied Croft for the rest of the journey in the third-class carriage reserved for 'non-whites'.

The incident caused great embarrassment to the apartheid government of the time, which was keen to counter the international sports boycott of the country by encouraging rebel tours. Apologies were issued, but Croft's belief that politics and sport should not be mixed had been severely tested.

Back in South Africa to write and commentate on the West Indies' first official tour of the country, Croft took the opportunity to relive the train journey from Cape Town to Newlands to experience a microcosm of the change that has taken place since the dismantling of apartheid. With the help of the *Sunday Telegraph*, he had even tracked down his white travelling companion of fifteen years ago, Raymond Roos.

The reunion provided an instant reminder of just how unlikely their original meeting had been – and not just because of their skin colours. The giant Croft, casually athletic and still the epitome of Caribbean cool at forty-five, dwarfed Roos, now seventy-two and looking rather stiff in his cricket club blazer and tie. They shook hands. 'Mr Croft, I never thought this would happen. After fifteen years ... this is beautiful,' said Roos and the two men, worlds apart but thrown together by a quirk of a reviled political system, headed for their train.

Cape Town station provided the first stark contrast. Gone were the sterile surroundings so typical of an authoritarian state. In their place was all the bustle and vibrancy of a developing country – ethnic music, fruit vendors, flower sellers, sprawling stalls of curios, fabrics, electrical goods.

'I don't recognise this at all. It was nothing like this. It's all very, very positive,' said Croft, as he bantered with the vendors and marvelled at how much his US dollars could buy.

Roos, a retired printer, had, like so many other Capetonians, warned us that the trains were not safe but, while the carriages were shabbier and seedier than they had once been, there seemed little threat as the two took up the positions they had occupied fifteen years before. It would, of course, be a brave man who took on the 6ft 5in Croft, though that did not save him from a mugging of a political kind in 1983.

'I just got on the train that day and sat down,' said Croft. 'I had no idea trains were segregated – it never came into my mind. I felt it was normal.'

Roos took up the story: 'Colin sat down opposite me. I didn't know him at all. To me he was just a person. We started talking about where he came from and about West Indian cricket when, a kilometre outside of Cape Town station, here came this little conductor. He was white, with scruffy hair, brown uniform, cap on his head … He told Colin to move because he was black.

'I thought: "No, wait a minute, as a Christian one can't allow these things." I felt like punching him. In those days it wasn't normal for black people to be thrown out of a whites-only carriage; by then things had started to change. You had to negotiate with a person, ask him if he didn't mind. But this conductor was a straight chucker-out.

'It was ignorance on his part more than anything else. The system was there but you could get around it – that's where human dignity comes into it. So I elected to stay with Colin and we both got off at the next station, Woodstock, and got into a third-class carriage, where there weren't any comfortable seats, just benches.

'Now the poor conductor didn't know what to do with me and there was a bit of apprehension from the other people in the carriage, but it was fine and they left us alone.'

Croft says he felt neither angry nor humiliated by the incident. 'I think the conductor was just doing his job,' he said. 'Perhaps he could have been a little bit flexible, but he didn't have to be. In his eyes I was just a black man.

He did what he was supposed to do. It could have been my fault, too. I should have been reading the 'whites only' signs, but not being accustomed to that sort of stuff I didn't worry about it.'

At least the 'whites only' signs at Newlands Cricket Ground had disappeared by then. 'But you never heard about that,' said Croft, who was banned for life by the West Indies for going on the tour. 'A lot of black people came to see our games, but the press never reported that. After the tour, I just went to Florida, went to university, did my own thing, because I can't deal with hypocrisy.

'I never considered myself a rebel. I was prepared to go against the boycott because of one man, Ali Bacher. He said he was trying to get normal sport in an abnormal society and that was good enough for me. I'm not into politics – I don't even vote in my own country – but that was naivety on my part. But I will say this: in retrospect, coming out here in 1983 did some good because, if nothing else, it showed that it's very difficult to have normal sport in an abnormal society.'

Two years later Croft, who was paid about US$30,000 for the tour, wrote to the United Nations and apologised, saying that his belief that sport and politics should not be mixed had been 'somewhat blind'. In 1986 his name was removed from the blacklist of people with sporting contacts with South Africa.

All of that is water under the bridge for him now. 'Fifteen years is a long time and things have changed in South Africa – and they've changed beautifully,' he said. 'I know people talk about the violence and the crime, but there's no developing country that doesn't have crime. The incident with Pat Rousseau [the president of the West Indies Cricket Board] being hijacked in Soweto was unfortunate, but it could easily have happened in Jamaica.'

In South Africa things are seldom entirely as they appear. There was even an extraordinary twist to the reunion with Raymond Roos. Croft remained diplomatically silent, but was noticeably uneasy when he discovered that in the intervening years Roos had joined the National Party, the party that invented apartheid and governed the country for forty-six years, and is now an active campaigner against Nelson Mandela's ANC.

'We are fighting their absolute incompetence and corruption,' said Roos. 'They say themselves that they were taken out of the bush and asked to govern a country. And it's very difficult for them. There is so much corruption now. Nothing is healthier now than it was in the past. They've made racism illegal but now there's affirmative action [positive discrimination]. That is entrenched in the law, just as apartheid was. The biggest mistake the previous government ever made was to entrench apartheid in law. We are deeply sorry for that.'

Fifteen years ago it was members of the same party apologising to Croft for his experience on the railways. This time his journey was incident-free, but as the train pulled in at Newlands station there was one more reminder that this was not the South Africa of 1983.

The white conductor, an Afrikaner called Willie van Zyl who admitted he ejected blacks from whites-only carriages in the apartheid years, approached Croft, shook him by the hand and said: 'It's a pleasure to meet you. And I hope your team win all their Tests.' A land of contrasts, indeed.

NECDET KENT

TURKISH DIPLOMAT WHO SAVED JEWS BY BOARDING A TRAIN TO THE CAMPS

(Extract)

Necdet Kent, who has died at Istanbul aged ninety-one, was a Turkish diplomat who risked his life to save Jews from Nazi concentration camps during the Second World War.

In 1943, Kent was the Turkish consul general at Marseilles. One evening, his assistant at the consulate alerted him that some Turkish Jews living there had been loaded into cattle cars bound for a German concentration camp. Kent immediately rushed to the Saint Charles railway station.

He approached the train and, as he later recalled: 'The one single memory of that evening which will never be erased from my mind was the inscription which I saw on one of the wagons: "This wagon may be loaded with twenty heads of cattle and 500kg of grass."'

Inside the wagons, as Kent soon realised, there were more than eighty people, crammed one on top of the other. The Gestapo commander at the station, having heard of Kent's presence, approached him and demanded that he leave the site at once. But Kent, forcing himself to civility, said that these people were Turkish citizens, and that there had been a mistake, which must be immediately corrected.

The Gestapo commander answered that he was merely following orders and that the people in the wagons were not Turks or anything of the sort, but just plain Jews. 'Realising that my threats were in vain,' Kent later recalled, 'I suddenly turned to my assistant Sid Iscan and said: "Come on, let's go. We, too, are getting on this train." And, pushing aside the soldier who tried to stop me, I entered one of the wagons. Now it was the Gestapo officer's turn to do the begging. I didn't respond to anything that was said, and the train began to move.'

At the next station the train stopped and German officers boarded and apologised to Kent for not letting him off at Marseilles. A Mercedes was waiting outside to take him back to his office. But Kent would not budge. 'I explained,' he said later, 'that more than eighty Turkish citizens had been loaded on to these animal wagons because they were Jews, and that I was a representative of a government that rejected such treatment.'

Dumbfounded by his uncompromising stance, the Germans let everyone off the train, thus putting an end to this drama. 'I would never forget,' Kent later said, 'those embraces around our necks and hands ... the expressions of gratitude in the eyes of the people we rescued ... the inner peace I felt when I reached my bed towards morning.'

CHUFF, CHUFF AND BASH, BASH

BILL POWELL JOINED A TRAIN-LOAD OF STEAM BUFFS ON A TRIP FROM KIEV TO SEBASTOPOL – AND GOT BETWEEN A 'GRICER' AND HIS HEART'S DESIRE

'Some people might think that I'd wasted my life,' says Mike Hudson as the maize fields of Moldova file past our carriage window in a haze of coal-smoke and steam. 'After all, I'm a fifty-plus trainspotter who still lives with his mum in Bognor!'

In fact, Mike's appreciation of the value of time – like that of many of his fellow enthusiasts – is finely tuned almost to the point of obsession. It is all part of what is probably the grandest passion, after the weather and angling, of the English-speaking world: railways.

'Interest seems to tail off the farther you go from the cradle of the Industrial Revolution,' says Mike. 'The French are more interested in food, and you just don't seem to find any Italian trainspotters ... of course it's very big in the old Brit colonies.'

I had fallen in with a trainload of British and Australian rail buffs. Night and day the corridors of our luxury special train, on its steam-hauled progress from Kiev to Sebastopol and back, were astir with stopwatches and timetables and tales of heavy metal. These folk were dedicated 'gricers' – a term, apparently, based on the word 'grouse' and signifying one who 'bags' things.

They are an instructive lot, and if the Russian engineers were thinking of swapping engines – an FD20-2714 Nemirov-built 2-10-2 loco for one of the equally old, equally scruffy TE 2-10-0s left behind in the German retreat of the Second World War, say – I was certainly going to find out all there was to know about it.

It was catching, this virus. Soon I was slipping along to the bar of an evening for two-bottle discussions on exotic gricer topics such as de-clink-ering procedures, slippage and momentum ratios on track gradients and curing leaks in steam boilers with potatoes.

I tutted with the best of them over the loss to world civilisation of British steam-age punctuality (spot-on to within a quarter of a minute, apparently). Before long I, too, fretted at yet another unexplained halt in some nameless ex-Soviet marshalling yard. I quietly pooh-poohed the official Russian assurance that the next type of engine put on would prove more serviceable than the last. I was to be heard speculating about the sort of bribe our trip organiser was having to employ to help local railway bosses remember where they kept the keys to their water towers. Over warm Crimean champagne I demanded to know why we weren't heroically on schedule like those tatty Moscow Expresses squealing past in the opposite direction.

Mike Hudson looked glumly at the bar's kitsch clock – in the form of a giant Rolex watch – and disclosed that wonky schedules were messing up his plans: 'I'm what they call a steam track-basher, which means that for me the whole point of coming on a trip like this is to observe the route.

'So long as we are moving, under steam, in daylight, I can draw a red line on the map which means I've 'done' that particular stretch ... at night I have to make a dotted line which I hope to convert to a red line on the way back.' Hang on, let's get this straight, I thought. You have actually to see the track unfolding beneath the train?

Correct. There were enthusiasts for every aspect of railwayana, said Mike. Some were devoted to cataloguing all those dismal little cast-iron wotsits you see beside the tracks. Some were rounding up every last rivet pattern around the world. Others felt the urge to eavesdrop with stereo sound recorders on assignations between engines and viaducts ... and there were those who awaited with their camcorders the fusion of sun angle, smoke direction and track curvature in one climactic train-filled 'glint' shot. But track-bashing is probably as close as anyone could come to a pure, unencumbered rail experience.

Such philosophising was all very well but wouldn't it need a team of Jesuits to figure out the minimum light conditions necessary to 'see' a rail journey? And wouldn't Mike's dawn-to-dusk red line on the map be compromised by, for instance, a visit to the loo? 'We say that being able to distinguish the colour of grass constitutes acceptable red-line conditions,' said Mike, 'although we still haven't resolved the difficult matter of moonlight. And as for calls of nature, I usually wait until the terrain is right – where I have a good far-ahead view.'

Mike has been through Peru's railway system a couple of times without ever finding time to visit the ruins of Machu Picchu, 'but I did manage to fit in the Taj Mahal once when I was track-bashing in India. It's a matter of luck – track comes before tourism, steam before stomach.'

For rail enthusiasts of all persuasions, it's the journey alone that matters. Quite a few that I spoke to on the Crimea Express had only a passing interest (literally) in what life was like beyond the world's rail networks. Mike Hudson – his regrettable snub to Inca architecture notwithstanding – is a notable exception. Not for him the hit-and-run gricing of Petey the Aussie number-cruncher, who told me: 'Get the serial-numbers and run, that's the ticket … the world's our olive, mate, and we're out to stuff it.'

Although he doesn't readily admit it, Mike can get by in most European languages. And he turned out to be a reliable source of background information on the ex-Soviet lands we were steaming through.

Throughout nearly all of his working life, starting as a ticket clerk at Barnham Junction until early retirement this year from the passenger train running section at Redhill, Mike has managed to fit in five two-week track-bashing trips every year, seeking out steam routes wherever time and money would allow. Last year he went to Germany, Austria, Switzerland, France, Belgium, Italy and southern Poland.

In winter, Mike looks farther afield – to South America, the Philippines, India: wherever steam engines still chuff. 'Maybe I'll go back to New Zealand – and I've always meant to look at the old French lines in Africa.'

Mike's unobtrusive style contrasted with some of the videoing-frenzies that went on when our train made one of its run-bys. We would stop in some picturesque spot where camcorder brigades could detrain and set up, while the engine retreated down the line before returning in a roar-past. Then it was woe betide anyone who got between gricers and their hearts' desires or, as in my case, inadvertently made some recordable aside.

Anxiously fiddling with their equipment, our video-ers held their breath as engine 16194 (a Voroshilograd-built LVOO62 2-10-2, if you must know) puffed itself up in a theatrical cloud of steam and smoke and charged, wailing in an Armageddon crescendo. In a cigarette-break afterglow we waited for the train to compose itself again. Petey from Ballarat was not best pleased. 'Very funny. Now it's on my tape – some drongo saying the earth was moving for him,' he fumed.

Mike said I was lucky to be allowed back on board.

CHAPTER 9
FAT CONTROLLERS, THIN EXCUSES AND RAILWAY RULES

———————

17 FEBRUARY 1980

LINES THAT CROSS FRONTIERS

BYRON ROGERS MEETS THE EDITOR OF ONE OF THE MOST ROMANTIC AND CIVILISED BOOKS IN THE WORLD – THE THOMAS COOK INTERNATIONAL TIMETABLE

At eight o'clock each morning a State Railway of Thailand train leaves a Bangkok suburb for the town of Nam Tok, 120 miles away. It is a slow train. The journey takes four-and-a-half hours, and there is one stop, at 10.34 on the River Khwae Bridge.

It is such a small entry in the timetable, and yet as you read on something nags at you until, suddenly, you realise what it is. Every day the 8 a.m. out of Bangkok stops on the Bridge over the River Kwai. (The local spelling is Khwae.)

But now all rails run to Peterborough. The headlines that once screeched around the world here subside into place names and times: yesterday's wars, today's timetables. At Peterborough John Horace Price edits the *Thomas Cook International Rail Timetable*. There is no other book like it in the world.

At 9.20 each night a train moves South from Hanoi. It takes three days to cover 880 miles: again a slow train and, again, that wash of strange familiarity. At 3.16 on the morning of the second day it leaves Hue. At 8.22 it leaves Da Nang. Seventy hours after leaving Hanoi it enters what was once Saigon.

Yesterday's lost world: the 6.55 from Puno arrives at Cusco at 17.35. Yesterday's gold rush: the morning train for the Yukon leaves Skagway at

10.00. At Peterborough John Price notes them down. For the trains arrive and the trains depart, and there is nothing else at all.

In his book *The Great Railway Bazaar* Paul Theroux records a conversation with a South Vietnamese stationmaster. As his country was falling apart the man talked thoughtfully of what would result if the line to Loc Ninh were reopened. Only lay a rail to Phnom Penh and South Vietnam would be linked to the world. For beyond Phnom Penh was Bangkok and beyond Bangkok was India, and beyond that Turkey. The man had heard that there was a railway in Turkey, and beyond Turkey was Europe.

In the world of the railway enthusiast there is no geography: the engineers have seen to that. There are no politics: in Price's timetable there are no frontiers on the maps, just railway lines. Wars are only a disruption: in the table for Phnom Penh to Kompong Sam the times are recorded but they come with the rider, 'service temporarily suspended'. That phrase more than any other sums up the timetable, for at some time things will come right. Political change just leaves a wake of inefficiency, but some day the trains will run on time again.

The timetable is one of the most romantic books in the world and, in an odd way, one of the most civilised. The five hundred pages of times breathe hope and continuity. There are no shades of meaning; no fudging of truth. As John Price put it, 'You either catch a train or you don't. A timetable cannot be other than right.' At Peterborough a man stands outside history like the guardian of a lost world order.

'Some of my earliest memories are to do with trains. I remember being held up to look out of a window in Balham at the bright lights very early in the morning. They were taking down the overhead wires of the old electric railway. And I remember the house I lived in as a child when my father was a policeman in south London. At the bottom of the garden there was a shunting neck. There was an engine there all day long. Simmering.'

John Price is only the fourth editor in the 106 years of the *Thomas Cook International Rail Timetable*. He has held the post for twenty-seven years, for twenty-five of which it covered only European railways. For the last two, under him, it has covered the world. He is fifty-two, a bachelor, a stocky, intent little figure, weighed down with carrier bags full of notebooks and maps and magazines. He has kept notebooks since he was a boy, filling two a year. He notes train times and rolling stock, and transport museums and the meals he eats in dining cars. He was just back from a visit to Poland. In the notebook, in a neat small hand, he had listed details of the transport system at Łódź. Today he still has the notebooks he filled as a boy.

This enables him to say that he joined Cook's on 16 February 1948; that it was a Monday; that it was raining. When he trained as a tank driver in the Second World War, he got 96 per cent for map-reading, for John Price can also memorise maps. The mark, he said, was considered 'very unusual'. There is no false modesty to him: there is no point in that.

'I once went to Blackpool to see the lights and to stay with a friend. But when I got there his house was empty. His mother had been taken ill. So I took a bus back to the town. Everywhere was full. It was midnight. But in the station there was a midnight excursion back to Coventry, wreathed in steam. I caught that. At a quarter to two it stopped at Crewe, but not at a platform. There was another train between it and the platform. I jumped on to that and through it to the platform. At 3.30 there was a sleeper coming through from Perth to London. They're not booked to stop at Crewe, but they do. I was home at 8.30.'

When he indexes the London-Scottish sleepers now it all comes back. He is proud of that night. 'Anyone who didn't know his railway system would have gone very badly wrong there,' said John Price.

The Second World War did not cause much of a disruption in his life: he did not allow it to. For most of it he was too young, and could note down, with enormous joy, the antique engines that had been pressed into service. When he finally got to Germany after the war he managed to get himself posted to the Hanover garrison. Hanover had a very large and undamaged tram system. He spent his time off learning German so that he could talk to tram operators. The army, he said, furthered his education.

At the same time he confused the British military authorities by writing letters asking what had become of requisitioned trams. He received in return stiff letters saying that this was a political matter. John Price grinned. 'Then I'd beaver around and write and tell them I'd got the information from the Model Railway Club.'

Leaves were spent in East Berlin riding happily on the Underground shadowed by Russian soldiers. His attitude to modern frontiers is much like that of a citizen of the Roman Empire. But they are of interest if the rolling stock is different.

There were no doubts as to a career. 'It had to be trains, or travel.' British Rail offered to start him as a booking learner, but Thomas Cook offered to push the horizons back by employing him to work on Continental routes. In June 1950 he joined the *European Timetable* as editorial assistant. He does not have the date for that. 'Black mark,' said John Price. Two-and-a-half years later he was made editor.

The timetable had begun as a handy alternative to *The Bradshaw Continental Railway Guide*, which by 1873 was a vast one-thousand-page volume attempting to cover every European line. From 1883 the Cook's timetable was published monthly. The First World War was marked only by an irritated reminder to its readers that the Belgian, German, Russian, Australian, Balkan and Turkish services were those in force before hostilities broke out. The editors of the timetable have always been aware of their responsibility. Publication was suspended during the Second World War, however, and only resumed in 1946. The European Bradshaw did not survive the war, and the British guide ended in May 1961.

On his appointment John Price discontinued the geographical maps used since the beginning. Under him there were to be no frontiers. And so time passed, interrupted only by the requests of writers for the menus, stops, rolling stock and engines of the Orient Express. In twenty-seven years John Price has had a bellyful of the Orient Express.

Then, in 1977, they went worldwide. A French company had tried it in 1949, but had failed. The French had to be dependent on what they were sent. 'But we had the offices abroad and we could check. I don't think there is anyone else in the world who can do this.'

Price and his staff of eight spent three-and-a-half years assembling the information. Things were complicated by the fact that Burma Railways were in the habit of amiably chalking up train times on a station board, and that Cuban Railways did not reply at all. Things are much improved now. For the past six months or so Burma Railways has owned a typewriter. 'With figures,' breathed John Price. An Embassy official sent a photocopy of the *Cuban Times*. From Angola came a wild 'revolutionary greetings' on notepaper with Portuguese Republic crossed out and Popular Republic of Angola typed over it.

The Mexican Chihuahua-Pacifico Railway sent every brochure they had, including menus. Some Indian railway even sent advertisements: 'It is only when you work pure and eat pure, that you live long and remain strong. Mustard oil produced by Young Oil Expeller has 100 per cent purity.'

Information poured in. Nigerian Railways boasted they had 219 steam and 101 diesel trains. Alaska Railways claimed passengers stood a better chance of seeing moose and grizzly bear from their cars than from those of any other line. Madagascar Railways helpfully sent details of their parcels organisation called EXTRA-MAD.

To qualify for inclusion a train must run at least once a week. They do not claim to include all the passenger trains in the world, only those the international traveller is likely to take. 'We are Thomas Cook and we know where people want to go,' said John Price loftily.

The South American trains are like an ulcer to him. There is Ecuador, which does not seem to know what times its trains leave, or where they go when they do. Price had again to enlist the aid of the British Embassy and received a mournful letter saying that the whole system was not long for this world.

Argentina looks good. Every December a long and detailed timetable appears: but things are complicated by the fact that the railway company spends the rest of the year crossing out services, often at a week's notice. It is hard when you are six thousand miles away and believe. John Price sniffs nostalgically about the good old days of Perón, when a general sat in the front room, but a Scottish engineer sat in the back making the whole show work.

There is never a breath of politics in the letter. 'We rely on radio and the press to know about the shootings.' But politics leave an echo. Recently the Barcelona and Bilbao timetables have come in with covering letters in Catalan and Basque. And in Mauritania the trains started running again from 1 November. 'Something must have happened to the Polisario rebels,' said John Price.

He grieves over Canada, where the state took over the passenger railways this year and is locked in conflict with the unions. Seventy hours before the new timetables came into force telexes went round the world cancelling them. The result was that trains left Montreal and Toronto and nobody knew what timetables would be in force when they arrived in Vancouver.

John Price has been watching events in Zimbabwe Rhodesia with great interest. On its outcome turns a whole new entry in his book, the passenger trains to the north – at present what he describes as a suspended service. A terrible silence hangs over that other suspended service, in Kampuchea.

Some countries have no railway systems at all: Afghanistan, Iceland, New Guinea, Mauritius, Honduras. Haiti has a railway but no trains. There was even a train that disappeared: the Italians built a line out of Mogadishu, but the tribesmen stole the rails. On the east coast of Africa, in the interior of Somalia, are mud huts with steel lintels.

The timetable has become so popular that of its annual sales of 167,500 two-thirds go overseas. 'We're in the export business,' said John Price. Because of the rising postal charges they use very light newsprint, and have even adopted the bizarre practice of cutting down on advertisements: 'It grieves our accountants.' But when you guard civilisation the message must get through.

'Any railwayman with a proper identity card can turn up on any railway in the world and travel at a privileged rate, provided the booking clerk can understand him. Railwaymen aren't politicians. Left to themselves they love to supply us with information, if only to see what's going on in the rest of the world, and whose trains are fastest.'

He spends all his holidays on trains. On the last steam trains of South Africa; on the narrow-gauge rails of the French Alps; in the Isle of Man when this year the island celebrated the centenary of its electric railway. 'Quite unrepeatable opportunity.'

And then perhaps he can forget the neat, cruel letters: 'Dear Mr Price, As an addicted and unashamed railway traveller of the world … I am pleased to write to correct an error in your South American section …. The error is on table 2212, Puno to Cusco. The times are right but now the trains run *every day* … '

A pea under the 18th-century mattress has nothing on an error in table 2212. For a moment in Peterborough a world order trembled.

But it was restored. John Horace Price amended table 2212.

SERIOUS REVISION

Peterborough

These are testing times for the compilers of the railway travellers' bible, the *Thomas Cook European Rail Timetable*, published since 1873. The changing face of the Continent means that the long-suffering editorial staff are rarely seen without a correcting pen in hand for last-minute alterations.

In what was East Germany, Karl Marx Stadt has become Chemnitz Stadt, while in Yugoslavia, Kardeljevo has become Ploce. Spain, Lerida, San Sebastian and Vitoria have been adjusted to accommodate Basque or Catalan equivalents.

'We've still got Leningrad in,' says Dave Gunning, one of the team. 'They've voted for a change but it hasn't happened yet.' But current concerns may pale into insignificance depending on events in Yugoslavia. 'Each state there once had its own railway company,' says Gunning. 'What would happen if the place broke up I shudder to think.'

YOU CAN TAKE IT BY RAIL

May Abbott

Mr Stanley Raymond, who took over this week from Dr Beeching, will no doubt quickly discover that railway passengers are an ungrateful lot.

During 1963 nearly 1,000 million passenger journeys were made. How many travellers paused in their endless grumbling to examine, not only their own responsibilities as ticket holders, but also the liberal privileges and 'concessions' available to them?

Ask a random sample, for instance, if they know in what circumstances they could take their canoe with them free of charge. How many could reply at once: 'Providing it is folded and packed in a kitbag or rucksack and weighs not more than 60lb'? How many appreciate that they can put their playpen in the guard's van at no extra cost, as long as it has no rugs or sawn-off shotguns or other articles folded inside it?

Railway travel, like marriage, is a matter of give and take. Each time a passenger buys a ticket he is, in effect, saying 'I will' by entering a contract to observe the by-laws ... only to flout them with contempt. For example, his accompanied luggage may look impressively 'one-up' when plastered with labels for Nassau and Syracuse, but he is in flagrant breach of the regulations ('all old or conflicting labels or addresses must be removed or entirely obliterated') if he is merely humping it from Nuneaton to Stoke-on-Trent.

One can only marvel at the tolerance of British Railways. It permits us to carry on to the train any article, possession, tool or thing used for the purpose of our profession, trade or vocation, in our free luggage allowance of 100lb (or 150lb, if travelling first). But there are provisos. It would be unwise to ask one's mother-in-law to help to carry the blowlamps, as tools must be carried by hand by the passenger himself. Nor should one's instrument or thing cause inconvenience to others, thus apparently excluding twangy wire lawn-rakes.

In any case, one should avoid taking tools of trade onto excursion trains, whose passengers are limited to a free luggage quota of 60lb on the return journey only, whether travelling first or second. An excursion train is a great leveller.

So is fish. Or, for that matter, fowl or good red herring. It is reassuring to know, when democracy is so often in peril, that a first-class traveller may take up to 60lb of his free luggage in the form of bloaters, or a second-class traveller up to 60lb in smoked salmon (or vice versa) if these are goods he is going to sell himself (but he must not sell them wholesale).

The more one studies the rules the more one appreciates the pains that have not been spared in meeting the needs of minority groups. Thus lecturers and people giving public or trade demonstrations, or representatives of religious, philanthropic, educational or scientific bodies, or theatrical companies, or equestrian performers leaping about in colourful breeches, each of these passengers may take 1.5cwt of masks or test tubes or saddles or bottles of carpet cleaner free (3cwt if he can afford to travel first). Lecturers, however, may not bring their cylinders containing gases.

It is heartwarming to picture these people, with their professional paraphernalia, traversing the realm quicker by rail while motorists and professors with their noxious gases are sweating it out in a five-mile jam on the Exeter bypass.

Yet a note of mild rebuke disturbs the otherwise harmonious theme. 'Theatrical groups or parties shall not combine to pay for more tickets than there are passengers in order to obtain an extra allowance of luggage.'

Railway benevolence is not confined to humans. Should you absent-mindedly leave your bird (feathered) on the luggage rack it will be fed, until reclaimed, for 3s a day – costly for a budgerigar, undoubtedly a bargain for a falcon or a macaw. The price of feeding a lost dog is 7s a day.

Is there one bowler hat on the 8.15 who knows that he may park his stove in the left-luggage department for the day for 1s, or his bedroll for 1s 3d? Is there one who is remotely grateful for the facility to leave his ice barrow there, or his tandem with sidecar, for 3s?

Most contingencies have been foreseen. If the length and girth together of any article exceed 25ft, a treble charge will be made. Officials possibly have in mind the wedding guest who takes his own marquee to the reception. But passengers who study the book of regulations, subject to which all tickets are sold, will appreciate not only that the onus is on them to get into the right train and to alight at the right station, but also that, although their alpenstocks and fishing rods in wooden cases could properly be despatched as luggage in advance, it would be absurd to expect the same arrangements for their camera stands and model yachts.

Here, however, a difficulty arises. Despite notices to the contrary at booking offices, the book of regulations is not always available for inspection. Inquiring at Waterloo, I was sent from pillar to post by officials struggling to live up to their own regulations. The book was not to be found.

INDIA TRAINS 'IN THE LAP OF THE GOD'

Peter Foster
New Delhi

India's railway minister has come up with a novel excuse for the appalling safety record of the world's largest railway network: he blames it on Vishwakarma, the Hindu god of machines.

'Indian Railways are the responsibility of Lord Vishwakarma,' said Laloo Prasad Yadav. 'So is the safety of passengers. It is his duty, not mine.'

India's 67,000-mile rail network, on which 1.4 million people are employed, suffers from decades of chronic underinvestment.

Accidents – three hundred a year on average – are a permanent hazard for the thirteen million passengers who use the railways daily.

Only last month twenty people were killed and about a hundred injured when a train fell off a bridge in western India, after hitting rocks on the line.

Mr Yadav, a low-caste activist who is a key ally of India's newly elected left-wing government, is not generally expected to improve matters. To date, his biggest policy initiative has been to order replacement of plastic cups on trains with earthen ones – a move calculated to benefit the potters in his home state, Bihar.

25 APRIL 2002

GERMANS RECREATE LITTLE BIT OF ENGLAND

Paul Marston

A German train manufacturer has spent £7 million damaging its test track to replicate the dilapidated network used by its British customers.

Siemens, which is building nearly eight hundred new vehicles for South West Trains, has deliberately inserted gaps between sections of rail, made track heights and gauge widths uneven and installed an erratic electricity supply to recreate the commuter routes of southern England.

The company says it wants to ensure there are 'no surprises' for its trains when they enter service in Britain over the next two years. Siemens invested £50 million five years ago in setting up the four-mile circuit at the former RAF base at Wildenrath, near Dusseldorf. Though the company makes trains for more than twenty countries, it has never previously had to downgrade the test facilities.

As the equipment was demonstrated yesterday, Hans Schabert, the company's vice-president, said engineers had run special data-monitoring trains over routes to and from Waterloo station in London to compile an exact picture of the network conditions.

Siemens has also placed blocks of dry ice and pieces of fibreglass resin on the tracks to simulate winter weather and 'leaves on the line'. Andrew Haines, managing director of South West Trains, said: 'It's a step backwards for them in technical terms, but the result should be better for our passengers.'

RETURN OF THE BRIGHTON BELLE KIPPER

Sir – What a way to run a railway! While I was abroad and thus not looking, a committee of catering executives at St Pancras (why St Pancras?) proved themselves utterly out of touch with the public taste by wiping kippers off the menu of the *Brighton Belle*.

Southern trains may occasionally run late; guards may want, as who does not, more money; and the trains themselves may split in half; but one thing, 'void of stain or smutch', the Southern did to a turn. They served a kipper cooked to perfection. When boarding the 11 p.m. *Belle* to Brighton I would inquire: 'Any kippers tonight?' Should the reply be 'Sorry, sir, we've run out,' or 'They went bad passing Haywards Heath on the way up,' my journey became a mockery.

Now, thanks to Sir Laurence Olivier and other kipper enthusiasts, the St Pancras executives have had a change of heart. They are forthwith reinstating the kipper on the *Brighton Belle*.

Not even when nightly strangling Desdemona at the National Theatre did Sir Laurence act to more noble purpose.

Collie Knox, Garrick Club

CHAPTER 10
GOING UNDERGROUND

---

14 JANUARY 1995

GREATEST SHOW UNDER THE EARTH

SO WHERE'S THE DANGER? IN NEW YORK, STUART REID BOLDLY GOES WHERE OTHERS HAVE WARNED HIM NOT TO TREAD

A woman with thick, pouting, purple lips is reading *Sex and Gender: An Introduction*, and highlighting passages with a yellow marker pen. By the door a Chinese man is earnestly studying *Wellness: 101 Tips for Health*. Next to me a blonde is picking over the food page of the *New York Times*. She looks up and says: 'What was that? A bird?' It certainly sounds like a bird. A black woman with orange hair sitting opposite us has a large plastic bag at her feet. She pulls back a corner to reveal a cage. 'Parakeet?' asks the blonde. 'Uh-huh,' says the woman with orange hair.

I am on the A Train, heading south on the 31-mile run from 207th Street on the northern tip of Manhattan to the beaches of the Far Rockaways on Long Island. I am among the Subway people: Hispanics, African-Americans, Indians, Chinese, Koreans, Italians, Hassidic Jews, Berbers, Samoans, Greeks, Aztecs, Tatars … plus people of no identifiable ethnic group: the sort of broad-faced, empty-eyed creatures you see confessing to incest on Oprah Winfrey's show. There are Wasps too (but not many): men in suits reading the *New York Times*; women in suits reading the *New York Times*.

Subway riders read a lot and care about their skin. Jonathan Zizmor, a dermatologist, has advertisements everywhere. 'Tired of that tattoo?' says one. 'Get rid of it with Dr Zizmor's NEW laser treatment. Great for brown spots too.' Another outfit, Manhattan Dermatology Associates, promises to treat ringworm, torn earlobes and skin cancer with 'a holistic approach'.

The Park Avenue Breast Center has a picture of a woman looking as though she is constipated. 'It's only 1.30 p.m.,' runs the copy, 'and already Gloria's neck and shoulders hurt ... She's one of many women who suffer needlessly because she's carrying too much weight up front. We have helped hundreds of women through breast reduction.'

Chinese traders hawk cheap clockwork toys from wickerwork baskets — performing seals, waggy-tailed dogs, pigs that skip, racing cars. The Chinese hold their wares aloft for general inspection, wind them up and then set them on the floor. 'Wun dolluh,' they say (a yo-yo); 'fi' dollah' (a performing seal). Their English is not good but they can add up fast — and they carry mobile telephones.

New York is the greatest show on earth, and you miss a lot if you don't ride in that hole in the ground. Most Englishmen therefore miss a lot, because most Englishmen, like most Americans, are scared of the subway.

But the only thing you have to fear is fear itself; and perhaps the occasional encounter with a knife-wielding psychopath. Your chances of being murdered, though, are slim. The subway carries 3.4 million passengers a day, and last year was the scene of a mere 11 murders. By contrast, in the city as a whole there were 1,600 homicides.

So, by New York standards, the subway is safe. The trains themselves are spacious, air-conditioned and reasonably clean. You use tokens for your ride. Each token costs $1.25 and is good for a journey of any length. The network seems dauntingly difficult but with a little goodwill you can master it in a couple of days.

That's not to say that everything smells of roses. Urine, carbolic and sweat, occasionally leavened by coffee and doughnuts, are the smells of the subway. The entrances to the stations remind one of public conveniences in the more run-down areas of British cities. In the summer it is disgustingly hot down there; even when the temperature is in the sixties above the ground it is uncomfortably warm.

But let's not be wimps: if you can't stand the heat you should stay out of the Big Apple. Besides, the subway takes you where you want to be far more quickly than bus or cab. Naturally, as in any jungle, it helps to employ guides. When I took the A Train from 51st Street to 207th Street I did so in the company of my wife, who was brought up in New York, and her elder brother, a former Jesuit seminarian and now a nightwatchman in Queens. My brother-in-law is 6ft 2in, not the sort of person to mess with. As it turned out, I needed no protection. It was a peaceful ride with only one incident, and that on the return leg.

At 200th Street three transit cops, hips heavy with night sticks, revolvers, radios and handcuffs, boarded our car. They looked casual, unconcerned, the way characters do in a Quentin Tarantino picture before something really dreadful happens. At 190th Street, they converged on an old black man with a hearing aid. 'Would you step off the train, sir,' they said. He looked bewildered. What could he have done? Maybe he was a drug dealer, or a child molester or, just as likely, a victim.

We came up for air in Brooklyn and made our way on foot and by cab to the East Village, where, in a small and noisy bar, we met my wife's other brother, an anthropology major from Fordham University, who works in a second-hand bookstore on Lower Broadway.

He refuses to join us on the subway. 'You've got to be crazy to go down there with those psychos,' he says. The bar itself seems to be full of psychos telling O.J. Simpson jokes, some of them very funny. But enough is enough. When a couple of girls from Newcastle upon Tyne, tight and giggling, start playing Abba songs on the jukebox my wife and I leave.

It is raining. Foolishly, we decide to take a cab rather than the subway. On Third Avenue a cab stops and two men get out. One is thin and unsteady and is carrying a Snapple bottle, though Snapple is not necessarily what it contains. His companion says to him: 'We'd better get that hand seen to.'

My wife and I get into the cab. There seems to be something shiny on the plastic seat cover. 'What's that?' I ask. 'Blood?' My wife jumps into my lap. 'Wassa goin' in da back?' says the driver, looking over his shoulder through the bullet-proof glass that separates us.

'Your last fare had a wounded hand, and I think there's some blood on the seat,' I reply sternly. 'Sheeze,' says the cabbie. 'Anything else?' My wife looks down. 'There's a shirt on the floor,' she says. The driver slams on his brakes.

Yellow cabs, limos, delivery trucks bounce over the potholes on either side of us. Rain soaks down. The driver gets out of his seat, opens the passenger door and, gingerly but with grim determination, hooks the shirt out of the back of the cab with his right shoe and kicks it into the street. 'Sheeze,' he says. 'There are some crazy people in this city. That's for sure.'

Over the next two days I stick to the subway. I go to Coney Island on the B Train: a dull and lengthy journey because of a fault on the line, but I enjoy a paddle at the beach (later, my sister-in-law, a psychiatric nurse in Albuquerque, New Mexico, says that she would not even put her pinkie in the water at Coney Island, for God's sake); and I go to 125th Street (now Martin Luther King Jr Boulevard) in darkest Harlem and walk four mean blocks to Malcolm X Avenue.

I am jumpy but no one bothers me. When I bump into a (black) man I apologise as though my life depends on it. He says: 'Sure', which is what checkout girls say when you thank them.

Nobody bothers me on the subway, either. But beggars can be tiresome. Some make their way up a carriage on their knees, hands clasped together, like holy Mexican women approaching a Marian shrine. Others announce: 'I take pennies', the idea being that no one can refuse to part with a cent; but they can, and do.

At 59th Street and Lexington Avenue a man with no legs is being pushed in a smart wheelchair by a friend, who takes him down the escalator to the E Train platform, then helps him out of the wheelchair, sets him on his stumps and leaves. On the train the man uses his arms to swing down the aisle. He bangs a tin. People look the other way but in a moment of disgust and guilt I give him some silver.

On my last night in New York it occurs to me I should go to the Bronx. But it is raining; I am tired; and my in-laws say that I must on no account go near the place. I weaken. 'Oh, very well,' I say. 'Let's send out for some more pizza.'

Or, as Ogden Nash put it: 'The Bronx? No thonx.'

LONDON ELECTRIC RAILWAY

Today his Royal Highness the Prince of Wales sets the seal of his presence on the formal completion of an undertaking the full importance of which will in all likelihood be gratefully remembered by the travellers of the coming generation.

The Prince will open the first electric railway constructed in the metropolis, and henceforth to be known as the City and South London. Here we have got another instance of the marvellous uses to which we have put our good friend the fairy Electra, whose headstrong ways and hitherto undisciplined waywardness have been so successfully conquered and disciplined by the wise men of science ... it is pleasant and comforting to record that under royal auspices she will make her debut in London this week as an underground traveller.

Of surface electric railways we have many examples, such as that at Brighton, and the pleasant little line that in noiseless security carries the tourist from Portrush to the Giant's Causeway in Antrim; but this is the first time we have applied the power to that ingenious invention of modern days – underground travelling. We were justly proud of ourselves when we first hit on the idea of borrowing a hint from our blind but astute friend the mole, and adopting his subterranean method of travelling; but every Londoner knows how, in spite of constant strenuous scientific effort, the discomforts of our habitual burrowings continue to vex under the rule of steam.

He who adventures passage by our justly popular 'District' or 'Metropolitan' must be prepared for much noise, smoke, evil smells, rattlings and grindings, and laborious descents and ascents at either end of his gloomy journey. It is brave news to hear that most, if not all, of these disagreeable features are expected by the experts to vanish, or at all events be reduced to a minimum, in the good time that is at hand.

It will be seen, from the accounts we recently gave of the new enterprise, what will be the lot of the traveller on the line which the Prince of Wales opens today, when he is borne under the bed of the Thames from the

Monument to that great and growing city over the water that we know as south London. Sinking into the earth on one of the lofty hydraulic lifts capable of holding fifty people – half a trainful – the passenger, having paid his twopence at the turnstile, for ticket-taking is to be happily abolished, will find himself at the bottom of a well, roofed by a comfortable red-brick dome.

Here in the pear-shaped arched station there will be waiting for him a dainty little toy train, consisting of three comfortable cars, open from end to end on the American plan, and lit by electricity. The ten-ton locomotive will set in action its 'motors,' and with its three 'brushes' begin in noiseless and decorous fashion to sweep up travelling force from the 'working conductor', which has been described as 'a steel channel or rail, resting upon glass insulators attached to the sleepers, and which looks to the untechnical eye like a third rail in the permanent way, and which absorbs electric energy at each station when the main cable is "tapped"'. The force once summoned into action, away slides the little train, and, as it 'sweeps up' energy and activity at every moment, it may fairly be said of it by any scholarly engineer on the staff: 'vires acquirit eundo'. The train enters an immense cast-iron tube, and, travelling at the rate of 15mph, plunges under the clay and gravel that lie at the bottom of the Thames, and in one short and, let us hope, by no means bad quarter of an hour the traveller will slow up on a slightly rising gradient and find himself at Stockwell, on the other side of the water, having thus, as it were, linked two great nerve centres of our vast Metropolitan system.

There can be no doubt but that many travellers more or less illustrious will follow the Prince's lead through this important three-and-a-quarter miles' dive, and admire the engineering skill that has, after four years of constant work, triumphed over so many difficulties, but the imaginative mind will go much farther than the recognition of English science and the closer connection now drawn between the City and the Clapham Road.

Poet and philosopher alike will look far away from the immediate practical boon conferred on the dwellers by the historic hostelrie of the Elephant and Castle, and the advantages offered to City men with a taste for cricket and football, who, it may be, will make hold to steal an hour from business, and be flashed, or 'brushed', or 'swept up' to their pet Oval to snatch a glimpse of some big game.

Far wider prospects develop themselves as we remember the oft-repeated Cassandra-like warning that one of these fine days our coal supply will be necessarily limited, and that consequently steam as a motive power will become abnormally expensive. How are we to get about the world and our business and our pleasure when we have dug up all our available coal and have not yet succeeded in extracting sunshine from cucumbers and turning it to a 'motor'? True, we constantly hear of mysterious 'motors' of transatlantic origin, but their secrets are as yet as indefinable and inscrutable as their solvency; and in such a far-off prospective dilemma as we imagine – it is only right to say that we have quite enough coal to last our time – it is comforting and logical to prophesy to posterity that they will find a firm friend and amiable ally in the pet child of the 19th century – electricity.

'The beginning is the half of all,' says Lucian, in his quaint personal 'dream dialogue,' and, as we have pretty little electric boats skimming through the reaches of our upper Thames, so some day we shall no doubt 'accumulate' ourselves across the Atlantic. As the heir apparent is now to be 'flashed' swiftly and safely from King William Street to the Clapham Road, so, before the ultimate decade of the looming 20th century we may hope for a condition of things that will enable the poorest mortal to post himself electrically, say, in the words of the poet, 'from Camberwell to far Cashmere'. No doubt a few old fogies in the coming race will continue to take pleasure in coaching and cycling and walking tours; but, if rapidity and ease of transit are to be among the necessary conditions for the existence of the forthcoming 'struggle-for-lifers', as the French have it, then we must give glad welcome to the latest onward move, and in all cordiality echo the prevailing sentiment of the scientific world, and cry long life to Electra!

LEARNING TO LOVE THE TUBE

THE BOMBINGS IN LONDON REMIND
ANDREW MARTIN OF HIS OWN INITIAL RELUCTANCE
TO VENTURE UNDERGROUND

When I heard about the bombs on a news bulletin, and how they'd been concentrated on the Tube, I thought of a boy I knew when growing up in York in the 1970s.

He was called Alistair. He would often go down to London but never used the Tube. 'You sit sideways on to the direction of travel,' he would say. 'It's not right – sets your head spinning.' On my own trips from Yorkshire to the capital I was also wary of the Underground, even though, as the son of a B.R. employee, I had an allowance of privilege tickets for Tube trains as well as ordinary ones. As far as possible I would navigate the capital on foot, marching wearily up to those street maps that used to dot the West End, only to discover that the crucial bit reading 'you are here' had been blotted out by vandals.

'Well, I'm knackered,' I'd think to myself, 'but at least I'm still alive, which I might not be if I use that Underground.' On arrival back in York I would return a full complement of unused Tube privilege tickets to my father, but he would not make any comment. He understood.

The defining quality of Londoners was that they were willing to ride on Tube trains. Did this make them more primitive, or more advanced? It certainly made them different, and if Tube travel was the price they were prepared to pay in order to live in London, then it might just be the wonderful place they all claimed.

Through a young northerner's eyes, the trains in which they travelled were entirely alien. There was no discernible locomotive; the front looked just the same as the back. The driver, often wearing a V-necked jumper, lacked all glamour; might even have been a filing clerk. He made incomprehensible announcements over the PA, and would drive in a series of mad dashes punctuated by abrupt stops, often in the middle of tunnels, at which point you would enter a limbo quite at odds with the raucous streets above.

There would be strange noises, the long, meditative whirring of the engine, the distant echoes of other trains in other tunnels, a sudden haunted-house whoosh of air. And the longer you waited, the more oppressive seemed the weight of earth above you.

As I willed the train to move I'd be thinking about the engineers who built the system. They'd been Londoners, yes, and therefore unknowable, exotic. But presumably they'd all been experienced men, with all the proper qualifications and certificates?

After university, I came to work in London as a journalist. At first my nervousness on the Tube persisted. I used to knock about with a bloke (also newly arrived in the capital from the provinces) who could mimic all the alarming Tube train noises with uncanny skill, and, knowing my nervousness, he would go through the full repertoire if we got stopped in the tunnel. But I tried to take my cue from experienced Londoners: the businessman in the corner who continued turning the pages of his newspaper as smoothly after the train had stopped in the tunnel as before.

I became used to the underground; and felt that I'd become a true Londoner when I instinctively moved down along the carriage without being asked. I began to read up on the Underground, and then an editor on a London magazine offered me a column on the subject. By now, my view of the system had been transformed. Far from being a series of anonymous conveyor belts, the Underground, if you used your eyes, was a repository of the charm and idiosyncrasy that has long since disappeared from the 'proper' railways. I had far more letters to my Tube column than to any other I've written, often putting questions expressive of affection tinged with cynicism and satire.

Was there ever a situation where the front of a Tube train was in one station, while the back was in another? (No, but you come close to that between Leicester Square and Charing Cross.) Why is there such a gigantic pipe across the platforms at Sloane Square? (It contains the Westbourne River, and it shakes in heavy rain.) How do Tube drivers obtain the cups of hot tea they often carry? (There are kettles waiting at 'tea points' around the network.) As you head west and face the direction of travel from Shepherd's Bush on the Central Line, the eastbound platform is on your right, but at the next stop, White City, the eastbound platform is on your left. Why? (The answer is far too fraught to set out here.) Is there really a man who goes around the system killing pigeons with a hawk? (Yes.)

I came to appreciate that riding on the Tube was not a mug's game, but a privilege. It was the oldest, largest, most complicated and beautiful system of urban transport in the world, full of surreal lacunae, which seem to be encapsulated in the famous warning 'Mind the gap'. If you look at a diagram showing the tunnels going into and out of Camden Town, it's like an Escher drawing, an optical trick. You can't trace the line of them with your eye. So complex is the Northern Line at that point that Harry Beck, designer of the Underground map, agonised for years about how best to depict the location of Mornington Crescent station.

I found that I could talk 'Tube' with a wide range of Londoners. A high percentage appreciated the art deco suburban stations of Charles Holden, which are like a series of space ships that have landed, for their own strange reasons, at Arnos Grove, Southfields, Cockfosters; people knew why there was a Mill Hill East station but no Mill Hill West. It wasn't like an interest in overground railways, which is something technical, entirely male-orientated.

And those who didn't know about the history could talk about the people. Londoners are not supposed to look at each other on the Tube, whereas in fact they pay extremely close attention, but furtively. After a while I stopped regarding the crowds flowing through Tube stations as a mass of transport consumers, so many victims – of delays or worse – in the making. I would look at the faces and think: the Tube is both because of them and for them. The Underground system is London, determining its very size and shape.

Sometimes I met Londoners who were refuseniks – those who boycotted the Tube, usually because of claustrophobia. One woman, who'd been involved in one of the very rare Underground accidents, told me that she could not even look at the page on which my column appeared. I felt sorry for her. It was one thing to be nervous of the Tube if you were from outside London, but these people had been denied their true birthright – and this because they were mired in strict rationality. If you stop to think about it, mass transit underground remains the startling, phantasmagorical concept it appeared when first introduced. In 1865 Lewis Carroll was going to call *Alice in Wonderland* 'Alice's Adventures Under Ground', but the recently opened Metropolitan line so horrified so many people that his publishers advised him to make this the subtitle.

The Metropolitan Line was a bold leap indeed, and Tube travel in general represents such a high level of imagination and civilisation that an attack upon it by the fundamentally jealous was inevitable. Every Tube user knew this, and yet continued to ride the trains. Was it because they had no choice? I'd rather say that the mysterious arteries of the system have become analogous to those within their own bodies. The Underground runs through the bloodstream of Londoners, and the terrorists will need to do more than they did on Thursday to change this.

DANS LA NUIT, SOUS LA TERRE

ANDREW MARTIN IS TRANSPORTED, IN MORE WAYS THAN ONE, UNDER THE STREETS OF PARIS

It was a Saturday night in January, and I'd been told to report to Porte des Lilas station, near the end of Line 11 on the Paris Métro, for 11.45 p.m. At 11.30 p.m., I was standing outside the station in a drizzle, reflecting that Porte des Lilas was analogous to Totteridge and Whetstone, a dullish sort of place.

After 11.40 p.m. I became aware that I was not the only person hanging about the station, and ten minutes after that I noticed I was the only person once again. Everybody had drifted off around the corner, where I saw a steel door: an elevator. I stepped inside, and descended to what I later discovered was the 'quai mort', or dead platform, of the otherwise fully functioning station.

The quai mort last saw regular passenger action in 1939, and accordingly was a little tatty. It corresponds to one of the two equally dead platforms on the London Underground at Aldwych, in that it impersonates other stations in films. Watching an excited crowd assembling there beside the special train, I was required to believe many impossible things.

First, there was a man in a straw hat playing a barrel organ. The tune, bizarrely, was 'New York, New York'. Farther along, some men were drinking beer and coffee at a portable mini bar that had been erected in the centre of the platform, as though in an attempt to contravene as many Métro by-laws as possible in one go – although I stress that the tour took place strictly according to regulations.

The 'Nuit en Métro' tours are organised by Ademas (Association d'Exploitation du Matériel Sprague), a society named in honour of Frank Sprague, an engineer who created the classic Métro rolling stock: spartan trains with hard wooden seats that served Parisians between 1908 and 1983, and were loved for the way they flickered and banged. During the tours (which happen every few months, and are advertised on the internet and by word of mouth) Ademas members wear straw hats, for a reason I never quite got to the bottom of. I should also mention that there is an overlap between Ademas and Parisians interested in old musical instruments, hence the barrel organ.

This may be just my Francophilia, but I would describe the Ademas lot as intellectual rather than trainspotterish, and whereas my previous guided tours of the London Underground have included a female quotient of approximately none, the crowd here was an equal mixture of men and women. Parisians have a reverence for 'les ingénieurs', and see the Métro for what it is: an efficient and beautiful utility. I asked one of the Ademas chaps – a classical pianist, unsurprisingly – how he explained the presence of the crowd of two hundred or so. 'This is their city, and they like to know how it works,' he said. I countered that in England an interest in the Underground is taken as proof of lunacy, and he frowned. 'Why?' he said.

At shortly after midnight, the shout went up that it was time to leave; the barrel organ and the portable bar were rolled on to the train, and we climbed aboard. As we began to move, the train tannoy crackled, and an Ademas man welcomed us in Latin. 'Jovis erepto fulmine per inferna vehitur Promethei genus,' he said, which means, 'Prometheus's children are transported in the underground inferno with the power of Jupiter.' These are the words of Fulgence Bienvenue, the engineer (and classical scholar) who built most of the Métro, beginning in 1900 with the line that is still marked number one; and 'Jupiter' means electricity.

I was wondering whether the whole commentary would be in Latin when the announcement came, in French, that we were heading along the surviving stretch of the abandoned extension towards Haxo station, which was completed in 1921 but never opened. It was dark, icily cold, graffiti-covered and sinister.

After ten minutes we were on board again and flying across Paris. The commentary was too fast for me to follow, but the spectacle made up for it: the tunnels of the Métro are not 'tubes' but wider, brighter, and more interestingly troglodytic, with dramatic flyovers or fly-unders that make for ease of signalling.

The Métro was built faster than the Underground – it was largely complete by 1913 – and more rationally. The wider tunnels also allow nocturnal maintenance to be done with the current left on, which in turn permits the all-night tours. The stations were all brightly lit, and some still contained stragglers from the late trains: 'Les voyageurs ordinaires,' as our guide haughtily put it. Then suddenly we were at Place Monge, on Line 7, where we reversed, in a northerly direction, onto Line 10.

This was the location of our next abandoned station: Croix Rouge, which was closed in 1939 as a war economy and never reopened, although in the early 1980s sand was spread across the platform, and it was decorated as a lit beach scene for the amusement of passing commuters. But there was no evidence of this frivolity, and the barrel organ was playing a blues to go with the ghostliness of the station, which was dominated by a huge ventilation fan. The portable bar was rolled out here too, and shouts of 'Le bar est ouvert!' echoed along the platform.

More dreamlike flying through stations, a few with tramps sleeping in them … Then, at 2.15 a.m., we pulled into Porte d'Auteuil – a depot on a spur of Line 10 – where we contemplated ranks of trains before going on to St Martin, a closed-down station between Strasbourg St-Denis and République. Here, we were guided along passageways boasting beautiful ceramic advertisements from the 1930s.

At 3.15 a.m. we pulled into a driver training depot directly under Gare du Nord. At each of our previous destinations, slightly gruff-looking Metro officials had been waiting to make sure nobody attempted to walk along the tracks, but here they were pouring Champagne. With our drinks in our hands, we were invited to file along underneath our train, which had been parked over an inspection pit, so that we might gaze upwards at its innards.

The final highlight came as we trundled along the overground portion of Line 2. It gave a panorama of Gare du Nord, which was empty of people but packed with slumbering trains; we then crossed back onto Line 3, as our guide recited a poem incorporating the name of every Métro station.

We arrived back at the Porte des Lilas quai mort shortly after 5 a.m., to be greeted with hot chocolate and croissants. I then made my way across to one of the working platforms of Porte des Lilas where I waited no more than ninety seconds for a train to take me back to the centre of town. The whole event – surreal, cerebral, replete with civic pride and masterly train craft – could only have happened in Paris.

114 METRO MILES – FOR JUST 7p

A retired railway planner from England claimed a new world record yesterday after travelling the entire Moscow Metro system – 114 stations and 184 kilometres (114 miles) – in 493 min 21sec.

Mr Eric Rudkin, of Lexington Road, Derby, made his trip on a holiday. He paid only 7p for the whole Metro journey. He said that starting at another station would have cut the cost by half.

SOZZLED IN THE SUBWAY

IN THE TOKYO UNDERGROUND, **HUGH FEARNLEY-WHITTINGSTALL** FINDS WELL-DRESSED DRUNKS ARE PART OF THE FURNITURE

There is a poster which you will encounter in almost every Tokyo underground station. It is a view of a subway platform, inevitably not vastly different from the one on which you are standing. But the picture is distorted, as if reflected in the kind of trick mirror that makes everything look bendy.

It is also out of focus. In the centre of the image is a man in a suit, also bendy and out of focus. The effect is somewhat disconcerting – the eye darts quickly back to the real platform for reassurance.

For several days, as I travelled the Tokyo underground, this poster bugged me. It had no text, so presumably delivered its message purely by means of this image. Yet I could not interpret it. Finally I asked a Japanese friend to decipher. 'It is a warning,' she explained, 'to drunk people on the subway. It means if they cannot see properly, they should stay well back from the edge of the platform.'

Shinjuku station, Friday, 7 p.m. From more than forty platforms, trains are leaving every few seconds, heading north, south, east and west to Tokyo's commuter belts. In the next five hours, nearly half a million people will pass through this labyrinth, the King's Cross of Tokyo.

At the bottom of the escalator, a man lies supine, motionless. In New York or London you would probably step over him. A bum, a casualty, what can you do?

In Tokyo no one helps either. Yet it is not a blind eye they are turning, but a seeing one. They have a word for his sort: salaryman. Look a little closer. His shoes are polished and new. He is wearing a belted fawn mackintosh, as are many of those who step over him. His suit may be crumpled, but it is not threadbare. And he is wearing a tie.

It is not that those who pass him by are indifferent. They simply assume that in a couple of hours he will wake up. He will have a headache, but he will catch the last train home – as they always do themselves.

On the London Tube, anyone clearly the worse for alcohol might be given a wide berth by other passengers. Come 10 p.m. on a Friday evening in the Tokyo subway, there are barely any 'others'. Most make it on to the train, but even there befuddled salarymen slump on the seats, the head of one on the shoulder of another. The sober minority raises no eyebrows. What may seem to us a gross invasion of personal space is to them just 'the way it is'.

It is a tolerance bred of security. Drunkenness may be rife, but subway crime is almost non-existent. In 1992 there were fewer than thirty serious assaults on the Tokyo underground, compared to London's eight-hundred-plus. Here in Tokyo alcohol does not spell danger. It does not even seem to predispose the drinker to anti-social behaviour. Inebriation is the socially acceptable pressure-valve for long hours, hard work and corporate loyalty.

The poster, then, is no big-brotherly admonition to lay off the booze – just a friendly reminder to the intoxicated not to stand too close to the edge. Nor is it the only thing to be found on the underground that is of express benefit to the sozzled salaryman. Vending machines, of which there may be half a dozen on one platform, specialise in extra-strong coffee, black and sweet, and antacid sodas. For the morning after, there are special 'stamina drinks' – concoctions with vitamins, caffeine, nicotine and other stimulants to revive the wobbly workforce.

The attitude of the subway staff towards their hard-drinking customers is at worst indifferent, at best sympathetic, even kindly. Most salarymen are left to sleep it off. Occasionally a pair of uniformed guards will remove a body causing an obstruction, and place it somewhere more convenient, more comfortable.

There is no shortage of personnel to perform such charitable acts. The reputation of Tokyo's underground for cleanliness and efficiency is unsurpassed. The fact is that it is also the most heavily staffed in the world. During the rush hour, as many as six uniformed and white-gloved inspectors may be employed on a single platform to shoehorn the mass of humanity into the carriages. For all its technological wizardry, Japanese management knows no better solution to a business problem than a hefty dose of man-hours.

Seven million Japanese spend up to three hours a day on the Tokyo subway. Occasionally, in this surreal atmosphere of cleanliness, security, efficiency and sanctioned inebriation, something extraordinary happens.

One evening at Roppongi station, some time close to midnight, I saw a portly, drunken salaryman stagger off a train. As the doors closed behind him, a tiny woman squeezed through them in the nick of time. She tapped the man on the shoulder, and stretched out her hand, palm up. He struggled to focus on it, then began nodding and smiling with animated delight. He took something pink, white and shiny from her hand, wiped it cursorily on his coat lapel, and placed it in his mouth. It was a set of false teeth.

CHAPTER II
STEAMED UP

---

4 JULY 1938

BRITISH TRAIN SPEED RECORD ·

A speed of 125mph – 11mph more than the previous British record for steam locomotives – was attained yesterday by an L.N.E.R. streamlined engine, *Mallard*, on a test run between Grantham and Peterborough.

Mallard, with tender, was drawing a streamline train of seven coaches, to which was attached a dynamometer car with instruments to confirm the speeds. The train carried only engineers and staff.

The speed of 125mph, registered when the train was approaching Peterborough, was maintained for 306yd.

Previously 120mph had been kept up for three miles beyond Little Bytham station.

The engine was driven by J. Duddlington and fireman T.H. Bray, of Doncaster. Locomotive Inspr J. Jenkins, of London, was also on the footplate.

The previous British record was held by the L.M.S., whose locomotive *Coronation Scot* attained 114mph on a stretch near Crewe on 29 June 1937, while the L.N.E.R. Silver Jubilee train registered 113mph on 27 August 1936.

The world record for steam locomotives is claimed by the United States with 127mph. Britain holds the record for the highest sustained speed, an average of 100mph for nearly 43 miles, set up by the engine *Silver Link*, drawing the Silver Jubilee train, on a test run in 1935.

'These tests are made to discover what locomotives are capable of doing,' Mr W. Whitelaw, chairman of the L.N.E.R., said to a *Daily Telegraph and Morning Post* representative last night.

'Such a test as today's shows how much power is held in reserve. I think the travelling public has the right to know how much there is in hand.'

THE FINAL MILEPOSTS

'You see something for your work on a steam engine,' said Alec Mackay, the fireman, as he prepared to shovel three tons of coal between York and Edinburgh. 'You go home tired from a diesel.'

Alec Mackay is an unshakable devotee of steam engines, like so many other railwaymen. But steam is fast disappearing from British Railways, and on Friday another chapter in railway history came to an end when the Elizabethan Express pulled into Waverley station, Edinburgh.

It was the last run of the world's longest and fastest non-stop steam-hauled express – 392½ miles from King's Cross to Edinburgh in 395 minutes. Soon the diesels will have taken over the East Coast route, rapidly becoming one of the most modernised sections of British Railways.

Appropriately the Elizabethan was hauled for the last run by *Mallard*, holder of the world speed record for steam of 126mph, and designed by the late Sir Nigel Gresley, the last of the long line of great British railway engineers that began with George Stephenson and *Locomotion* at Darlington.

For many people British Railways are unfortunately personified by the unhelpful porter on a city station. But what of the operating railwaymen, on the footplate, in the lonely signal box, or maintaining the track, the men who keep the wheels turning night and day to carry more than 1,000 million people a year in almost total safety?

They are none-too-well paid; a driver may average £17 a week over the year, a fireman £13, though top men can make more. But almost all in my experience are men with a pride in the job too rarely found elsewhere today. Railway work – significantly, the men always refer to the 'service' – calls for steadiness, reliability and integrity of character. It is no coincidence that the railwaymen of France provided the most trustworthy element in the Resistance during the war, or that the months-long strike of Dutch railwaymen was one of the greatest collective acts of defiance of the Germans.

Travelling to Edinburgh in *Mallard's* cab, I saw something of British railwaymen and their work. Our two crews – a corridor through the tender allows them to change over without stopping – were as typical as you could find.

From London to York the driver was Harold Birkett, a quiet, unshakable man with forty-seven years' service behind him, yet still basically a countryman, and his fireman John Thorne. At twenty-two, Thorne is unusually young to be working a crack express. He is passionately interested in railways; modernisation made him redundant at Nottingham, but he moved to London rather than leave the service.

At York Alec Mackay and Bob Currie, the driver, came on to the footplate. Currie, who began as a train register boy in 1913, shared his fireman's enthusiasm for steam. 'It's a real pleasure to step on to an engine in good form like this one,' he told me.

Their two London colleagues preferred diesels. 'But,' said Driver Birkett, 'it's not so easy when you're turned sixty to go back to school and learn about electricity, wiring and all the other details.'

There are other snags, too. 'You can always keep a steam engine going and you can always get a bit more out of it. But when a diesel stops, it stops.'

It is the steam engine that is the more sensitive machine, and part of the satisfaction of driving one lies in its responsiveness to the crew's skill. A computer can calculate the performance and timing of a diesel engine; its maximum load and speed is pre-ordained. The machine is master. The diesel driver merely releases the power already there. Steam is a craft, the crew jointly creating and utilising power.

'No two drivers are alike,' said Mackay. 'A fireman can soon tell the difference between a driver and a hash … ' 'And a good fireman knows just when his driver needs that little bit more steam,' added Currie.

I saw the partnership between crew and machine at close quarters in the cab of *Mallard*. From the moment Birkett opened the regulator at King's Cross there was unceasing activity on the footplate. A footplate rocking and vibrating, heat blazing from the firebox, one's ears deafened by a continual roar broken every few minutes by the automatic warning system – a bell as we approached a signal at green, a siren for caution.

For the fireman it is an endless round of stoking, adjusting the injector to keep the right water level in the boiler (*Mallard* consumed 40lb of coal and 35 gallons of water a mile), and watching for signals on the driver's blind side. Between shovelfuls there is the footplate to be hosed and swept to keep the dust down. Six times between London and Edinburgh we dropped the scoop to pick up water.

For the driver it is a matter of unceasing vigilance for signals, speed restrictions and timekeeping – supplemented nowadays by the automatic warning system. This vigilance, the signalmen checking the train past en route and the gangers inspecting the track, all combine to give a striking sense of security, even in the rocking cab.

There's an eleven-mile climb out of King's Cross, and Harry Birkett took it quietly, conserving his steam. We had left two minutes late, but it was not until Potter's Bar that we touched 60 mph and began making it up. Hitchin, thirty-two miles, was passed at 80 mph and on time.

But soon after we had the first check – caused by modernisation work, a long stretch at 20mph over relaid track, which set us back three-and-a-half minutes. Then there was the slow crawl through the sharp curves at Peterborough and the hard climb up to Stoke Summit, the highest point on the line. But in between Harold Birkett had our 359-ton load of ten coaches travelling for long periods at up to 88mph. York was passed at 12.37, three minutes early.

Neither of our drivers used a watch much or relied on the speedometer. The speedometer has only recently been fitted and, for some reason deep in history, watches are issued only to guards.

Most drivers have an instinctive knowledge of the speeds required by the timetable. Likewise their bump of locality is either instinct or something that's meaningless to the traveller: the feel of the line, the sound of a bridge or tunnel. Station names aren't much use in the middle of a stormy night.

At York we entered the heart of modern railwayland, where the signalmen control trains they don't even see; then on to Darlington, the railways' birthplace; Newcastle, home of George Stephenson's original locomotive works and of his son Robert's cast-iron high-level bridge over the Tyne; and so to the magnificent sweep of the Royal Border Bridge, also by Robert.

As we came in sight of Edinburgh Castle and Bob Currie closed his regulator and gently applied the brakes, I wondered whether all this was just a sentimental reverie. Great men, great engines, great records – all of the past. What of the future, with air and road transport expanding so rapidly?

Across the English Channel the French have no doubts. French Railways, given high priority in modernisation under the Monet plan, are booming with the rest of the nation and leading the world in speed and technical development.

My companions had no doubts either. 'In a few years' time it will be a great job,' said Mackay. Bert Dixon, chief motive power inspector, who travelled with us, told me that improved wages and the chance of working on a modernised system were already attracting a better type of young entrant, although wages, many may think, have still a long way to go to be a just reward.

The next few months will see twenty-two English Electric 3,300-horse-power diesels replace fifty-five steam locomotives on the East Coast Main Line (the diesel can work twenty-two hours out of twenty-four, compared with steam's eight hours). The Deltics are the world's most powerful single-unit diesel engines. Their rapid acceleration and powerful braking will allow faster timings than is possible with steam. Leeds in three hours, Newcastle in four and Edinburgh in six is the target, a level reached only by the short and specially built Coronation and Silver Jubilee trains.

Steam may have its charms, but it could never achieve this as a regular service with a standard train. The next few years may well see a second railway revolution.

LAST PUFF OF STEAM

PAUL JENNINGS BIDS A SYMPATHETIC FAREWELL TO THE IRON HORSE

It seems unlikely that when the very last steam train runs on British Railways some day next year there will be much of a ceremonial. For one thing, unless something special is laid on, it will be a goods train, perhaps into Preston, where the largest steam concentration is centred, serving the area between Crewe and Carlisle, but already accounting for less than 1 per cent of total passenger traffic. For another, this age would be presumptuous to think it could write a funeral march to compare with the marvellous, brilliant, mad overture with which steam began.

Music, fireworks, cannon, huzzas, broken legs, banquets, floods, battles with landowners – steam began its career in an atmosphere of passionate human involvement. Paradoxically, people reacted to this first technological triumph with an earthy vitality which the subsequent 130 years of technology have perhaps dulled in us.

The firing of guns at 9.30 a.m. on 18 June (anniversary of Waterloo) in 1838 announced the arrival of the first of six trains from Carlisle for the opening of the Newcastle-Carlisle Railway. The mayor of Carlisle and some directors boarded a state barge to go and have breakfast with the mayor of Newcastle. Passengers from the second train crowded onto the gangway of a steam packet. The gangway broke, and they fell in. When these guests went back to the station for the return procession (all the company's locomotives were in it, led by the *Rapid*, travelling light with the Union Jack) they found their reserved seats occupied, although Gateshead Corporation, arriving prudently early, had secured theirs.

The procession consisted of 13 trains with 3,500 passengers. Following the *Meteor* (four carriages with the mayor of Newcastle and the Allenheads band) were *Victoria* and *Wellington* (each with nine coaches), *Nelson* (seven, these two engines ornamented with shields bearing portraits of the heroes of Waterloo and Trafalgar), *Lightning* (ten coaches and the Carlisle town band), *Tyne* (nine, with a steam organ), *Carlisle* (eight), *Eden* (ten), *Atlas* (no fewer than seventeen, with the Newcastle and Northumberland Volunteers' band), *Samson* (eleven), *Newcastle*, *Hercules* – all names of immense masculine strength and confidence.

Soon thick fog, in which bands and steam organ had been booming and pooming away to the echoing hills of that Hadrian's Wall country, gave way to steady rain. Early comers bagged the covered carriages for the return to Newcastle; ladies in summer dresses got wet; there were accidents.

'At Greenhead we were run into again with full force ... Strange to say, our wagon suffered no harm, but the truck in front was broken into matchwood, and a young man had his arm mangled while a gentleman had a leg broken. The collision threw us into a state of terror and we seriously thought of leaving the train and making the best of our way home by road ... but it was some satisfaction afterwards to be able to say I was one of the passengers on such a memorable journey.' Alderman Thos. Wilson of Gateshead celebrated the whole occasion in verse.

With due respect to Charles Parker of BBC Birmingham and his poetic radio documentary on the making of the M1, we can't match this kind of thing with the first flight of Concorde, let alone the opening of a new diesel or electric service. Nor can today's corporate research-and-development projects show individuals like the first great steam heroes – Daniel Gooch, Brunel (heroic seven-foot gauge, Clifton Suspension Bridge, first England-America steamboat, atmospheric railway which reached 80mph in Devon in 1847, but rats ate grease sealing the vacuum tube along which the train was pulled), Brassey, whose navvies on the Paris-Rouen line astounded the French, J. Hughes from Ebbw Vale, who founded a whole Russian iron town for making rails (Hughesovka, or Yuzovka, later Stalino) – or old Stephenson himself, knighted by the first Belgian king, ending his days trying to grow straight cucumbers.

Somehow one has the idea that the r-and-d boys know what they're going to do before they do it; there isn't this pioneering feeling, the air of 'well, let's try this' that so humanises steam history. When Stephenson was building the Liverpool-Manchester line over boggy Chat Moss he was forced to use wooden sleepers instead of the heavy stone blocks which on normal ground were dropped from a height thirty or forty times while ballast was packed underneath, and he was rather peeved when everyone said the wooden part was much smoother.

Why is it that everyone with a spark of poetry feels an obscure regret at the end of steam? This is not the mere nostalgia-aestheticism that gathers round anything once it ceases to be crudely modern and functional; there

have been poets of steam from the very beginning, ranging from Alderman
Thos. Wilson and T. Baker –

Through striving to avoid it, Huskisson

By unforeseen mischance was over-run.

That stroke, alas! was death in shortest time;

Thus fell the great financier in his prime!

– to Tennyson, who was mistaken about the rails, thinking they were
hollow, like tramlines, but nevertheless got his image about the great world
spinning down the ringing grooves of change from the same source.

Nor is our regret entirely caused by the curious embryonic personality of
any steam engine, so different from the shut-in, mind-your-own-business
diesel. To the actress Fanny Kemble, who rode on Stephenson's *Rocket* at the
world's first locomotive race, the famous Rainhill trials of 1829, at which he
was the runaway winner, it was the 'iron horse' (one entry, the Cycloped,
was a horse, clumping away on a treadmill geared to the wheels).

'The reins, bit and bridle of this wonderful beast is a small steel handle,'
she wrote of the *Rocket*, 'which applies or withdraws steam from the legs or
pistons so that a child could manage it ... this snorting little animal, which
I felt rather inclined to pat ... '

To others it has seemed a half-conscious creature with its own nature,
undoubtedly male, drawing calm female carriages behind; snorting, fussy,
extrovert – yet also big, open, noble, simple; rather like Elgar.

But there is something more fundamental. Steam is innocence, it is the
childhood of industrial man. The railway age, in which England led, but
only just (by 1850 we had 6,658 miles, the United States had 9,072; in 1836 an
American engine, the *Columbus*, was supplied to Germany for the Leipzig-
Dresden line), was the beginning of industrialism's total change from the
static agrarian order based on land and house ownership to the (as yet quite
unachieved) fluid, mobile, egalitarian and ordered society of the future.

Travel and motion, hitherto the privilege of the aristocrat on his horse
(look at the very names for aristocracy: the equitatus of Rome, the French
chevaliers, the Spanish caballeros, the German ritter or rider, all to do with
horses) were now every man's privilege. We tend to think that steam began
as an extension of mining, and so it did technically, but nobody was prepared
for the public's instant enthusiasm for travelling; it was not until 1862 that
freight revenues caught up with those from passengers.

Steam, therefore, has in it the first primary magic of travel. Steam is the
mysterious and romantic smell and sound from brick and fretwork stations
with clomping wooden bridges, big clocks, men in blue-black uniforms,

with big old turnip watches, twanging wires operating the signal on the curve connecting this dozy provincial town with the world – with the seaside terminus of childhood, with London, with the other.

Take, for instance, the city of Coventry, now (unbelievably to one who grew up in it) a place on the tourist route. It has a smart new station with lots of glass in modern impersonal expanses, an ornamental fountain and pond; all perfectly attuned to the anonymous diesels roaring effortlessly across the grey plains of a distance further annihilated by the cars made in Coventry.

All that remains of magic childhood steam is the curious cul-de-sac air of the road leading to it. The old station, all sooty fretwork, iron pillars, draughts and the noisiest iron trolleys in the world, had much more of this outskirts feeling – indeed it was also a tram terminus, an official end of the town. In this road strangeness was already in the air: the immense clanking engine with a cardboard-looking number on the front, in a summer dawn, that would take us on a day excursion to Llandudno and an unimaginable western sea; the single line to Kenilworth, where a baton was solemnly handed over at signal boxes; familiar streets and parks, already extraordinary as seen from the bright rails to London, because seen from the wrong side, in another light, from high-arched bridges; all forever associated with that chuffing sound from ahead ...

Such personal memories, in anyone over thirty, are supported by some deeper, dim, corporate memory of steam as the harbinger of an immense confident picnic; it was through steam that man, in real numbers, escaped from his age-old localisation and ventured into bright new world landscapes. Steam in locomotives – it was the poet Claudel who pointed out the curious pictorial aptness of the written word locomotive even if written on one line; but it looks even better like this:

$$l_{oco}{}^m{}_{otive}$$

Steam in the boilers of the great calm 19th-century British Navy. Steam making the American continent into a country. Steam performing incredible feats of clambering up the Alps and the Andes.

We know, after 1914 and 1939, that mobility brought us more than a picnic; all that machinery and metal and science can do is help good men to do more good, but equally, bad men to do more bad; and perhaps Dickens was a prophet as well as a brilliant impressionist in the famous passage in *Dombey and Son*, published in 1848:

'Away, with a shriek and a roar, and a rattle, from the town, burrowing among the dwellings of men and making the streets hum, flashing out into the meadows for a moment, mining in through the damp earth, booming on in darkness and heavy air, bursting out again into the sunny day so bright and wide; away, with a shriek, and a roar, and a rattle, through the fields, through the woods, through the corn, through the hay, through the chalk, through the mould, through the clay, through the rock, among objects close at hand and almost in the grasp, ever flying from the traveller and a deceitful distance ever moving slowly within him: like as in the track of the remorseless monster, Death!'

That is one of four such wonderful paragraphs, each ending with the same words about 'the remorseless monster, Death.' Even so, it is shot through with glimpses of that timeless, innocent pastoral through which the first steam trains passed. Steam is ambivalent, Janus-faced. When it goes we shall be totally industrialised, we shall have lost our last contact with the unique moment when the modern and the medieval looked at each other with mutual surprise, and man thought he had not changed.

The 20,000-odd steam locomotives which British Railways took over in 1949 have now nearly all been sold as so much scrap steel (and a little copper), usually for something around the £1,000 mark. There has been no steam at all in Scotland since last April. Mr Alan Pegler, a Leeds business-man, bought the *Flying Scotsman* and keeps it at Doncaster; but soon even 'memory trips' for enthusiasts will not be possible because there will be no stocks of coal or even water supplies, on any route. We are relentlessly approaching that as yet unnamed day next year when the last steam train runs.

The very last? Well, no. After that mournful but inevitable day it will still be possible to go on a dreamlike steam voyage such as the one I enjoyed with my family and about two hundred other people only two weeks ago.

We got into little open trucks in a sunlit little station that seemed to have been invented by Walter de la Mare. An engine, 4ft high but a real steam engine making all the right noises and smells and smuts, pulled us over a bridge, a salty, sunny wind on our faces, past a wide estuary, through woods where the line was bordered by waving, shiny marsh grasses and was drenched with the smell of meadowsweet, alongside magical, clear streams, through fields containing an old man with a scythe, two foals, a waving rubber-booted girl on a tractor, through cuttings of pink granite, seven miles up into rich private valleys dominated by the majesty of Scafell and other Cumberland peaks.

The Ravenglass and Eskdale Railway, like the Tal-y-Llyn, the Bluebell, and several others, is now run by a society of enthusiasts. It was built with a 30-in gauge, to serve long-since defunct iron ore fields in the hills, and relaid in 1915 by Bassett-Lowke with a 15-in gauge. This is just large enough not to be a mere toy, for it carried mail, much freight from Eskdale and, until 1953, granite, that beautiful pink granite.

Now it is free from economic dependence on such imponderables, and we can see, as it were, the pure form of steam – we can see steam in its last days with something of the surprise of its first, when people clambered on and swamped the freight; a long train of open carriages in the sunlight, full of waving, huzzaing human beings in an innocent summer landscape. It's a good way to go.

ON THE FOOTPLATE TO HEAVEN

MINTY CLINCH DISCOVERS WHY BRITISH TRAIN BUFFS ARE
THUNDERING OVER TO POLAND

There was always a possibility that a Polish train driver would not want to hand over a 100-ton locomotive hauling a string of double-decker coaches to a rookie driver. Then again, I did have some experience: nearly ten minutes of forward and reverse on a branch line at Wolsztyn station. I had been promised that would qualify me to drive OL49, the engine hauling the 5.05 commuter service into Poznań station in time for the Monday morning rush hour.

But I knew my drive was in jeopardy when I clambered on to the footplate. At that crucial moment, the group leader, Howard Jones, disclosed that seven out of the twenty-one drivers on this line – the last mainline standard-gauge steam service in Europe – refuse to allow his clients to take the throttle. This one was scowling in the reflected light from the furnace and it didn't take a genius to recognise which side of the divide he was on.

Jones, forty-six, wanted to be an engine driver when he was a boy. Nothing original about that, but he did break the mould last year when he resigned as director of a travel company and sold his house in Burgess Hill, West Sussex, to move to Wolsztyn, a tranquil town set among lakes and woods in western Poland. 'It was bar talk that did it. I was going on about my romantic dream of owning a loco and I realised that I'd had enough of the stresses and strains of modern life. What I really wanted to do was revert to childhood and play with trains.'

As the last steam train in Britain ceased regular service in 1968, this was not an easy midlife crisis to resolve. It is also debatable whether setting up Steam Breaks in Wolsztyn has been less stressful than running a travel company. But Jones has given himself five years to find out, and initial progress is encouraging.

Although he speaks little Polish, Jones is now a qualified engine driver and has persuaded railway officials to allow two clients a week to take driving lessons on the steam network. 'The bureaucrats were a bit edgy and a lot of people said it couldn't be done,' he says, 'but commercial steam is in jeopardy here. The majority of the drivers were very enthusiastic because my custom means their jobs are virtually guaranteed for the next five years.'

The first client to grasp the regulator – the long lever that controls power by increasing and reducing the supply of steam – was Ralph Thomas, a local government worker from Birmingham. He had signed on as soon as he read about Jones's scheme in a railway magazine. The week cost him £500, but he has the option of converting it into a £2,000 share that will allow him to come annually for five years.

Thomas could imagine no better holiday than spending up to eighteen hours a day on the footplate, including twelve to fourteen hours of actual driving during his six days on the job. Polish commuters may be relieved to learn that he started on a freight train, but by Thursday, he was rattling the commuters into Poznań.

Engine driving is simple enough to learn – our non-English-speaking hosts used sign language – but it does require a certain amount of strength to operate the heavy forward and reverse gear wheel. The great knack, however, is in precision braking – too much steam and you crash through the barrier; too little and you undershoot the platform, earning glares from passengers who might be forced to walk those twenty extra yards in a bitter Polish winter.

In addition, a driver must maintain commercial speeds of up to 70mph, because there are bonuses for timekeeping which the Polish drivers are not about to sacrifice. 'I was apprehensive the first time the driver handed over to me on a passenger train,' Thomas admitted. 'But I knew I'd cracked it when he offered me a cigarette while I was at the controls.'

He took a long pull on his Polish draught beer and smiled beatifically. 'A steam engine is the nearest a machine can come to a living being – temperamental like a woman, but more reliable.'

David Leyland had no such doubts. He had already driven a steam train once, when his mother and sister gave him a footplate ride on the *Sir Nigel Gresley*, on the Mid-Hants line, for his fiftieth birthday. 'Steam trains are definitely alive,' he told me. 'You can take my word on that.' When he took early retirement from his job as a local government solicitor in Matlock eighteen months later, he signed up for a timeshare with Howard Jones. 'I took a lot of mockery from my colleagues, but I know I made the right decision,' he said after his first day's training.

The second string to Jones's bow is his 'train addict's weekend', which takes place either in Woltszyn or the Harz Mountains in Germany, where steam locos still operate on narrow-gauge track for tourist purposes. We were a baker's dozen when we met at Tegel airport in Berlin, all with serious cameras and video equipment concealed in shoulder bags that had seen better days.

Jones's elder brother, Trevor, guided us through the Berlin subway to the starting point for the mainline service to Rzepin on the Polish border. The party greeted the venerable orange underground trains from the former East Berlin with enthusiasm, but that was nothing compared with the paroxysms of delight at Rzepin. 'Steam on the line!' shouted Ken – or was it Bill? – and eleven spotters took up the cry. Pointing fingers converged on a large black engine with red trim sitting on a plinth at the end of the platform. 'T151, a Polish development of USTY246,' they chorused.

This particular weekend coincided with the ninetieth anniversary of the Wolsztyn depot. Along with the officials who had come in on a VIP train from Poznań, we watched a parade of locos steam past – initially one by one, then in twos, fives and, climactically, all ten in a row.

By now I had learned that train buffs divide into 'linesiders' and 'footplaters', albeit with quite a lot of overlap between the two. The linesiders spent their time alighting at stations – often no more than a bus shelter – when a steam train was due so as to film it. The footplaters preferred to ride the locos, taking their turn at the regulator whenever a driver would allow.

Most had driven engines on preserved railways in Britain, deemed an inferior experience, not least because safety regulations confine speeds to 25mph. Britain may have ruled the rails in the early part of the century, with prestige trains like the *Flying Scotsman* 'doing the ton' on a regular basis, but only politically incorrect Poland allows that kind of thrill today.

'They are oblivious to danger,' said Scottish John, suggesting that the national spirit that persuaded Polish cavalry officers to charge German tanks in September 1939 was not yet dead.

Nor, it would seem, is the nation's love of steam. The Wolsztyn parade was cheered on by crowds of families; the drivers tooted their horns merrily as black smoke mingled with low scudding clouds in the fleeting autumn sunshine.

Five past five on Monday morning was another matter, damp and black, but Jones's boyish enthusiasm was undimmed as he took the regulator that should have been mine. It may be that driving is not women's work, but shifting coal is, apparently. The stoker was more than generous with the offer of his shovel. Would the traditional steam loco practice of cooking breakfast on the shovel also be something a woman could participate in? I mimed a fry-up – but old surly shook his head.

CHANGE AT VENICE FOR ATHENS

CHRISTOPHER FILDES STEAMS THROUGH AN OBSESSIVE'S
ACCOUNT OF RAILWAYS THEN AND NOW

Review of Platform Souls: the Trainspotter as Twentieth-Century Hero *by Nicholas*
Whittaker (Gollancz)

I had forgotten about the machine that made your feet tingle. There used
to be one on Shrewsbury station. It looked like a weighing machine, but if
you stood on it and fed it money, it would start to vibrate. Nicholas
Whittaker enjoyed it: 'You felt as if your feet had been turned ino a kind of
goo and your legs were sliding away from under you, rather like the watch
in Salvador Dalí's painting.'

Shrewsbury was a junction, with lines coming in from six different directions. So passengers from Leominster might change there for Pwllheli (they
still can) and stand around for hours, waiting for their connection, with
their feet killing them. Then the soothing touch of the machine would be
well worth the coin in the slot. The railways were a world of their own,
with a reason for everything.

Mr Whittaker came to it in the final years of steam, and in his heart has
never left it. Perched on a level crossing gate in Burton-upon-Trent, he
would spot the surviving giants – Jubilees, Black Fives, the odd Scot – as
they clattered from Derby to Birmingham. He scrawled down their
numbers and marked them off in his spotter's handbook: 'I prided myself
on my neatness.' He would bunk into engine sheds, note the numbers of
their inmates and bunk out again.

Trainspotters are obsessives. Mr Whittaker resents the stereotype that fits
them out with anoraks, ballpoint pens and inadequate sex lives. He and his
friends wore parkas and were interested in girls, although trains came first.
When he went on holiday he took a train from Charing Cross to Athens
(changing at Venice, which was interesting as a junction) and Elaine was
left behind.

Some obsessives just like railways, old and new. What a pleasure, recently,
to go tearing down Brunel's main line from Paddington to Kingswear on

the Dart Estuary, with three changes, the last stage hauled by Great Western steam. I was proud of that. Mr Whittaker loves railways but is unhappy to think what has become of them.

Beeching hacked them back. Diesels replaced steam and boring diesels replaced quirky diesels. Trains went faster (except on the old Southern Railway, still stuck in the 1930s) but that did not endear them to him. Modern railwaymen, he says, are squeaky clean in corporate uniforms designed by marketeers, but proper railwaymen wore shiny caps and carried cans of cold tea, to be warmed on the firebox.

I like Mr Whittaker's theory that they and their iron steeds are not scrapped, only resting. Trainspotters checking their lists – locos withdrawn, locos broken up, locos preserved – could not make the numbers tally. So there must, they thought, be a strategic reserve of steam engines, perhaps concealed in that mysterious siding at the east end of Box Tunnel. In the nation's hour of need they will emerge, like Merlin from his cave.

He may well be right. In any case, he and I and the Welsh poet R.S. Thomas would agree:

It is too late to start

For destinations not of the heart.

HOW *DID* THE PUFFER TRAINS GO?

PETER CLAYTON MUSES ON WHAT WE'RE LOSING AS BRITISH RAIL RUNS ITS LAST STEAM TRAIN.

New Cross Gate station lies at the London end of a long cutting which, walled with false countryside, funnels the old Brighton line up the slope to Forest Hill, on its way to clattering Norwood, past the insurance company skyscrapers of Croydon, and out through a tenacious suburbia to where the real countryside begins at last on the far side of the North Downs.

The line was electrified in the late 1920s, and to my certain knowledge no regular steam service has run through there for years. Yet less than a month ago I watched a mother hold up her little boy, still in his waddling clothes, to look from the train window out over the forlorn sidings where the engine shed used to be. 'How does the puffer train go, Alan?' The response was as automatic and perfunctory as Amen. 'Ch-ch-ch-ch,' obliged Alan without much conviction. 'That's right,' said his mother.

As soon as he is old enough to think about it, Alan will be forced to conclude that his mother's hearing is seriously defective, because no train he has ever heard is likely to have gone anything remotely resembling ch-ch-ch-ch. A combined humming and grinding sound, perhaps, accompanied by a peculiar spur-like jingling; alternatively the same sort of noise as a bus or an outsize farm tractor, but definitely no ch-ch-ch-ch.

For, unless he's been taken to one of those carefully pickled private concerns like the Bluebell Line, he hasn't seen a steam train – only electrics and diesels. And with British Rail running its last steamer today, in Carlisle, he has lost his chance. As he grows up learning about electronics or computer programming he won't agree, but I think he's missed something.

I'm not sentimentally attached to smoke and soot; I don't think it's particularly ennobling for a man to have to shift three or four tons of boulder-sized coal with a hand shovel just to get me from London to Exeter; I can't say I'm favourably impressed – apart from the sheer spectacle of it – by the idea of a portable furnace and several hundred gallons of boiling water rushing overhead on rumbling iron bridges.

But with the drawing of that last fire in that last firebox today, I feel as though somebody had finally raked out the embers of my childhood.

Electric trains were for my father to go to work on, later for getting me to school. Steam trains were for holidays – holidays we could afford only because my father worked on the railway himself, a member of the second generation to seize that little crumb of security – and the bigger one of cheap travel – that the railway offered.

And holidays meant the long journey to Cornwall, to a bleak row of one-time tin-miners' cottages up on the stinging Perranporth sandhills. Best of all, it meant travelling on that most immaculate of railways, the Great Western, where it was all kings and castles and halls and manors, those surpassingly handsome locomotives with their copper-trimmed chimneys and devices like upturned brass buckets on top of their boilers.

That I should refer to them as 'devices' and not by their correct technical name is typical of my relationship with the steam engine. I never collected locomotive numbers. Although I tried, I failed utterly to understand those meticulous anatomical drawings of the insides of engines, all plumbing and bolts, that used to appear in boys' magazines.

And not even prolonged study of the diagrams of locomotive controls – another magazine favourite – would have prepared me for stopping a runaway train.

Luckily, railway engines didn't run away, except in films. They took you on holiday, and that helped to make them beautiful. They were beautiful, anyway, most of them, but because of my associative, highly subjective reasoning, they became more beautiful the further west you went, which means that the most beautiful of all were the tiny tank engines that worked the single-track branch on the last few miles of the journey.

Unlike the more objective railway enthusiasts, I can't tell you who built them (it's rather like cherishing a jazz record without wanting to know who is on it), and if I had known I should almost certainly have assumed that he'd done it specifically for my delight.

What I did know was that they were sturdy – an emotive word applied in railway literature to all tank engines – and that they smelled delicious, giving off an aromatic warmth which I have always assumed was made by combining steam and hot oil in the right proportions.

I know also that the characteristic Great Western noise, which you could imitate to perfection by going through the motions of spitting out apple pips, was made by the valves. I got to know the drivers, too – gentle Cornishmen with accents so far west as to sound practically mid-Atlantic.

Year after year they would help me up into their cabs, where I would stand awkwardly, flinching at the fire (suddenly they were big engines) and longing for an engineman's shiny-crowned cap in place of the peaked acorn cup I suffered as a schoolboy.

The line itself followed an improbable course, full of impetuous right-angled changes of direction, across the Cornish plateau from just west of Chacewater, to St Agnes. Then came the crazy poetry of Goonbell and Mithian, the tortuous clamber down the side of Perran Coombe, and the hairpin cutting, which I always tried to reproduce in mashed potato at lunchtime, into Perranporth itself.

As so often on the Great Western, the station stood aloof from the town. With a farmyard as its only neighbour – one looked very like an extension of the other – and with its long vista up the aisle of another coombe, it made a separate place to go. There, in the long drowsy silences between trains, you could dangle your legs over the edge of the flagged platform and watch dragonflies, the colour of spilled oil, rise menacingly from the reed beds in the river at the foot of the bank.

And when you'd stayed too long and the unaccustomed rich cream had done its work and you were caught short, Mr Miners, the signalman, would come down out of his box and unlock the toilet for you so you didn't have to squander a penny on inessentials. To be on those terms with a vast railway company meant you were in.

Although it had its share of unmanned halts, lit at night by oil lamps in handsome goblet-shaped glasses (the guard of the last train of the day had to turn them out as he went through), the line was not ultimately primitive. There was enough traffic to require passing loops, and it was never worked on the push-and-pull principle.

At each end the engine would run formally round its two-coach train, and would always be facing the same way – boiler first going towards Newquay, bunker first going to Chacewater. How, during the decade or so that I knew the branch, an engine never did a working that brought it round the other way, I don't know. Perhaps it was the Great Western's passion for order.

It all had to go, of course – not just the little steam engines, but the line itself. I suppose we couldn't really afford the Edwardian leisureliness of it even in the 1930s, let alone the 1960s. We now have a more ruthless system – sometimes ruthlessly efficient, often enough ruthlessly inefficient; but ruthless.

After today's tears at Carlisle have been wiped away (and there will be tears, surely) things will go just as wrong, but they'll go wrong in a different way. There'll be no chance, for instance, of seeing a porter dash off the platform at St Agnes and along the track after an animal, shouting 'Stop that dog! He's a parcel!'

One day Alan, or some little boy like him, will probably ask me, 'Well, how *did* the puffer trains go?' I'll tell him all right, but it will be much more than just the noise.

GOING LOCO FOR A VANISHED AGE

JAMES BEDDING REKINDLES SOME CHILDHOOD MEMORIES
WITH A RATTLING TOUR OF NORTH WALES

Flames licked at the door of the firebox at the engine driver's feet. 'Oh yes, we still do cremations, for those who are really keen on steam,' he said. 'We'd use a bigger engine, with a bigger firebox, mind.' Some years ago, according to my guidebook, Llangollen Railway in North Wales had dreamt up the ultimate send-off for steam fanatics taking that last train to the great terminus in the sky. But residents of the quiet, leafy Dee Valley had kicked up such a fuss at the thought of their gardens being coated in anorak ash that the plans had been shelved. So the book said, anyway – but I'd wanted to make sure first-hand. Or was that the flicker of a smile around the engine driver's lips?

Just playful boys' talk, perhaps, between men who really should act older. But if we're allowed to be boys anywhere, then Llangollen – home not only to the BBC *Doctor Who* exhibition, but also the terminus for North Wales' only standard-gauge preserved steam railway – is a pretty good place.

On this trip, reliving childhood memories of a tour of steam railways of North Wales, I'd brought along seven-year-old Marco, hoping to share with him some of the pleasure I'd had as a child. Though as the burly engine chuffed steadily up the wooded valley, Marco showed no interest whatsoever in sticking his head out of the window next to mine, my eyes watering as they filled with smoke and specks of coal. 'It's a bit slow, isn't it?' he muttered, doodling on a piece of paper.

At the little village station of Carrog, the end of the line, a small crowd huddled admiringly around the black, spluttering engine. At least the men were admiring; fathers and grandfathers were forcing scared children to pose in front of the footplate for pictures ('Say steeeeeeeeeam!'), while their young charges snivelled and stole anxious glances at the roaring blaze behind them, and the whistling, hissing black pipework on either side.

Inside the restored, 1950s ticket office, I asked the stationmaster if this was the inspiration for *Ivor the Engine*. 'Oh no,' he said, 'you need to go to the narrow-gauge railways for that. This is just a load of middle-aged men who got together to buy their own train set.' And he explained how they started restoring the Beeching line in 1975, steadily extending the track over the years, reaching Carrog, seven-and-a-half miles up the valley, in May 1996.

'Have you got a train set, young man?' the stationmaster asked Marco. 'Sure, I used to play with it when I was little,' was the casual reply. 'Bet mine's bigger than yours,' said the man. 'Yeah, but you have to share yours, don't you?' said Marco smugly.

On our loco, the heaviest job of all – that of fireman, shovelling coal into the firebox – fell to the only volunteer woman in sight. I asked her how much shovelling she had to do on each trip and she had to ask the engine driver. He leant back and sucked his teeth while she carried on shovelling in the blazing heat. 'Ooh, that's a good question,' he said, scratching his head. 'We do four trips a day, that's sixty miles. In that time we use half of that,' he said, tapping the bunker at the back of the loco, 'and it holds three tons. Ooh yes, hard work, that is.'

Women firemen weren't quite what I expected to find, but everything else about the railway was reassuringly familiar. It dawned on me that there was more to steam preservation than just putting clapped-out steam locos on life support; it's about keeping our childhood alive, saying, in the midst of the stresses of modern life and the responsibilities of adulthood, that it's all right, innocence still exists. Whether Marco would ever value the pleasures of oily, wheezing steam engines above slick PlayStations is entirely another question …

That night we stayed in a former railway station converted into a b and b – at Eyarth, on the old Denbigh-Ruthin-Corwen line, another Beeching casualty. The ticket office window is still there, as is the edge of the platform – but the breakfast room has been built beyond the platform edge, so where you munch your toast, bleary-eyed, steam locos once thundered. The walls are lined with black-and-white pictures of huffing, puffing dinosaurs of a vanished age; pride of place goes to a photograph of Margaret Thatcher presenting a commemorative plate in 1996 to the b and b's owner, Jen Spencer.

'We're not railway fanatics, really,' said Jen at breakfast. 'But we do get them coming to stay. They're always telling us how we should be running the place – you know, wearing railway uniforms, putting up loudspeakers and playing steam loco sounds during breakfast.'

There was no shortage of steam fanatics at our next stop: the harbour town of Porthmadog, terminus of the Ffestiniog Railway, and my favourite memory of Welsh steam. The little station beside the harbour, the miniature carriages pulled by a locomotive that seemed to be made of two sawn-off engine front ends welded together back to back and the magical journey that begins with a clickety-clacking rattle along the mile-long causeway across the Glaslyn Estuary are everything that a miniature railway should be.

Once across the Cob, the train chugged through farmland, before starting a steady climb, revealing increasingly expansive views across the Vale of Ffestiniog and to the coast. As we puffed through woods of larch, oak and conifer, an attendant came through the packed carriage, taking orders from the mostly adult passengers for snacks and drinks such as Ffestiniog Railway House wine (25cl, £2.95). It all felt very grown-up compared with my last visit.

Back then the line stopped at a halt in the middle of the woods, called Dduallt. This time, the little train launched itself just after the halt into an extremely tight loop that crossed back across the line, and continued climbing above the edge of a reservoir – where we could see the bed of the original line blocked by a hydroelectric power station. We chuffed along the new, volunteer-built line until finally, seventy minutes and just over thirteen miles after setting off from Porthmadog, we pulled into the slate-quarrying village of Blaenau Ffestiniog, sitting uneasily at the foot of towering, fragile-looking hillsides of menacing grey slate.

We walked along the platform to chat to the driver as he climbed down from the footplate of the symmetrical, two-faced *Lloyd George*. With two front ends to the loco and no back ends, I wondered where the firebox was, and was shocked to learn that the loco was powered by oil. 'Sure, this was built as an oil burner,' he said. 'Others have had to be converted. You couldn't burn the rubbish coal they give you these days in one of these. It's all right for the big steam engines on broad-gauge lines, they are only doing a fraction of the work they used to. This line only ever used to have a couple of slate wagons, running at 8mph or 9mph. Now we pull a whole string of carriages at up to 20mph. If you tried to do that with a coal fire, you'd blow the engine apart.'

I smiled weakly at Marco, but he clearly wasn't worrying too much about the authenticity of his steam experience. And he seemed far more at home than I was in the station shop back in Porthmadog, where they were selling imitation sets of fir trees, or cows, or 'working people', or 'city people', for train sets, as well as all kinds of Ffestiniog souvenirs and toys, not to mention *Thomas the Tank Engine* mugs, flags, footballs, torches and jigsaws. By then I wasn't surprised to be given a leaflet on how to apply for a Ffestiniog Railway Visa credit card; or to find a window in the station called Ffestiniog Travel where a woman said she could book us tickets on virtually any train from Eurostar to the Trans-Siberian, and gave us a copy of a glossy brochure that climaxes with a Millennium round-the-world rail trip for just £4,600.

Reeling from the novelty of it all, I headed back on to the platform, where our engine driver was preparing for another trip. I was relieved to see that some things in the world of boys' toys were becoming reassuringly predictable. Even oil-fired engines, I discovered, need a fireman; and who was doing the dirty work? A woman.

DIRTY FACES, WIDE SMILES

TO MARK THE 200TH ANNIVERSARY OF STEAM RAILWAYS, **SUZY BENNETT** JOINS THE 'PUFFER NUTTERS' ON ONE OF BRITAIN'S LONGEST AND MOST SCENIC ROUTES

It all happened in a flash. One minute I was wandering by myself along the platform, the next I was caught up in a jamboree of forty or so rail enthusiasts. Some wore grins as wide as their faces, others looked distinctly feverish. All wore goggles and carried clipboards, and for a second I feared kidnap at the hands of genetic scientists.

In fact, the object of their ardour was the 34067 *Tangmere*, a 1947 racing-green steam locomotive that was now sliding regally into the station. It was barely visible beneath the clouds of steam billowing from its chimney, but when the smoke slipped away, and the cloud of ash that followed settled, we stood in collective, open-mouthed awe.

In front of us were two brightly polished locomotives: the *Tangmere*, an engine once used to pull prestigious Golden Arrow trains, and in front of it, a jet-black ex-British Rail Standard Class classic. Weighing in at 100 tons each, they towered above us at the height of a first-floor bedroom.

Their massive bellies glistened with oil and steam as delicate plumes of smoke curled around their smooth curves. 'Magnificent,' muttered someone behind me. There was urgent scribbling on clipboards of numbers and symbols I didn't understand. Cameras, camcorders, stopwatches and – strangely – Global Positioning Systems appeared from nowhere. Trainspotting had certainly come on since I was a girl.

These two majestic locomotives, and thirteen maroon-coloured 1960s carriages behind, were to take us on a journey along one of Britain's longest and most scenic steam rail routes: a seventy-two-mile stretch from Settle, North Yorkshire, to Carlisle in Cumbria.

Over the next four hours, the engines would haul us up to the Yorkshire Dales through a world of peat and heather, time-warp towns, mighty viaducts and little rushing rivers, before sweeping us through the heart of Cumbria with its lowering fells and baize-green fields.

This was a charter train, one of hundreds run each year across Britain by private companies with the help of misty-eyed volunteers. Many run on specially preserved tracks; others, like this, are given regular slots on everyday routes.

This year is the 200th anniversary of the world's first moving steam engine, Richard Trevithick's *Pen-y-Darren*. In 1804, at Merthyr Tydfil in Wales, it wheezed its way over nine miles of track, carrying five wagons, ten tons of iron and seventy passengers at the breakneck speed of five miles per hour. Little more than a boiler on wheels, it was a gloriously Heath Robinson contraption, and the event was largely ignored by the general public. But the *Pen-y-Darren* was to herald a railway era that helped build the British Empire and, within a hundred years, would span the globe.

Steam is in my blood – my father was a 'puffer nutter' and my great grandfather a stationmaster – yet I'd come hopelessly badly prepared for the journey. This was my first such trip and everything about me said 'rookie'. Within seconds of the train's lurching out of Preston station – the nearest embarkation point to Settle – the crisp white shirt I'd put on that morning had turned mottled underpant grey. My face was covered in soot, and a smote – a tiny hot cinder from the chimney – had lodged itself in my eye. Lesson one: never lean out of the window of a moving steam train without adequate protection. I spent the rest of the journey begging to use the very goggles I had earlier made fun of.

As the train eased into a slumbrous chuffety-chuff sound straight out of *Thomas the Tank Engine*, I took my seat, a luxuriously fleshy affair of red and orange moquette with a white linen antimacassar. The carriages were panelled in wood, and the tables clothed in crisp white napery, each with an elegant lamp.

Highly polished silver cutlery and glasses were laid out to geometrical perfection; I felt like minor royalty. Corks popped, glasses tinkled and strangers struck up conversations. This is the life, I thought.

The train was full of families and railway fans; the latter identifiable only by their anorak-clad bottoms that spent the entire journey bent over windows. Next to me sat Michael and Lesley Perkins, who had come up from Gloucestershire. 'I just love the smell and the smoke of steam engines,' said Michael. 'I've come to see into people's' back gardens,' said Lesley. 'You can't do that in a car; all you see are hedges.'

We were travelling uphill at a stately 45mph, a speed at which I could pinpoint the unfolding scenery: church spires in tiny villages, picture-perfect granite-and-slate cottages, enormous fluffy sheep and centuries-old stone field barns. After an hour in which we had travelled due north, the Dales' famous three peaks appeared in the distance: the sharp nose of Pen-y-Ghent on the right, Ingleborough on the left and, just visible in a thin mist, Whernside in front.

We could feel every bump in the track as the train lurched from side to side, each jolt sparking laughter from the passengers. Everyone was entering into the sepia-tinged spirit of the day, aided by the drivers, who seemed to pull the whistle at every passing sheep.

Still climbing, we rattled slowly over Ribblehead Viaduct, a twenty-four-span testimony to Victorian engineering, and trundled through the one-and-a-half miles of Blea Moor tunnel. The scenery was bleak now, treeless and barren. As we passed Dent station – at 1,150ft, the highest in England – we were treated to an expansive view of Dentdale, one of the most remote and dramatic northern dales, before making a (relatively) rapid and exhilarating descent towards the lush Eden Valley in Cumbria.

Completed in 1876, the Settle-to-Carlisle route was one of the last mainline steam routes to be built in Britain and was constructed almost entirely by hand. Used by the Victorian and Edwardian public as a route to Scotland, and by freight carriers to transport goods from the Dales, it was – until faster electric and diesel routes took over – the lifeblood of the north. A proposal to close the line in the late 1980s was fiercely resisted by locals, and it now runs more passenger and freight trains than ever.

Steam rail travel is ludicrously inefficient. For this 72-mile journey, 10 tons of coal and 13,000 gallons of water are required – that's enough water to keep you or me abluted and hydrated for a year and a half. Appleby station was a scheduled refuelling stop. Up front, a small army of blue-overalled, stout-bodied, coal-faced men attended to the puffing engines.

Bob Hart, a steam veteran and driver of the *Tangmere*, invited me onto the footplate. Inside, the heat from the white-hot furnace was intense and as humid as a tropical rainforest. Within seconds my eyeballs felt skinned and my face seared like a slab of tuna. Pies stood sizzling on a ledge. The roar from the engine was deafening. 'It's noisy, hot and dirty, but it's fantastic,' shouted Bob, as I turned my left cheek towards the fire. If I was going to get cooked, I wanted to be done evenly.

'It makes me so proud that steam engines are still popular,' Bob went on. 'To me they are alive – you have to feed them and treat them properly to get the most out of them. There's a technique to it – it's an art form. Here's to the next two hundred years.' And he began shovelling coal into the fire for the final leg of our journey.

Arriving at Carlisle late that afternoon, and watching passengers disembark, I noticed a trend: the dirtier the face, the wider the smile. Catching a glimpse of myself in a window, I saw that my skin was encrusted in black grease fit for a chip pan. Great-grandfather Bill would have been proud.

A NEW WINDOW ON WALES

SOPHIE CAMPBELL, WITH THE RESTORATION TEAM,
ENJOYS AN INAUGURAL RUN ON A FRESHLY COMPLETED
STRETCH OF THE WELSH HIGHLAND RAILWAY

Sarah and Alex Bell are holding hands over a train table. 'I liked trains, but I was far more interested in Alex,' remembers Sarah fondly, as her husband of two years looks suitably bashful. 'It was only when we were overlooking the track, with a Garratt engine coming towards us, that the power and glory of steam suddenly converted me. We married a year and a day later.'

Blimey. What is it about steam trains? What on earth is a Garratt engine? And why do I think I'm about to find out? Sarah and Alex are sitting in the first carriage of a train on the newest railway in Wales, where the only thing that stops them gazing at each other is the sight of something really sexy: a newly restored engine, say, retrieved from South Africa, where it has done a million miles or so lugging timber across the veld; or a particularly shiny, well laid set of rails. Oh, and a front window full of rural Wales, passing in a glorious blur of bluebells, spring woods and sheep Velcroed to the green skirts of Snowdon.

At the rear of the train, in first class, where there are free-standing armchairs and the observation car has a single pane of glass carefully curved to avoid unwanted reflections, are the Gold sponsors; people who have given £6,000 or more to make this day happen. In between are 150 Silvers (£200 or more) and volunteers who have given not only money but days, weeks, sometimes years of their lives, grabbing weekends and holidays, often travelling from other parts of Britain or abroad, to shovel coal, lay track and lug sleepers. They are all bonkers, obviously. I don't think I've ever been on a happier train ride.

The new Welsh Highland Railway, which runs down the western edge of Snowdonia National Park in North Wales, has been creeping towards this moment for the past twelve years. It went south from Caernarvon to Dinas in 1997, Waunfawr in 2000, and Rhyd Ddu in 2003, minutely observed by the railway press, the government, local residents and landowners, the national park and Visit Wales.

Now it is open to Hafod-y-Lyn and later this year it should complete the missing link into Porthmadog. Not only will train buffs and tourists be able to transfer to its sister route – the 13.5-mile Ffestiniog Railway, from Porthmadog up into slate country at Blaenau Ffestiniog – it will also open up Snowdonia to cyclists (the trains have bike wagons), walkers and the carless.

As we pull out of Waunfawr and start climbing, there are exclamations of pleasure. Not just at the scenery, as the great mountain rears up above us with its broad summit lost in cloud and little grey farmhouses balanced on its lurching fields, but because nobody can quite believe it's happening.

The leaders of the track gangs – groups of volunteers who laid the 25 miles of steel rails and sleepers – josh each other over who holds the top-speed record of half a mile in two-and-a-half days. 'There's Roland's Runner!' the cry goes up as we pass a contraption invented by a volunteer to move rails. Everyone winces as we scrape against granite rubble dumped too close to the rails: they're worried about Gary, who painted the livery and crests and tricked out the interiors in cream and coral.

The Welsh Highland Railway has cost £28 million so far and needs another £300,000 to reach Porthmadog. The five engines – double-ended, designed by a bloke called Garratt, I now discover – were shipped back from Africa and Tasmania and restored. All the carriages, bar two originals, have been made from scratch by full-timers and volunteers at the engineering works, Boston Lodge. It's smart, comfortable, and deliberately designed to be a different experience from the Ffestiniog, with its Victorian heritage carriages.

'These were always private railways, they were never nationalised,' explains Stuart McNair, one of the supervising engineers. 'In the Twenties, Porthmadog was like Spaghetti Junction. It was littered with railways, all narrow-gauge, all owned by Ffestiniog Light Railways, all bringing slate and minerals into the port.'

The Ffestiniog itself opened in 1836. Slate had previously left the mountain on donkeys, but the new narrow rails could cope with the terrain. Still, carriages were horse-drawn until it became the first narrow-gauge railway in the world to use steam, with spectacular results. 'There was a massive slate boom in the 1860s and '70s,' says Stuart. 'The North Wales slate barons became some of the richest people in the country.'

The poor old Welsh Highland Railway, completed in the Twenties, missed the boom and limped along for 17 years before closing. Fortunately for the post-war preservationists, neither railway disappeared.

The Welsh Highland, too costly to remove, gradually gave way to walking and cycling paths and people's gardens. The Ffestiniog, established by an Act of Parliament, could not be demolished without legislation, so it was mothballed. According to Paul Lewin, the general manager of both railways: 'They flung open the doors to Boston Lodge and all the engines were still sitting there, untouched.'

Paul is sitting one carriage up from first class, chewing the fat with engineers, volunteers and board members. His father built miniature steam railways for amusement parks: 'I've got pictures of me aged five, going around and around in circles. You ran them in, like cars.'

All day I hear similar stories: people whose fathers worked on trains; people whose families holidayed in North Wales and went on the Ffestiniog for a treat; and people who started at the annual August Kids' Week. About half the 7,600 members and half the management team are women: one female Kids' Week alumnus now drives trains for London Midland.

Outside, we have reached the high point of the railway at Pitt's Head, 650 ft above sea level. It's steep, a 1-in-40 gradient – where a mainline track would rarely be more than 1-in-100 – with sinuous 'S' bends. That means it can't be used in winter; even now, in spring, it's tough on the engine. But we're over the hill and running for the Aberglaslyn Pass, the first time any passengers have travelled this far, and all attention turns to the landscape.

We follow the pretty Glaslyn River as it makes its way down to the Porthmadog flood plain through mixed woodlands smudged with bluebells. Hills and escarpments erupt to the south. Meadows nod with ladies' smocks and buttercups. We pass the village of Rhyd Ddu, one of several places where hikers can leap out and make for the summit of Snowdon and Beddgelert Forest Campsite, one of the biggest in Wales and an important market for the train. Gelert was the hound of Prince Llewellyn and Beddgelert is famous as the site of his grave; a corking story made up by the landlord of the Royal Goat Hotel to drum up custom.

As we pass an osprey's nest belonging to Wales's first breeding pair – all paths nearby close during the breeding season, so the train is a useful vantage point – the day is coming to an end. Or it is for the triumphant passengers, who have just seen a dream come true. I, on the other hand, am going to make a mad dash across country to catch the last train of the day on the Ffestiniog Railway. The steam, the soot, the Garratt engine … Really, I could get into this.

CHAPTER 12
FIRSTS AND LASTS

---

7 MAY 1994

ENTENTE CORDIALE CLOSES
THE GREAT DIVIDE

ROBERT HARDMAN ON THE
CHANNEL TUNNEL INAUGURATION

The spirit of controlled chaos that accompanied the construction of the most ambitious engineering project in European history continued to the end. But the Queen and President Mitterrand emerged into an overcast Folkestone afternoon and the history books ahead of schedule.

The delays, the Kentish revolts, the spiralling costs were all brushed aside in a flamboyant celebration of entente cordiale. As the Queen observed in her speech: 'The mixture of French élan and British pragmatism, when united in a common cause, has proved to be a highly successful combination. The tunnel embodies that simple truth.'

The diplomatic niceties of the occasion meant that the protocol was as complex as the technology – not least because the celebrations had contrived to bring Mr John Major, Lady Thatcher, Lord Howe and M. Jacques Delors, the president of the EC, together in several confined spaces.

The Queen began the first of several ribbon-cuttings and unveilings at 9.30 when she opened the new Eurostar passenger terminal at Waterloo. M. Mitterrand did the same at the Gare du Nord in Paris. The royal party then travelled in a first-class carriage at a sedate 80mph to Calais.

Champagne was served as the train entered the tunnel seven minutes late thanks to what British Rail called 'congestion in the south-east' – but it emerged on time. At the same time the presidential party sped north to the coast at 186mph and the trains met nose-to-nose in Calais at 11.28 a.m. The two heads of state cut another ribbon to signal the opening of the tunnel and unveiled a plaque at the Coquelles terminal.

The Queen, speaking in untroubled French, reflected on the unique nature of the occasion: 'This is the first time that the heads of state of France and Britain have been able to meet each other without either of them having to travel by sea or by air.' Despite the way in which Anglo-French relations had 'fluctuated violently through the ages', the tunnel would represent an enduring bond.

'The French and British peoples, for all their individual diversity and ages-long rivalry, complement each other well – better perhaps than we realise.'

M. Mitterrand expressed his belief in the tunnel as a monument to European unity. Afterwards, Lady Thatcher preferred to see it in technological terms. 'Every generation has to do something exciting that will affect the future,' she said.

Following a French banquet, both parties boarded Le Shuttle, the train service for vehicles. The heads of state, travelling in the Queen's Silver Jubilee Phantom VI, had one of the spotless mobile garages to themselves. Behind them, the heads of government and VIPs embarked in a bus.

The train arrived at Folkestone three minutes early at 2.52 p.m. and spared the Queen the effort of another ribbon-cutting by driving through a large, ceremonial tape across the track.

Before the last plaque unveiling at Folkestone, M. Mitterrand spoke about the historic symbolism of the tunnel. The Queen remarked that it had been a Frenchman who first flew across the Channel and a Briton who first swam it. 'What could be more appropriate, therefore, than a Frenchman and a Briton shaking hands under the middle of the Channel in December 1990.'

An explosion of balloons provided the last signal that the Channel Tunnel was open for business. And so it will be – in October.

The eyes of the world were on the inauguration of the tunnel – but it was business as usual on more conventional means of travel from England to France. One direct competitor to Eurotunnel, P&O European Ferries, helped the celebrations by taking the Queen's Rolls-Royce to Calais.

FRENCH TOAST BRITISH LIFE WITH BOWLERS AND BROLLIES

SUZANNE LOWRY REPORTS FROM CALAIS

It wasn't quite a public holiday in France but it had much of the mood of a fête. Window displays, flags, live television coverage and radio devoting half the day to English composers.

In Calais, they celebrated with jokes and parodies of British life. It seemed almost as if the town was once again ruled from London. A British bobby dragged a wooden dog on wheels through the streets and gentlemen in bowlers carried rolled umbrellas.

The town that once fretted that the tunnel would take away its ferry trade was thrilled by its new contact with England, although this may have more to do with the cheap price of supermarket booze than the new mode of transport.

Back in Paris at the newly spruced-up Gare du Nord, the Eurostar train was lined up at dawn and the blue carpet rolled out for the President of the Republic, who was off to meet France's first official visitor through the tunnel. Curious commuters leaned on the barriers as guests filtered through. The first thing they were given, apart from a badge, was a full-length see-through plastic raincoat. Someone had obviously read the weather forecast. 'I thought the tunnel was supposed to do away with weather,' I heard an English voice complain.

The French press united to celebrate the end of island life: 'It's the end of British insularity,' proclaimed *Le Figaro*. It may not be as easy as that, although French passengers on the train that took an hour and a half to cover the 180 miles to Calais speculated that British attitudes would change.

It was in France a very French event; the train, the construction, the motivation, were all seen as French with Britain as the lucky beneficiary. Before meeting the Queen, President Mitterrand made a quasi-royal progress across northern France to Lille to open the terminal that links Belgium to the network.

Nevertheless, the Queen's arrival gave the event an extra edge: 'It is the royal track,' announced *Le Parisien*. President Mitterrand told the Queen with some pleasure: 'From now on we have a land frontier,' adding that when Britain and France worked together they achieved great things but they could be more united and 'solidaire'.

An argument still rages about whether or not Le Shuttle should be called La Navette in France. Robert, the dictionary publisher, took out advertising explaining that the word 'tunnel' was originally from the French tonnelle. Then there was the vexed question of the fox. The opening of the tunnel coincides with a campaign to wipe out the disease called 'la rage' from Europe. As the Queen and President Mitterrand greeted each other, six million chicken heads impregnated with anti-rabies vaccine were dropped from helicopters across the countryside.

All magazines carried features on Britain. One hailed Eric Cantona as the first 'cross-Channel hero'. Television channels played romantic footage of old English trains chugging through lush countryside, with the occasional close-up of rusty rails covered with leaves.

TUNNEL VISION A TROUBLING SIGHT

Stephen Pile

This week saw the opening of an underwater passage joining together two nations who cannot stand the sight of each other. To mark this happy occasion, BBC2 presented *Going Underground*, a wilfully bizarre season that was weird from start to finish and seemed a very odd way to celebrate our transmanche triumph.

The Great Escapers (BBC2, Sunday) described how fifty men were shot after tunnelling out of Stalag Luft III. *Death Line* (BBC2, Sunday) was a horror film about something nasty lurking on the London Tube system. And *Notes From the Underground* (BBC2, Saturday) was a dark and powerful documentary about life in the fetid tunnels beneath Moscow in which 7,500 inhabitants died last year. All in all, tunnels sounded nothing but trouble.

CHUNNEL TRAIN FAILS TO START

The Eurostar passenger train broke down before it had even started on an inaugural trip from London through the Channel Tunnel to Paris yesterday.

A substitute train loaded with journalists eventually left Waterloo one hour late and, though it arrived twelve minutes ahead of schedule, its two hours and forty-eight minutes trip failed to prevent the incident from wiping ten pence off the Eurotunnel share price.

NEW PULLMAN TO BRIGHTON

LUXURIOUS TRAVELLING

With the inauguration of the *Southern Belle*, the new Pullman Limited express between London and Brighton, almost the last word has been said on luxury in railway travel. Search the world, and it would be impossible to find anything quite up to the level of this, the latest train-de-luxe of the London, Brighton and South Coast Railway Company. Its introduction is due to Mr Davison Dalziel, chairman of the Pullman Company, and the expense of building the seven cars which make up the train has been something like £40,000. There is seating accommodation for 219 persons. Each car has a distinctive name, and a different colour scheme, which will be especially appreciated by ladies, who have a pardonable horror of an unsuitable setting. There is diversity in other directions. The woodwork, for instance, in some cases is of mahogany, and in others satinwood or oak, the finest materials in every instance being used. All is richly and beautifully inlaid, while the mouldings, friezes and cornices are of the most elegant work-manship. The ceiling of each car is completely symmetrical and decorated in bas-relief. The upholstery of the easy chairs and settees, which afford a maximum of comfort, is very tasteful. The shade of the pile carpet blends with the surrounding colours, and the effect of the whole compartment is pleasing in the extreme. The electric lighting will satisfy the most fastidi-ous, and in this connection one of the many novel features is the dainty standard lamp which adorns every table. There is a buffet-car, and meals will be served in the train.

Among the inducements which have led the railway company to run this expensive train are the great success of the Sunday Pullman Limited, and an improving Brighton traffic. The journey will be performed each way in sixty minutes, the train leaving Victoria at 11 a.m. on weekdays and Sundays, returning from Brighton at 5.45 p.m. on weekdays, and 9 p.m. on Sundays. The price of the day return ticket is 12s.

At the invitation of the London, Brighton and South Coast Railway Company, and the Pullman Company, a number of representative gentlemen of Brighton and others, including press representatives, accompanied *Southern Belle* on its inaugural trip on Saturday, and were able to test the comfort and convenience of the train, and the easy travelling which is afforded. Both journeys were accomplished in the good space of fifty-seven minutes, or three minutes below the scheduled time. At the Hotel Metropole, Brighton, the party had luncheon. The Earl of Bessborough (chairman of the London, Brighton Company) presided, and was supported by Mr Davison Dalziel, Mr E.A. Villiers, MP, the Mayor of Brighton (Alderman Roberts), Viscount Duncannon, Sir F. Laking, Sir C. Furness, Sir V. Caillard, Sir F. Blaker, Sir W. Bell, Mr W. Forbes (general manager), and others.

In submitting the loyal toast, the chairman expressed his pleasure that his Majesty's visit to Brighton had done him so much good. From that time the Brighton traffic began to improve, although a great deal more was wanted. Lord Bessborough afterwards proposed 'success to the *Southern Belle*', and mentioned that they were encouraged to try the experiment by the success which had attended the running of a somewhat similar train between Paris and Trouville. It showed that they were doing their best to encourage first-class traffic to Brighton and they hoped this would not be the only train of its kind. (Cheers.) The Mayor of Brighton, responding to the toast of 'the Mayor and corporation', hoped the new train would be followed by many of the same sort, because they would bring to Brighton the class of passengers that place wanted. The visit of the King was of immediate benefit to the town. Houses had let better, and would continue to do so, because the King expressed his intention of coming there again. (Cheers.) They all hoped his Majesty would come again, and he (the Mayor) hoped it would be by train (laughter).

EXEUNT AUDREY AND VERA,
BEARING KIPPERS

Peter Clayton

It is almost forty years since Audrey and Vera, twin sisters, left their Birmingham home and came to work in the south. They were a couple of strapping young girls, but they had elegance enough in their way, and most people grew inordinately fond of them once they got to know them.

Indeed, they rose so high in the affections of those who came into regular contact with them that even when, old enough to know better, they became increasingly boisterous and given to horseplay and practical jokes, they were invariably forgiven. They were entitled to take a few liberties, of course, because they worked so hard; nobody could begrudge them the occasional lapse. Now that they are about to retire we are all torn between relief that at last they are going to get some rest and sorrow at seeing them go.

I travelled up from Brighton with Vera last Wednesday for the sake of spending an hour in her company for the last time. She was still the same exhilarating, unpredictable companion but outwardly she had changed a good deal, and to tell the truth, she was beginning to show her age. By present-day standards she has a weight problem, too; but then, at 43 tons since birth, I suppose she always had.

At one time I presume most of the Pullman cars on the *Brighton Belle* had names, but of the ten cars which had been working the train during this final week of its existence, all are anonymous except Vera and Audrey. Not that you will see their names on the outside; doubtless that kind of nonsense was obliterated when British Rail blue-and-dirt replaced the chocolate and cream livery of the Pullman Car Co. You will find them inside, however, on small roundels up near the ceiling.

But you had better be quick. Tonight, the *Belle* makes its last run, amid libations of the most potent cocktail known to man: Champagne and tears. Both ingredients will be liberally spilled – the tears because that's the way people get on these occasions, the Champagne because that's the way the

Belle has always dealt with liquid refreshment. Always, that is, to my recollection, though I have to admit that where I come from meals on trains were largely a matter of paper bags, vacuum flasks, crumbs in the lap and forgetting to bring the salt; I first attempted to eat aboard the Belle comparatively late in its career.

By common consent it was the roughest ride since four-wheeled trams. A place setting was the conventional knife-fork-spoon, but bib, spoon and pusher might have been more practical. Six years ago I took two children for a teatime ride on it, as an experience not to be missed, like going down a mine or seeing the Taj Mahal by moonlight. We had medium-rare toast, which my daughter – a connoisseur – rated as perfect; the tea was good, too, what we had of it. The spilled-to-swallowed ratio was about 4:1 in favour of spillage for the children, 2:1 for adults.

Last week at lunch I did much better. Of the soup of the day – out of the can of the day – not a drop was lost, largely because it was cunningly served while the train was still at the platform. A quarter bottle of wine is too small to have time to get spilled; and by good timing there was nary a slip twixt pot and lip (and double handling doubles the risk, naturally) when it came to the excellent coffee. Some of the cucumber from the salad went astray, but cucumber does that anyway, even after you've eaten it. The track is mostly welded now, of course, and I was near the centre of the car, not over one of those massive, lurching bogies; nevertheless I was agreeably surprised.

According to the guard, this special stock was designed for a working life of twenty-five years, and the fact that it is still sound after thirty-nine years of bludgeoning speaks well for it. Obviously it had to go, and I can't get very worked up about its not being replaced. I feel very sorry for all Brighton's showbiz personalities, the Alan Melvilles and the Lord Oliviers, who won't get their ritual kippers any more, but the fact that the train has become an autograph album on wheels is not necessarily an argument for keeping it going. In these times I'd be happy to settle for a clean, fast, all-day train service that you could count on.

It has been a good week for nostalgia, nonetheless. At least half Wednesday's passengers had cameras; two boys persuaded the driver to photograph them on the running board of his cab. NBC television had a cameraman aboard and a helicopter and camera crew overhead. All the way up, sad, sniping photographers lurked in the lineside bushes.

Audrey and Vera and the other now-nameless old ladies showed their mettle as they pranced through Three Bridges at a fraction over 77mph.

Horley and ham salad, Croydon with the coffee. Then the long trundle over Grosvenor Bridge and into Victoria two minutes early. It was as if they were keen to get their feet up.

TRAIN HAIRDRESSERS

L.N.E.R. INNOVATION

A hairdressing saloon, where not only may the male passengers have a shave or a haircut, but where the women passengers may have their hair shingled, bobbed, or Eton-cropped, will be one of the novelties introduced on the L.N.E.R. on Tuesday next, when the twin *Flying Scotsmen* commence their service as non-stop expresses between London and Edinburgh.

In addition to the saloon the expresses will also have a men's waiting room and a women's retiring room, the latter being in charge of a woman, who will have for sale perfumery, toilet articles and restoratives. These facilities will be available for third- as well as first-class passengers.

'Is it easy to shave on a moving train?' a representative of the *Daily Telegraph* yesterday asked one of the men who will be on duty in the saloon. 'Perfectly simple,' was the reply. 'But suppose the train sways while you are shaving?' 'We sway with it,' he declared. 'But is there no risk of you swaying the wrong way?' 'None whatever,' was the answer. Moreover, no safety razors will be used. 'We should never dream of using them,' said the hairdresser. 'The honest open blade for us.'

India's first air-conditioned train, in which a constant temperature of 72°F and a 55 per cent humidity are maintained, has made its inaugural run from Delhi to Agra and back.

TRAVELLER'S JOY

Peterborough

'We are now travelling at 90mph; I hope you are having a comfortable journey.' The calm voice, from discreet loudspeakers, the contemporary decor and the gliding motion reminded me of a modern airliner. But in fact I was railborne on British Railways' latest effort to woo the traveller. This is the new diesel-electric Pullman which made a demonstration run yesterday from Marylebone to High Wycombe.

Five of these trains, painted Nanking blue, are to ply between London and Manchester, Birmingham and Bristol. The first, the Midland Pullman, comes into service on 4 July.

In my experience they will be as good as anything on the Continent. I was particularly taken yesterday with the air conditioning – the first on British trains. It can be varied from semi-tropical to cocktail temperatures.

Also with the driving cabin, fitted with an electric cooker. But Mr Tom Stevenson, the driver, assured me there was no question of driving with one hand while grilling a chop with the other. The cooker, he said, was strictly for use between runs.

HIGH-SPEED TRAIN STOPS FOR ISLA ST CLAIR

The Advanced Passenger Train is expected to be back in use today despite the embarrassing failure of its tilting gear on its first run from London to Glasgow with paying passengers on Monday night.

A fault in the electricity supply triggered a circuit-breaker and locked the train in an upright position instead of allowing coaches to tilt when taking curves at speed. The sudden locking movement sent food and drinks splashing across the floor.

The fault arose just north of Preston, and the train was twenty-eight minutes late arriving in Glasgow. But yesterday it was revealed that five of those twenty-eight minutes were spent on an unscheduled stop at Penrith, in the Lake District, to allow Isla St Clair, the BBC's *Generation Game* girl, to get off.

Miss St Clair emerged from a part of the train normally sealed off for engineers to monitor the train's performance. A B.R. spokesman said they had been told the stop at Penrith was for technical reasons, but if it was true that Miss St Clair had been allowed to get off it was 'highly unofficial' and an inquiry would take place.

The spokesman said the train had stopped at Penrith because a brake warning light started flashing and engineers wanted to investigate. He added, 'Miss St Clair chose to alight there.'

Last night Miss St Clair, appearing on the *Russell Harty Show*, said she had been due to be in the Lake District to film the *Pebble Mill Christmas Show*, but arrived ten minutes late at Euston station. 'I had no money and I have lost my cheque book. I didn't know what to do, then suddenly a crowd of heavy gentlemen approached me. One said, "We're from the APT. Can we help you?"'

Miss St Clair said she had not even realised what the APT was, but when they turned out to be members of the design and project team and offered her a lift she said: 'That's wonderful.' She added, 'On we went and they dropped me off at Penrith.'

Her problems did not stop there. Back at her hotel she realised she had left a small plastic bag with her underwear on the train and last night on television she appealed to the design and project team, 'Please send it back to me. I can't imagine what you're doing with it. I dread to think.'

Meanwhile, it has not yet been discovered whether the failure in the tilting gear came from within the train or from the electricity supply through the overhead wires. The train was not due to run yesterday, being timetabled only for Mondays, Wednesdays and Fridays in its first fortnight with customers.

Almost anything that happens to, or on, a foreign train has always been sure-fire success stuff in the cinema. From the earliest years on, the titles have promised breathtaking moments – *The Great Train Robbery*, *The Iron Horse*, *The Lady Vanishes* (the original: I have no time for remakes), *Night Train to Munich*, *Murder on the Orient Express*, and hundreds more.

The excitements have been varied: bullion at risk in the luggage van, prisoners of war escaping and seated next to German officers, mackintoshed figures moving menacingly down corridors, dead bodies dotted here and there in the couchettes. Even when somebody went ('excuse me') to the lavatory, it looked tremendously suspicious.

English trains wouldn't somehow quite fill the bill dramatically, the only sensational happenings to, or on, the 10.42 a.m. stopping train to Bournemouth being its late arrival (signal failure at Brockenhurst) and the closing of the buffet, advertised as being open. Angry British faces, robbed of their Krunshybicks and expensive cups of coffee and loudly complaining ('I say, look here!') are not really good cinema box office.

In the theatre, trains have always been rather scarce. However, in plays and whenever anybody is either eating or telephoning, audiences are perfectly happy to sit and watch and an absorbed hush falls.

With the telephoning, even the dialling (the old-fashioned twirling finger sort rather than this modern jabbing kind) enthrals and is keenly watched, with always the right number resulting and something interesting to overhear ('Sylvia? Listen dear, Enid has found out about … us! Oh, my darling, please don't cry …'). Incoming calls cut sharply across the dialogue and are usually rewarding in one way or another: 'That will be Gustave! He said he would ring if they had had any … trouble. We shall have to answer …' In real life it would be a wrong number and an eager voice saying, 'Is that Macfisheries?'

And now for thrilling news! The dramatic possibilities of both foreign trains and telephones are to be combined in West Germany where express trains are to be equipped with coin-box telephones, on which local and foreign numbers can be obtained. So now in films, fugitives escaping from the secret police can rush down the corridor to cries of 'Let me pass!', dash to the Wagon Restaurant coin-box, wait their turn, carefully read the directions, lift receiver, wait for the dialling tone, insert two marks, dial number, press Button A as soon as they hear their number answering, and gasp out 'Fritz, they've got me …' before the crack of the Luger, the bullet, the cry of 'Ahhhhhhhh …', the slump to the floor and the ejection of the body ('Ah good, here comes a tunnel') onto the permanent way.

Perhaps, by way of making extra profit, Sir Peter Parker will arrange similar telephone facilities on British trains and encourage vandals to buy tickets and board trains where such a challenging new field of destruction awaits them.

TELEVISION ON A TRAIN RECEIVED AT 60mph

A party of radio and television experts yesterday received on a moving L.N.E.R. train the normal television transmission broadcast through the Brookmans Park BBC station by means of the Baird process. No special apparatus was necessary.

The train touched speeds up to 70mph between Sandy and Huntingdon, but the dancer at the studios at Long Acre could still be seen. This is the first time that television broadcast by wireless has been received on a rapidly moving railway train, no experiments of this nature having been tried elsewhere in the world.

23 OCTOBER 2003

NO ESCAPE AS TV IS TURNED ON IN COMMUTER TRAINS

Neil Tweedie

Commuting by train is often an unpleasant business, but it can also offer a kind of agreeable limbo. Time to reflect on the working day ahead or just ended, to dream of Caribbean shores, or to catch up on the dog-eared novel in the briefcase.

Most wonderfully of all, it provides a period of enforced abstinence from television, that constant invader of the senses. Until now.

Yesterday, Thameslink passengers between Bedford and Gatwick Airport had a trial run of a television service designed just for them. TNX could soon be a feature of trains across the country, providing bite-sized news and 'lifestyle' programmes interspersed with advertisements. It will be regularly updated so passengers need no longer be unaware of a breaking news story, or the signal failure that is about to prolong their viewing experience.

TNX claims that the travelling public is dying for the chance to watch thirty-minute loops tailored for the time of day: news at rush hour, and comedy and DIY in the afternoon. But those watching the screens in a test carriage yesterday had mixed feelings.

Jeremy Brinley Codd of Haywards Heath, West Sussex, appeared unimpressed as the Duke of Marlborough expounded the delights of Blenheim Palace on a vandal-proof screen above him. 'It would be OK as long as there were designated carriages where people could escape it,' he said. 'There is enough noise with stereos and mobile phones, but I would be interested in news – probably as an alternative to the *Evening Standard*.'

TNX believes that providing television-free carriages would be a problem, forcing commuters to run along platforms in an effort to find or avoid a screen. It proposes quiet zones in each carriage where travellers can escape TNX, taking up about a quarter of the seats. The other three quarters will have it whether they like it or not.

Geraldine Wilson from Brighton, liked the idea. 'It's good. I don't like to read on the train because it makes me sick.'

If TNX is right, the peaceful crossword, the snatched teach-yourself-Italian session and the right to come to terms with the day quietly and grumpily may soon be at an end.

LAST TRAIN FOR TROUBLE HOUSE HALT

A country tavern that had its own railway station, where the last customers at night could stop a train by waving lighted matches at the driver, had its last train at the weekend.

The line, a seven-mile stretch between Kemble and Tetbury in Gloucestershire, came under the Beeching axe on Saturday. It was a line that Lewis Carroll and Emett between them might have devised.

It had British Railway's one and only portable station, known as Beercrate Halt, invented by an enterprising guard for passengers who found the first step too steep. It had diesel rail cars instead of engines and coaches. It had the most versatile and obliging crews, men who could drive a stray cow off the line, stop to pick pussy willow for a passenger or back up a few yards to collect a housewife waiting at the bottom of her garden.

Sadly, but perhaps not surprisingly, it did not make a profit and it had to go.

On Saturday night, bowler-hatted mourners loaded a flower-decked coffin aboard the last car at Trouble House Halt, just opposite the 17th-century inn with the same curious name.

The coffin was plastered with notices such as 'Urgent, in a state of decay,' addressed to Dr Beeching. It contained, symbolically, the Tetbury line's corpse and physically a dozen empty gin bottles.

Mr William 'Laddie' Peare, licensee of the Trouble House, was one pall-bearer. His brother, George, an undertaker, who knocked up the coffin in his spare time, was the other.

There were mournful cheers from Trouble House customers and the camera-carrying train-spotters who packed the forty-five-seater car. There were black crêpe and ivy trails on the bumpers and sad posters: 'Did you support this railway? Why come now, it's too late.'

There was hardly room to stand on the last train out of Kemble. Someone had lit a bonfire on the track near Culkerton and the crew had to stop and put it out. A last stop at Trouble House, cheers from the packed public bar ringing across the railbus. Fog detonators and cheers and 'Auld Lang Syne' on the last run.

Once they said the railway would make Tetbury prosperous and important. But that was in 1889, before Dr Beeching was born.

RAIL ENTHUSIASTS GATHER FOR THE DAWN OF A NEW ERA

AS PRIVATISED TRAINS RUN FOR THE FIRST TIME, FOLLOWERS OF THE TRACK JOIN FORCES ON A TRIP INTO HISTORY

Toby Moore

Nine fare-paying train-spotters were joined by one secretary of state and his wife in a cold west London dawn yesterday to mark the first privatised passenger rail service since 1948.

Philip Bedford, who spends most weekends roving the London and suburban bus network on discounted tickets, pedalled hard from East Sheen to make the 5.10 a.m. from Twickenham to Waterloo. He was anxious to earn his footnote in history: the first person to take a bicycle aboard a privatised train. He set off early.

Mr Bedford, forty-three and unemployed, was planning a day trip to Clacton anyway. Catching the thirty-seven-minute service into town seemed the practical solution to combining immortality with his day by the sea. 'I thought this was a bit of history and the chance to save some cycling at the other end. The arcades are cheaper off-season, you see,' he said.

Another keen cyclist, Sir George Young, sat further down Stagecoach One, racily named after the bus company that runs the South West Trains franchise. 'This is a momentous day for the railways,' intoned Sir George, extolling the benefits of privatisation with at least one reference to the word renaissance.

A Gatwick Express service passed as Stagecoach One drew out of an unlit Clapham Junction. 'It's empty,' one of the five-dozen reporters on board noted sullenly. But he proved only how hard it is to bait a battle-weary Tory Cabinet minister these days. 'Ah, but it's not in the private sector yet,' Sir George replied with a wan smile. A quirk of accounting procedure required British Rail to hand over control formally to Stagecoach at 2 a.m., making the 5.10 from Twickenham the first true moment of change in nearly fifty years. The new owners of the train – anticipating 550 passengers – doubled the length of the normal Sunday service, but only a particularly hardy species of train-spotter turned up.

John Bird, a retired RAF officer and anorak wearer, drove from Faringdon, Oxon, to be the toast of the thousand-strong Branch Line Society. 'I just had to be here. Simple as that,' he said, confidently breaching a clutch of protective civil servants to get Sir George's autograph. Not to be outdone in what turned out to be a competitive day for students of the surreal, the Labour Party sent a team into Hampshire to support its assertion that the first privatised train was, in fact, a bus.

Engineering works had forced South West Trains to take to the road on the final leg of the 1.12 Waterloo to Southampton Central. Glenda Jackson and Brian Wilson, Labour transport spokesmen, were there to meet the train at the switchover. They were not alone. News of the spoiler leaked and the Conservatives rustled up Stephen Reid, their prospective parliamentary candidate.

He insisted that because the train left London before 2 a.m. the revenue would go to B.R. and the train was not the first. 'What they thought was the first private train service was in fact the last nationalised service,' he said.

LAST POST FOR THE NIGHT MAIL

THE TRAVELLING POST OFFICES IMMORTALISED BY AUDEN'S POEM WERE MAKING THEIR FINAL RUNS. **ADAM EDWARDS** JOINED ONE OF THEM – AND REMEMBERED TO TAKE HIS OWN TEA MUG

In the 1950s, the Ace Café in the London suburb of Stonebridge Park was a favourite of the hardest bikers, a place so rough that the plastic spoons were chained to the tables and the tables chained to the floor. Nowadays, it is more genteel. It has been revamped as a nostalgic themed bar for geriatric mods and rockers, with monthly rallies of classic English motorbikes, American hot rods and other forms of dated tearaway transport. It's where the ageing go to remember their wheels.

Sadly, it is unlikely that any of the crash-helmeted 'faces' at the café know or care that directly above them is the sixteen-acre Princess Royal distribution centre, where another set of twentieth-century wheels is about to be consigned to the history books – the travelling post offices.

The dark red Royal Mail trains that have set off every night from the biggest privately owned station in Europe, rattling through the darkness sorting first-class mail for the nation's far-flung towns and villages, have finally been killed off.

The last T.P.O. from Stonebridge Park will leave for Newcastle at 11.18 p.m. next Friday. (The last of all will leave Bristol for Penzance seven hours later, at 6.30 a.m. next Saturday.) It is the end of an extraordinary service that started 166 years ago.

A few weeks ago, I was offered the chance to take one of the T.P.O. trains that service the north. It was a ride redolent of post-war Britain, belonging to an age of saucy seaside postcards, rust-coloured tuppenny stamps and prison mailbags. It evoked memories of a simpler, more austere life, particularly when James Eadie, the press officer for Royal Mail, phoned me on my mobile an hour before I was due at the terminal to remind me to bring a mug if I wanted a cup of tea. 'There's always a shortage of spare mugs on board,' he said.

I arrived at the depot at 10 p.m. with my snapping tin and Diana, Princess of Wales souvenir — the only mug on sale late at night in central London. Scores of lorries from post offices all over the south-east were queuing to get into the floodlit sorting office at the back to dump bags for electronic sorting.

They included the mailbags for the Plymouth and Carlisle trains, which were being loaded on to the windowless carriages from York Mover trolleys. They skidded about the platforms like Daleks in a terminal that looked and sounded like a proper train station, with its clocks and incomprehensible PA system, but had the aura of a B-movie science-fiction set, with no passengers, ticket offices or fast-food suppliers.

I stepped into the bare-boarded carriage 80428. It was empty except for a small table and mean office chair at one end. The sliding door clanged as it was pulled shut and the train, pulled by an E.W.S. electric engine, left for Rugby and points north on the dot of 11.02 p.m.. 'The T.P.O.s always leave on time,' said James Eadie, as it lurched forward into the night and we tumbled backwards, with no hanging straps or seats to hold onto.

The carriages at either end of me contained postmen wearing Royal Mail red cotton tops. There were thirty-five sorters on the eight-carriage train and each stood at his post at the long, low table that ran the length of each carriage. Each emptied out a sack of mail that had already been sorted according to postal regions, breaking it down into smaller areas by slotting the letters into one of forty wooden pigeonholes directly in front of him. The letters were then bundled up and put into bags that would go to individual postmen. Those postmen in turn would arrange the bundles into streets and numbers and deliver them to our homes.

The men stood underneath the naked light bulbs, legs apart to steady them and rocking while they worked to the rhythm of the train. Sometimes, it pitched or lurched with a sudden lateral swing. If it shook from side to side, the men said it was 'hunting'. If the driver took a bend too fast and the letters shot out of the cubby holes and spun across the carriage like Frisbees, the description was so colourful that it is unprintable.

They could tell a good driver from a bad one and knew by instinct at any given moment where they were on the line, despite the windowless rolling-stock. At various stops along the way, at Rugby and Warrington, for example, the smokers among them drifted on to the platform for a quick fag while the sorted postbags for that area were chucked out and new bags thrown on. (The old net 'apparatus' made famous in the Ealing comedy *Two-Way Stretch*, which was introduced in 1852, was abandoned in 1971.)

The brilliance of the T.P.O. was that it utilised the dead time when mail was moved. If the bags had gone by road, as they now must, they would have needed a sorter at the delivery end. It was a system that worked well for more than a century and a half.

The first travelling post office was a converted horsebox that left London for Birmingham on 20 January 1838. It had only one sorting clerk and a red-coated mail guard who had been recruited from the Royal Mail's horse-drawn carriages. Such was its success that within a couple of months a government bill was passed obliging the railway companies to provide a separate carriage for sorting letters en route. The establishment of new rail routes and the heavy increase in mail confirmed the travelling post offices as an integral part of the Royal Mail system and by the beginning of the First World War there were 139 T.P.O.s that made up the web of interconnecting routes.

Even in those early days, there was a romance about the trains that would slip through the night while we slept. The G.P.O. recognised this fact and made a powerful documentary in the 1930s called *Night Mail* to celebrate the centenary of the T.P.O.. It concentrated on the London-Scotland run and was shown in cinemas across the country. Benjamin Britten composed the music and W.H. Auden was commissioned to write an accompanying poem, which has been in most children's lexicons ever since.

This is the Night Mail crossing the border,
Bringing the cheque and the postal order,
Letters for the rich, letters for the poor,
The shop at the corner and the girl next door.
Pulling up Beattock, a steady climb;
The gradient's against her. But she's on time.
Past cotton grass and moorland boulder
Shovelling white steam over her shoulder,
Snorting noisily as she passes
Silent miles of wind-bent grasses.

Yet despite the nation's constant love, the service has been consistently downgraded. After the Second World War, only forty-three trains were reinstated. The introduction of the two-tier postal system in 1968 slimmed down the T.P.O. service so that only first-class mail would be sorted on the trains. Twenty years later, a revamp of the Royal Mail distribution system saw further reductions. No T.P.O. has crossed the Scottish border and pulled up Beattock in a decade: the mail for Scotland goes by plane.

Perhaps the saddest moment was in 1996 when the trains were moved from the main-line railway terminals and ordered to leave from the Royal Mail's soulless Rail Net distribution centre at Stonebridge Park.

But even then, in fact until the very end, it was still possible to post a letter on a T.P.O.. Every carriage had its own postbox. When a letter was dropped through the box, it would be franked on the train with a T.P.O rubber stamp. In recent years, the postboxes were used only by philatelists, who posted first-day-issue stamps on the trains for a more interesting post-mark, and the sorters, who used the boxes to keep their cans of beer cold in the summer.

Now the travelling postboxes and the trains that carried them are finished. It cost £16 million a year to run the T.P.O.s. At the final count, there were 18 trains with 420 staff running from Carlisle and Newcastle in the north to Penzance in the south-west. Between them, the trains handled 15,000 bags, ensuring that the most remote farmhouse would receive its mail the morning after it had been posted from anywhere in the country.

The Royal Mail claims it would have needed a further £30 million invest-ment to keep the T.P.O.s going – in part because of new health and safety regulations, but also because the poor state of our railway system made continuation of the T.P.O.s economically impossible.

According to Steve Griffith, the Travelling Post Office manager at Stonebridge: 'The Post Office is trying to run a business that is as cost-effi-cient as possible.

'Our aim is to save £90 million a year by transferring the mail from rail to road and plane. The T.P.O.s were a Victorian answer to a Victorian problem to moving post in a pre-motorway era. But they have become inefficiently priced and the inconsistency of the railways has meant it has been difficult to keep to our target of more than 92.5 per cent of deliveries next day.'

Dave Dennerley, a sorter from east London, told me when we were stuck outside Warrington: 'We don't get leaves on the line on this train – we get engineering works. And if a T.P.O. train is only half an hour late, the whole system goes up the spout. The post won't get delivered until the following day.'

From next week, the engineering works, heatwaves, cold snaps, autumn leaves and spring flocks of sheep that have combined to make our rail system a Third World joke will be a thing of the past for the Post Office. All mail criss-crossing the country will be sorted at a variety of distribution centres, in particular at Daventry in Northamptonshire, and delivered by lorry and plane. There will, of course, be fog and traffic jams to cope with in the new streamlined system, but there will be no expensive sorters on the roads or in the air.

The end of the T.P.O. will leave behind a group of semi-skilled workers who are no longer needed. The postmen – there was only one female sorter on the T.P.O.s – have always been considered the elite. They claimed they were twice as fast as their office-based colleagues and could sort 3,000 letters an hour (a machine can sort 25,000), and as they got a working night premium of £70 and a travel subsidy of £50 they earned considerably more.

It was, though, a rough, anti-social life in primitive conditions. In summer, the trains were boiling; in winter, they were either too cold or, if the heating was on, too hot.

'It's not everyone's cup of tea,' said Bob Bates, who has been sorting on the T.P.O.s for twenty-two years. On the other hand, it has been a most clubbable way of working. The crews always work the same trains to the same destination. 'We see more of each other than the wife,' said one, with perhaps rather more cheer than he should have done.

Between Warrington and Carlisle I finally got to talk to the veteran sorter Dino Howell. He joined the T.P.O.s in 1962 and remembers being on the 'down' train to Carlisle (all the trains heading away from London are 'down' trains, while those heading towards the capital are 'up' trains) when John F. Kennedy was assassinated. 'I'll never forget it – we were late into Carlisle,' he says without a smile. Dino was also on the 'up' train that was robbed by Ronnie Biggs and his gang in August 1963.

'In those days, we would have 150 men on the train,' said Dino, as he started on the story of the great train robbery that he has told many times in the 40 years since its execution. 'None of us were aware that there was so much money being transported. And when the train stopped, most of the sorters didn't know what was going on. The money was in the front carriage.

'The only reason most of us knew something was wrong was because the train shouldn't have stopped there for that length of time. And by the time we did know something, it was all over.'

But the robbery gave the boys on the T.P.O.s a cachet. It was something else they could be proud of. We crawled into a pitch-black Carlisle at 5 a.m. The sorters checked for any mail that might have been mislaid, packed up their Thermos flasks and, when the train pulled in, they slipped from it into the inky morning without a backward glance. That evening they would be working the 'up' train to London.

'It's not a job, it's a way of life,' said Dave Dennerley. At least it was. Dave, like most of the sorters, will retire next week. The T.P.O.s will be scrapped or given to railway museums. There will never again be a night train crossing the border delivering the cheque and the postal order.

A TRAIN-SPOTTER TO THE END

STEAM TRAINS WERE FRED NORMANTON'S LIFELONG
HOBBY; FITTINGLY, ONE CARRIED HIM TO HIS GRAVE.
GARETH PARRY ATTENDED HIS EXTRAORDINARY FUNERAL

Until quite recently it was a privilege granted only to the great and the good. Queen Victoria, George VI and Sir Winston Churchill all made their final earthly journey by rail, surrounded by all the pomp and circumstance of a state funeral. Now it was the turn of an ordinary working man: Fred Normanton, born 30 April 1936, died 1 February 1999 – and a dedicated train-spotter all his life.

Fred was granted his final wish when the elderly London, Midland and Scottish Railway's engine No. 47327 puffed out of Butterley station in Derbyshire, carrying his mortal remains, as well as his family and his friends in a dining car for the wake.

He would have loved the billowy smoke with its core of orange and red flame, the infernal clanking of connecting rods, the ear-splitting shrieks as scalding steam shot from safety valves, and the shouts from the footplate crew for more water and yet more tea.

It was a fitting farewell. While the conventional funeral procession begins when the glossy black Daimler's engine purrs into life, Fred's started much earlier, for it had taken four hours to raise steam. Overnight LMS No. 47327, herself a seventy-three-year-old maid of all trade – freight, passenger and shunting – had suffered frozen tubes, which had to be thawed.

It was only after a wreath of red carnations (Fred was a proud Lancastrian) was tied on to her smoke-box door that she nudged up to the three coaches and the guard's van in which Fred already lay, a dark-blue velvet cover and a white fleece softening the austere lines of his biodegradable cardboard coffin.

Fred's sixty-two years were celebrated with affection, humour and happy memories, as he and his family and friends travelled sedately through a threadbare wintry landscape to his woodland grave on the side of the track at Swanwick Junction near the Midland Railway Centre in Ripley.

There are more than 120 preserved railways in Britain and Fred had visited every one during half a century of spotting, photographing and cataloguing locomotives and railway-stock. But now it was his turn to enter the record books as the first full railway burial at Ripley, a train-spotter's nirvana of restoration workshops, hands-on footplate courses, and a unique collection of locomotives and rolling stock from the 1860s to present times.

The non-religious funeral, organised by Peace Burials of Ormskirk, Lancashire, was what he and his wife, Maureen, decided on after Fred's cancer was diagnosed last August, on the eve of a railway holiday of a lifetime. Fred and Maureen had taken a railway holiday every year of the thirty-two they had been married, and this one was to have been to Holland, France and the Harz Mountains in Germany.

Fred Normanton and railways went back a long way. He was born close to the line at Littleborough, Lancashire. As a boy, he would spend hours with his uncle in the signal box there – this was often the way in railway families, uninhibited by rules and regulations, and it was also the manner in which future railwaymen were nurtured and recruited.

But Fred's short-sightedness, in an era when uncorrected twenty-twenty night-and-day vision was obligatory for railwaymen, consigned him for ever to the platforms, embankments and bridges still visited by thousands of enthusiasts.

His fascination for steam and its fundamental organic power possibly led to his second-choice career as a research chemist. In the 1950s, university places were still too often out of the reach of working-class families. But the clever grammar-school boy won his Licentiate of the Royal Society of Chemistry in day-release courses and evening classes.

He worked mostly in industrial laboratories, and it was as a researcher in the government's quixotically named Unit of Nitrogen Fixation, based at Sussex University, that he met and married Maureen, a mathematics graduate. They had two sons: Andrew, a computer consultant, and Derek, a civil engineer.

The couple lived in the south until three years ago, when Maureen's job with the Inland Revenue was relocated to Manchester. It was a heaven-sent opportunity for Fred to return to his Lancashire roots, with its brass bands and, more importantly, its railway preservation societies – there are dozens in Lancashire, Yorkshire and Derbyshire.

The choice of a new home was easy: it had to be near a railway. It did not take Fred long to find a comfortable, three-bedroom semi in Bury, which had the irresistible feature of the East Lancashire Railway at the bottom of the road. He took two jobs, one as a chemist in a thread-dyeing factory and another as a part-time volunteer repairing and maintaining the signals on the East Lancs.

'We could have lived anywhere,' said Maureen, perhaps a little wistfully, 'but Fred was Fred and his whole life's hobby was steam trains and only steam trains. We've had a railway holiday every year either in Britain or abroad. We've stayed in old stations converted into b and bs, self-catering ex-stationmaster's houses and I think we once stayed in a converted signal box. I grew to share an interest, but never became an enthusiast. On holiday, Fred would go looking at trains, taking their photographs and recording their details – he was still cataloguing all those thousands of pictures to the end – and I'd go and do some shopping.

'At weekends, we would make up sandwiches and a flask and go to a preserved line or a rail museum. There was always a good selection of special outings and these I enjoyed. On the day of the Princess of Wales's funeral, we went up to Carlisle to photograph a special steam train arriving there. They had debated whether to run it in view of the circumstances, but they did. It was a way of life and it worked for us.'

Fred was one man who would never have been late for his own funeral, and Peace Burials had drawn up a timetable so precise it was reminiscent of an era when 'leaves on the line' was an undreamt-of excuse, when one minute adrift was a matter for report and five minutes could be a sacking offence. This is how it went:

10.10 Fred's family and friends – fifteen people in all – arrived at Butterley station where volunteer staff had just finished scraping ice off the carriage windows.

10.15 The mourners were served tea and coffee in the dining car.

10.30 precisely. The guard – Gordon Johnson, a sixty-two-year-old retired coalface worker – waved his green flag. 'I'm really the stationmaster, but somehow I've done 257 guard's turns,' he said, with the relaxed air of someone who knows his place in the pecking order of railways. The driver – Steve Hill, aged fifty-eight, a retired policeman – drew four long blasts on his whistle and the train moved off on its seven-mile journey.

11.05 (to the minute on the guard's fob-watch). The train arrived at Swanwick Junction. Fred's coffin, his two sons among the pall-bearers, was carried from the train to the funeral service at the railwaymen's chapel, one of the so-called 'tin tabernacles' put up by railway families when the main lines were laid in the 19th century.

St Saviour's, as it was originally consecrated, is clad economically with corrugated iron sheet on the outside and mellowed pitch pine within. As the mourners entered, a brass band recording of Gershwin's classic *Rhapsody in Blue*, one of Fred and Maureen's favourites, filled the air.

Then, relatives and friends recalled memories of the blunt-spoken Lancastrian. Others read pieces of poetry, concluding with Maureen's recitation of W.H. Auden's 'Funeral Blues', the poem made famous as 'Stop all the clocks ... ' in the film *Four Weddings and a Funeral*.

It was the most poignant moment of the day, but instantly the tears it provoked were mixed with laughter as John Mallatratt of Peace Burials proposed 'a toast to Fred with Tesco's whisky' – clearly an in-joke among the family.

Then we all filed out into the thin February sunshine to Bette Midler's *My One True Friend*.

At noon, as Fred's coffin was lowered into his clay grave at the Golden Valley Woodland Burial Ground, LMS Engine No. 47327, standing swathed in steam and smoke just a few yards from the plot, gave three blasts of her whistle in final farewell. Someone, perhaps overtaken by the moment, clapped his or her hands.

They said afterwards that the wake back aboard the train was Fred's party, and it was terrific. Vegetable soup, roast beef and gateau, coffee, cheese and biscuits, and a generous bar service. The train had stopped for the wake on a large stone embankment overlooking Butterley Reservoir, where ducks and drakes and a lone swan skidded and stumbled around on its deep-frozen surface.

'It was exactly what I wanted and, I know, what Fred wanted, too. It might seem a strange thing to say, but I thoroughly enjoyed it,' said Maureen.

NOTES ON CONTRIBUTORS

MAY ABBOTT was a journalist and, from 1978 to 1985, a crossword compiler for the *Daily Telegraph*.

JOSIE BARNARD is the author of two novels, *Poker Face*, which won the Betty Trask Award, and *The Pleasure Dome*, and two travel guides – to New York and London – that were translated into five languages, all published by Virago. She is writing a new book for Virago to be published in 2011.

GODFREY BARKER is best known for his writing about the art market. Between 1972 and 1997 he worked on the *Daily Telegraph*, where he was variously parliamentary sketch-writer, arts editor and leader writer on political and home affairs.

JAMES BEDDING's great-grandfather built the railway line through the marshes fringing Lake Maggiore in Switzerland, his foreman giving him a daily tot of rum to ward off malaria. Many years later, James's father worked for British Rail as an architect; he now runs the family train set. James, meanwhile, is a journalist who hopes that the Swiss Federal Railways clock on his desk will one day improve his relationship with deadlines.

GAVIN BELL is a former foreign correspondent of the *Times*, who has found that travel writing makes an agreeable change from reporting on wars and *coups d'état*. He won the Thomas Cook/*Daily Telegraph* Travel Book of the Year Award with *In Search of Tusitala: Travels in the Pacific after Robert Louis Stevenson*, and his latest book is *Somewhere Over the Rainbow: Travels in South Africa*. He is still travelling hopefully.

SUZY BENNETT is a self-confessed railway geek who has a passion for long-distance and adventurous train travel. She works in London as a freelance travel and news journalist and is a regular contributor to the travel section of the *Daily Telegraph*. She spends her free time in Dartmoor, Devon.

ADRIAN BRIDGE, a former Berlin correspondent of the *Independent*, is a commissioning editor on the travel desk of the *Daily Telegraph* and takes the train as often as possible.

CRAIG BROWN's parodies of modern life appeared for 14 years in the *Daily Telegraph*. He is a columnist for *Vanity Fair* and *Private Eye* and chief book reviewer for the *Mail on Sunday*.

ERICA BROWN is a writer and editor who lived in Provence for five years either side of the Millennium and is the author of *Provence Gastronomique* (Conran Octopus). Having started in journalism at the *Sunday Times*, she spent a decade in New York, where she edited the lifestyle section of the *New York Times Magazine*. Returning to England, she wrote features from the *NYT*'s London bureau before creating magazines for Diners' Club, the Roux Brothers and Egon Ronay.

TOM BRUCE-GARDYNE, still being nibbled at by the travel bug, has recently succumbed to the demon drink, which he writes about regularly. Countless wine articles have sent him all round Europe and South America, while three books on Scotch whisky have kept him closer to his home town of Edinburgh.

SOPHIE CAMPBELL has been a freelance journalist for 15 years and writes a monthly heritage column for the *Daily Telegraph*. She is currently researching a book on the rival postal routes to the Indian Empire, which involves just as much minute detail as anything she has written about the railways.

JEREMY CLARKE writes the weekly 'Low life' column for the *Spectator*.

PETER CLAYTON (1927–91) was jazz correspondent and later radio critic for the *Sunday Telegraph* and a presenter of jazz programmes for the BBC.

ALISON CLEMENTS has reported for the *Daily Telegraph* from Italy and Thailand.

MINTY CLINCH, a long-time contributor to the travel pages of the *Daily Telegraph* and the *Sunday Telegraph*, has written biographies of Robert Redford, James Cagney, Burt Lancaster and Harrison Ford, and a novel, *Clean Break*.

JULIET CLOUGH, while on the staff of the books page, wrote her first travel piece for the *Sunday Telegraph* 40 years ago, bursting with the conflicting impressions left by a return to India, her birthplace. Her highly individual accounts have appeared in the travel pages of all the leading British broadsheets and won her several journalism awards.

GRAHAM COSTER is the author of two travel books, *Corsairvile: The Lost Domain of the Flying Goat* and *A Thousand Miles from Nowhere*, about riding with long-distance truck drivers. His fiction has appeard in the *New Yorker*, *Granta* and the *London Review of Books*. He is now Publisher at Aurum Press.

NICHOLAS CRANE is a writer and broadcaster. *Clear Waters Rising*, his account of a mountain walk from Finisterre to Istanbul, won the Thomas Cook Travel Book Award in 1997. He has written a biography of the map-maker Mercator and presented two television series for BBC2: *Coast* and *Great British Journeys*.

JANET DALEY spent 20 years in academic life, teaching philosophy while also writing art and literary criticism. She was a columnist and leader writer on the *Daily Telegraph* from 1996 to 2005, then wrote for other titles before returning to the paper.

CAROLINE DAVIES followed the Royal Family for six years for the *Daily Telegraph*, battling valiantly to keep up with them on her economy-class tickets. Though she never managed to hitch a lift on the royal train, she was given a tour while it was resting in a shed somewhere outside Milton Keynes.

ANDREW EAMES is the author of four books, including *Blue River, Black Sea* (Bantam Press), a journey down the Danube in the footsteps of Patrick Leigh Fermor, and *The 8.55 to Baghdad*, for which he set off in pursuit of Agatha Christie. He has edited *Great Train Journeys of the World*, due to be published in October 2009 by Time Out.

ADAM EDWARDS is a freelance journalist who has worked in Fleet Street most of his life and, with the notable exception of the *Sunday People*, written for every national newspaper in Britain. In 1996 he was voted Newspaper Magazine Editor of the Year. He recently published his first, and probably his last, book: *A Short History of the Wellington Boot*.

HUGH FEARNLEY-WHITTINGSTALL is a writer, broadcaster and campaigner, widely known for his uncompromising commitment to seasonal, ethically produced food. His books, journalism and series for Channel 4 have earned him a huge popular following.

CHRISTOPHER FILDES, who lists his recreations in *Who's Who* as 'Racing, railways', was a columnist for the *Daily Telegraph* and 'City and Suburban' columnist for the *Spectator* from 1984 to 2006. He is a member of the Railway Heritage Committee. He is also the only financial journalist whose copy has ever made the editor of this anthology want to turn to the City pages.

TREVOR FISHLOCK is a writer and broadcaster. He was staff correspondent of the *Times* in India and New York, and Moscow bureau chief for the *Daily Telegraph*. He has worked on assignment in more than 60 countries and has written books about Wales, India, America and Russia. He wrote and presented the popular *Wild Tracks* series for ITV and *Fishlock's Sea Stories* for BBC Wales.

MICHAEL FLEET covered Wales and then the Thames Valley for the *Daily Telegraph* but now runs a small B&B in Cornwall. He enjoys the train journey from St Erth into St Ives, but his favourite railway recollection is hearing a stranded bishop tell striking 1980s train driver, 'If you dropped dead now, I'd refuse to bury you!'

PETER FOSTER joined the *Daily Telegraph* in 1999, reporting on home and foreign affairs as a London-based correspondent. His assignments included the September 11 attacks in 2001 and the post-conflict arenas of Afghanistan and Iraq. In 2004 he was posted to New Delhi as South Asia Correspondent, covering the Boxing Day tsunami and the Kashmir earthquake of 2005. He is currently China correspondent.

DAVID GRAVES, a *Daily Telegraph* reporter from 1984 to 2003 (when he died at 50 in a diving accident in the Bahamas), was the epitome of the London-based newspaper 'fireman', ready to be dispatched anywhere at a moment's notice. He covered warfare in the Falkland Islands, Angola, Zimbabwe, Sri Lanka, Sudan, Kashmir and the Middle East, saw famine in Ethiopia and reported on the Union Carbide catastrophe in Bhopal, the 1986 Soweto schools uprising and terrorist attacks in continental Europe and the United Kingdom.

ROBERT HARDMAN, formerly at the *Daily Telegraph*, now at the *Daily Mail*, has been, among other things, a political sketch-writer, a diarist, a sports columnist, a restaurant critic and a royal correspondent. He was the writer and associate producer of the BBC1 series *Monarchy: The Royal Family at Work* and *The Queen's Castle*.

MARTYN HARRIS (1952–96) was a brilliant reporter, columnist and critic for the *Daily Telegraph* for 10 years. Some of his best work is collected in *Odd Man Out*, including excerpts from his novels, *Do It Again* and *The Mother-in-Law Joke*, and the article 'Something Understood', an account of how cancer had caused him to think again about Christianity, which prompted hundreds of letters from readers.

RONALD HASTINGS (1922–97) worked for the *Daily Telegraph* for 35 years, successively as reporter, theatre correspondent and television previewer. After joining the paper in 1955 he established himself as an expert on railways, sealing his reputation in December 1957 with an article that analysed the causes of the terrible crash at Lewisham only 24 hours before. He was an expert on long-case clocks, of which he owned several notable examples. He also gave up a room of his house to a model railway.

IVAN HEWETT writes about music for the *Daily Telegraph*, broadcasts on BBC Radio 3 and teaches at the Royal College of Music. He is the author of *Music: Healing the Rift* (Continuum), a very personal view of 20th-century music.

SEAN HIGNETT, a long-time contributor to the travel pages of the *Daily Telegraph* and the *Sunday Telegraph*, is the author of *Brett: From Bloomsbury to New Mexico*, a biography of the painter Dorothy Brett.

PETER HUGHES was founding editor of ITV's *Wish You Were Here...?* Since turning from television to full-time travel writing, he has received three Travel Writer of the Year awards, although his first foray into travel journalism was nearly his last. In 1968 he attempted to drive a family car from London to Timbuktu and back in a fortnight. The journey took a month and the car was abandoned in the Sahara.

MICHELLE JANA CHAN says there is no better place to gather stories and write them than in third class on a long-distance train. She writes, films and broadcasts everywhere from Antarctica to Zanzibar, preferring to be on the move rather than stay somewhere called home

PAUL JENNINGS (1918–89) was best known as a humorist. He was on the staff of the *Observer* from 1949 to 1966. Later he was a regular contributor to the *Daily Telegraph* and the *Sunday Telegraph*. His many books included *The Train to Yesterday* (for children) and *My Favourite Railway Stories* (which he edited).

BORIS JOHNSON is mayor of London. In a previous incarnation he was on the staff of the *Daily Telegraph*, for which he still writes a weekly column. He has published six books: *Friends, Voters, Countrymen, Lend Me Your Ears*; *Seventy-Two Virgins*; *Dream of Rome*; *Have I Got Views for You*; *Life in the Fast Lane: The Johnson Guide to Cars*; and *The Perils of the Pushy Parents: A Cautionary Tale*.

P.J. KAVANAGH is the author of eight books of poems, a columnist, essayist and travel-writer, a novelist, and editor of the poems of Ivor Gurney. He has received the Cholmondeley Award for Poetry, the *Guardian* Fiction Prize, and the Richard Hillary Prize for his memoir *The Perfect Stranger*. His latest books are *A Kind of Journal* (collected essays, 2003) and *Something About* (poems, 2004).

LEE LANGLEY is the author of nine novels, short stories and screenplays. Born in Calcutta of Scottish parents, she spent a nomadic Indian childhood and travel has always been part of her life. She is a Fellow of the Royal Society of Literature. Her tenth novel, *Butterfly's Shadow*, set in Japan and America in the middle of the 20th century, will be published by Chatto & Windus in 2010.

JAMES LANGTON has been a news editor of the *Sunday Telegraph* and New York correspondent. He now works for the *National* in Abu Dhabi.

SUZANNE LOWRY has worked for nine newspapers, including the *Guardian* (where she launched the *Guardian* Women page). She was Paris correspondent of the *Daily Telegraph* and the *Sunday Telegraph* for more than eight years. She has written four books: *The Guilt Cage: Housewives and a Decade of Liberation, The Young Fogey Handbook, The Cult of Diana: The Princess in the Mirror, La Vie en Rose — Living in France*. She now lives in the south of France.

PAUL MANSFIELD (see Introduction) said of himself in the yearbook of the British Guild of Travel Writers: 'Former backpacker, layabout, teacher, farm labourer, encyclopedia salesman, musician, arts writer and celebrity interviewer — all of which have proved invaluable during 15 years' full-time travel writing.'

ARTHUR MARSHALL (1910–89) was probably as well known for his appearances on the BBC's panel game *Call My Bluff* as he was for his humorous columns for publications from the *New Statesman* to the *Sunday Telegraph*.

PAUL MARSTON, formerly education correspondent and then transport correspondent of the *Daily Telegraph*, is now media relations manager at British Airways.

ANDREW MARTIN is the author of a series of thrillers set on the railways in the early 20th century, featuring the young railway policeman Jim Stringer. The first in the series was *The Necropolis Railway*; the latest is *The Last Train to Scarborough*. Forthcoming (2010) is *The Somme Stations*. All are published by Faber.

SUKETU MEHTA is the author of *Maximum City: Bombay Lost and Found*, which won the Kiriyama Prize and the Hutch Crossword Award, and was a finalist for the 2005 Pulitzer Prize, the Lettre Ulysses Prize, the BBC4 Samuel Johnson Prize, and the *Guardian* First Book Award. He is associate professor of journalism at

New York University. He is currently working on a non-fiction book about immigrants in contemporary New York.

CHRISTOPHER MIDDLETON writes for the *Daily Telegraph*, the *Sunday Telegraph* and other newspapers and magazines on everything from travel to etiquette. He is the author of *Behave! Tiptoeing through the Minefield of Human Conduct*, a collection of his 'Modern Manners' columns from the *Daily Telegraph*.

PETER MITCHELL was born in South Africa and grew up there. He is sports editor of the *Sunday Telegraph* and, if not quite in the same class as Colin Croft, a fine cricketer.

MARTIN MOORE (1904–91) served the *Daily Telegraph* for more than 40 years, first as a special correspondent and then as a leader writer. He covered the Italian colonisation of Libya, from which was to emerge his book, *Fourth Shore*.

TOBY MOORE, a former transport correspondent of the *Daily Telegraph*, has also been New York correspondent of the *Daily Express* and worked for the *Financial Times*, the *Sunday Times* and the *Evening Standard*. His novels include *Sleeping with the Fishes* and *Death by Chocolate*, both published by Penguin.

MICHAEL PALIN, one of the founders of Monty Python, always wanted to be an explorer, but says that until 25 September 1988 he was 'doomed to be nothing more than a very silly person'. That was the day he set out to make *Around the World in Eighty Days* — the first of eight series for the BBC that have brought him a half-dozen very full passports and personal acquaintance with more than 80 countries.

TIM PARKS has written 11 novels, including *Europa*, *Destiny*, *Cleaver* and, most recently, *Dreams of Rivers and Seas*, as well as three non-fiction accounts of life in northern Italy (most recently *A Season with Verona*), a collection of 'narrative' essays, *Adultery and Other Diversions*, and a history of the Medici bank in 15th century Florence, *Medici Money*.

GARETH PARRY was a reporter for the *Daily Express*, the *Daily Mail* and latterly *The Guardian* for 17 years. He covered conflicts in the Congo, Indo-Pakistan, the Middle East, Vietnam, Cambodia, Uganda, Cyprus – where he was wounded – and the Falkland Islands. 'Freelance writing about such things as railway journeys seemed a safe thing to do in my retirement,' he says.

ANTHONY PEREGRINE left Lancashire for Languedoc 20 years ago and has since travelled, eaten and drunk his way round Europe for a living. His work has appeared in the *Daily Telegraph*, the *Sunday Times*, the *Daily Mail* and other publications too obscure to mention. Some still owe him money. He reckons there's nothing more exciting than settling into a first-class seat on the TGV – unless it be the exploring of a new destination at the other end.

JIM PERRIN, a leading rock climber of the Sixties and Seventies, has twice won the Boardman Tasker Award for mountaineering literature, first for *Menlove*, his biography of John Menlove Edwards, then for *The Villain: The Life of Don Whillans*. *Travels with the Flea* and *Other Eccentric Journeys*, one of his several collections of essays, contains many articles that first appeared in the *Daily Telegraph*.

STEPHEN PILE has been a television critic for the *Daily Telegraph* and is the author of *The Book of Heroic Failures: Official Handbook of the Not Terribly Good Club of Great Britain*.

BILL POWELL is a long-time contributor to the travel pages of the *Daily Telegraph* and the *Sunday Telegraph*.

STUART REID is a columnist for the *Catholic Herald* and the *American Conservative*. He was deputy editor of the *Spectator* and before that comment editor of the *Sunday Telegraph* and a regular contributor to the *Telegraph* travel pages. He lives in Balham, London, with a wife and a three-legged cat, but really wants a dog.

NIGEL RICHARDSON was on the staff of the *Daily Telegraph* for 13 years. He has written five books, including a bestselling travelogue, *Breakfast in Brighton*, and a critically acclaimed novel for teenagers, *The Wrong Hands*, as well as radio drama. He continues to contribute to the *Telegraph* and to other leading publications.

FRANK ROBERTSON was a foreign correspondent for the *Daily Telegraph*.

BYRON ROGERS has been a feature writer for the *Daily Telegraph*, the *Sunday Times*, the *Guardian*, the *Evening Standard* and *Saga* magazine. His eight books include several which collect his journalism, such as *An Audience with an Elephant* and *The Bank Manager and the Holy Grail*, and two acclaimed biographies, of the idiosyncratic novelist and publisher J.L. Carr and the Welsh poet and vicar R.S. Thomas. The latter, *The Man Who Went into the West*, won the James Tait Black Biography Prize. His most recent book is *Me: The Authorised Biography*.

BARNABY ROGERSON is co-publisher at Eland, home to many of the classics of travel literature. He has written half a dozen guidebooks, as well as *A History of North Africa*; *The Prophet Muhammad: A Biography*; and *The Heirs of the Prophet Muhammad: And the Roots of the Sunni-Shia Schism*. His latest book is *The Last Crusaders: the Hundred-Year Battle for the Centre of the World*.

JONATHAN ROUTH (1927–2008) was an author, an artist and the deadpan agent provocateur of *Candid Camera*, Britain's first television prank show.

JOHN SIMPSON is world affairs editor of the BBC. His books include an autobiography, *Strange Places, Questionable People* (1998), and several accounts of his journalistic experiences: *A Mad World, My Masters* (2000); *News from No Man's Land* (2002), *The Wars Against Saddam* (2003) and *Days from a Different World* (2005).

ELISABETH DE STROUMILLO is a former travel editor of the *Daily Telegraph* and author of many guidebooks.

LIZ TAYLOR has suffered from wanderlust since the age of three, when she first took off and was found three miles away sitting under a tree with her dog. Her travels were financed by journalism and novels written under the name of Elisabeth McNeil. Trains are her favourite means of travel, closely followed by cargo boats.

NEIL TWEEDIE, a feature writer for the *Daily Telegraph*, is the son and brother of railwaymen and grew up to the sound of midnight freight trains crossing

Stockport Viaduct. So great is his love of the iron road that he took his wife by train from London to Istanbul on honeymoon. Ten years later she is still getting over the Bucharest-Istanbul leg.

IAN WALLER (1926–2003) was the political correspondent and then columnist of the *Sunday Telegraph* from its foundation in 1961 to his retirement in 1986. Railways were a lifelong passion and he had strong views on how they should be managed. In retirement, he bombarded newspapers, particularly the *Daily Telegraph*, with letters expressing his objections to the mode of privatisation adopted by the government.

ACKNOWLEDGEMENTS

My thanks to Graham Coster, who first wondered whether there might be material for a *Telegraph* book of great railway journeys; to the staff of the *Telegraph* library, particularly Gavin Fuller and Nick Alexander, who told me in which manilla envelopes I might find it; to George Newkey-Burden and Martin Smith, who downed spades from their own time tunnels to help me start digging mine; to Caroline Buckland of Telegraph Books, who steadied wobbles along the way; and, as always, to my wife, Teri, who has been persuaded, by the writing of Byron Rogers, that even timetable-compiling can make for a good read.